Big Data Forensics – Learning Hadoop Investigations

Perform forensic investigations on Hadoop clusters with cutting-edge tools and techniques

Joe Sremack

[PACKT] open source*
PUBLISHING   community experience distilled

BIRMINGHAM - MUMBAI

Big Data Forensics – Learning Hadoop Investigations

First published: August 2015

Production reference: 1190815

Published by Packt Publishing Ltd.
Livery Place
35 Livery Street
Birmingham B3 2PB, UK.

ISBN 978-1-78528-810-4

www.packtpub.com

Credits

Author
Joe Sremack

Reviewers
Tristen Cooper

Mark Kerzner

Category Manager
Veena Pagare

Acquisition Editor
Nikhil Karkal

Content Development Editor
Gaurav Sharma

Technical Editor
Dhiraj Chandanshive

Copy Editor
Janbal Dharmaraj

Project Coordinator
Bijal Patel

Proofreader
Safis Editing

Indexer
Priya Sane

Graphics
Abhinash Sahu

Production Coordinator
Komal Ramchandani

Cover Work
Komal Ramchandani

About the Author

Joe Sremack is a director at Berkeley Research Group, a global expert services firm. He conducts digital investigations and advises clients on complex data and investigative issues. He has worked on some of the largest civil litigation and corporate fraud investigations, including issues involving Ponzi schemes, stock option backdating, and mortgage-backed security fraud. He is a member of the Association of Certified Fraud Examiners and the Sedona Conference.

About the Reviewers

Tristen Cooper is an IT professional with 20 years of experience of working in corporate, academic, and SMB environments. He completed his BS degree in criminology from Fresno State and has an MA degree in political science from California State University, San Bernardino. Tristen's expertise includes system administration, network monitoring, forensic investigation, and security research.

His current projects include a monograph on the application of Cloward and Ohlin's Differential Opportunity to Islamic states to better understand the group's social structure and a monograph on the international drug trade and its effects on international security.

I'd like to thank Joe Sremack for giving me the opportunity to work on this project and Bijal Patel for her patience and understanding during the reviewing process.

Mark Kerzner holds degrees in law, math, and computer science. He is a software architect and has been working with Big Data for the last 7 years. He is a cofounder of Elephant Scale, a Big Data training and implementation company, and is the author of FreeEed, an open source platform for eDiscovery based on Apache Hadoop. He has authored books and patents. He loves learning languages, currently perfecting his Hebrew and Chinese.

I would like to acknowledge the help of my colleagues, in particular Sujee Maniyam, and last but not least, of my multitalented family.

www.PacktPub.com

Support files, eBooks, discount offers, and more

For support files and downloads related to your book, please visit www.PacktPub.com.

Did you know that Packt offers eBook versions of every book published, with PDF and ePub files available? You can upgrade to the eBook version at www.PacktPub.com and as a print book customer, you are entitled to a discount on the eBook copy. Get in touch with us at service@packtpub.com for more details.

At www.PacktPub.com, you can also read a collection of free technical articles, sign up for a range of free newsletters and receive exclusive discounts and offers on Packt books and eBooks.

https://www2.packtpub.com/books/subscription/packtlib

Do you need instant solutions to your IT questions? PacktLib is Packt's online digital book library. Here, you can search, access, and read Packt's entire library of books.

Why subscribe?

- Fully searchable across every book published by Packt
- Copy and paste, print, and bookmark content
- On demand and accessible via a web browser

Free access for Packt account holders

If you have an account with Packt at www.PacktPub.com, you can use this to access PacktLib today and view 9 entirely free books. Simply use your login credentials for immediate access.

To my beautiful wife, Alison, and our new bundle of joy, Ella.

Table of Contents

Preface

Forensics is an important topic for law enforcement, civil litigators, corporate investigators, academics, and other professionals who deal with complex digital investigations. Digital forensics has played a major role in some of the largest criminal and civil investigations of the past two decades — most notably, the Enron investigation in the early 2000s. Forensics has been used in many different situations. From criminal cases, to civil litigation, to organization-initiated internal investigations, digital forensics is the way data becomes evidence — sometimes, the most important evidence — and that evidence is how many types of modern investigations are solved.

The increased usage of Big Data solutions, such as Hadoop, has required new approaches to how forensics is conducted, and with the rise in popularity of Big Data across a wide number of organizations, forensic investigators need to understand how to work with these solutions. The number of organizations who have implemented Big Data solutions has surged in the past decade. These systems house critical information that can provide information on an organization's operations and strategies — key areas of interest in different types of investigations. Hadoop has been the most popular of the Big Data solutions, and with its distributed architecture, in-memory data storage, and voluminous data storage capabilities, performing forensics on Hadoop offers new challenges to forensic investigators.

A new area within forensics, called Big Data forensics, focuses on the forensics of Big Data systems. These systems are unique in their scale, how they store data, and the practical limitations that can prevent an investigator from using traditional forensic means. The field of digital forensics has expanded from primarily dealing with desktop computers and servers to include mobile devices, tablets, and large-scale data systems. Forensic investigators have kept pace with the changes in technologies by utilizing new techniques, software, and hardware to collect, preserve, and analyze digital evidence. Big Data solutions, likewise, require different approaches to analyze the collected data.

In this book, the processes, tools, and techniques for performing a forensic investigation of Hadoop are described and explored in detail. Many of the concepts covered in this book can be applied to other Big Data systems—not just Hadoop. The processes for identifying and collecting forensic evidence are covered, and the processes for analyzing the data as part of an investigation and presenting the findings are detailed. Practical examples are given by using LightHadoop and Amazon Web Services to develop test Hadoop environments and perform forensics against them. By the end of the book, you will be able to work with the Hadoop command line and forensic software packages and understand the forensic process.

What this book covers

Chapter 1, *Starting Out with Forensic Investigations and Big Data*, is an overview of both forensics and Big Data. This chapter covers why Big Data is important, how it is being used, and how forensics of Big Data is different from traditional forensics.

Chapter 2, *Understanding Hadoop Internals and Architecture*, is a detailed explanation of Hadoop's internals and how data is stored within a Hadoop environment.

Chapter 3, *Identifying Big Data Evidence*, covers the process for identifying relevant data within Hadoop using techniques such as interviews, data sampling, and system reviews.

Chapter 4, *Collecting Hadoop Distributed File System Data*, details how to collect forensic evidence from the Hadoop Distributed File System (HDFS) using physical and logical collection methods.

Chapter 5, *Collecting Hadoop Application Data*, examines the processes for collecting evidence from Hadoop applications using logical- and query-based methods. HBase, Hive, and Pig are covered in this chapter.

Chapter 6, *Performing Hadoop Distributed File System Analysis*, details how to conduct a forensic analysis of HDFS evidence, utilizing techniques such as file carving and keyword analysis.

Chapter 7, *Analyzing Hadoop Application Data*, covers how to conduct a forensic analysis of Hadoop application data using databases and statistical analysis techniques. Topics such as Benford's law and clustering are discussed in this chapter.

Chapter 8, *Presenting Forensic Findings*, shows to how to present forensic findings for internal investigations or legal proceedings.

What you need for this book

You need to have a basic understanding of the Linux command line and some experience working with a SQL DBMS. The exercises and examples in this book are presented in Amazon Web Services and LightHadoop—a Hadoop virtual machine distribution that is available for Oracle's VirtualBox, a free, cross-platform virtual machine software. Several forensic analysis tool examples are shown in Microsoft Windows, but they are also available for most Linux builds.

Who this book is for

This book is for those who are interested in digital forensics and Hadoop. Written for readers who are new to both forensics and Big Data, most concepts are presented in a simplified, high-level manner. This book is intended as a getting-started guide in this area of forensics.

Conventions

In this book, you will find a number of styles of text that distinguish between different kinds of information. Here are some examples of these styles, and an explanation of their meaning.

Code words in text, database table names, folder names, filenames, file extensions, pathnames, dummy URLs, user input, and Twitter handles are shown as follows:

"The following command collects the /dev/sda1 volume, stores it in a file called sda1.img".

A block of code is set as follows:

```
hdfs dfs -put ./testFile.txt /home/hadoopFile.txt
hdfs dfs -get /home/hadoopFile.txt ./testFile_copy.txt
md5sum testFile.txt
md5sum testFile_copy.txt
```

When we wish to draw your attention to a particular part of a code block, the relevant lines or items are set in bold:

```
hdfs dfs -put ./testFile.txt /home/hadoopFile.txt
hdfs dfs -get /home/hadoopFile.txt ./testFile_copy.txt
md5sum testFile.txt
md5sum testFile_copy.txt
```

Any command-line input or output is written as follows:

```
#!/bin/bash
hive -e "show tables;" > hiveTables.txt
for line in $(cat hiveTables.txt) ;
do
hive -hiveconf tablename=$line -f tableExport.hql > ${line}.txt
done
```

New terms and **important words** are shown in bold. Words that you see on the screen, in menus or dialog boxes for example, appear in the text like this: "Enter the **Case Number** and **Examiner** information, and click **Next.**"

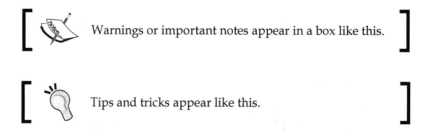

Warnings or important notes appear in a box like this.

Tips and tricks appear like this.

Reader feedback

Feedback from our readers is always welcome. Let us know what you think about this book—what you liked or may have disliked. Reader feedback is important for us to develop titles that you really get the most out of.

To send us general feedback, simply send an e-mail to feedback@packtpub.com, and mention the book title via the subject of your message.

If there is a topic that you have expertise in and you are interested in either writing or contributing to a book, see our author guide on www.packtpub.com/authors.

Customer support

Now that you are the proud owner of a Packt book, we have a number of things to help you to get the most from your purchase.

Downloading the color images of this book

We also provide you a PDF file that has color images of the screenshots/diagrams used in this book. The color images will help you better understand the changes in the output. You can download this file from: `http://www.packtpub.com/sites/default/files/downloads/81040S_ColorImages.pdf`.

Errata

Although we have taken every care to ensure the accuracy of our content, mistakes do happen. If you find a mistake in one of our books—maybe a mistake in the text or the code—we would be grateful if you would report this to us. By doing so, you can save other readers from frustration and help us improve subsequent versions of this book. If you find any errata, please report them by visiting `http://www.packtpub.com/submit-errata`, selecting your book, clicking on the **errata submission form** link, and entering the details of your errata. Once your errata are verified, your submission will be accepted and the errata will be uploaded on our website, or added to any list of existing errata, under the Errata section of that title. Any existing errata can be viewed by selecting your title from `http://www.packtpub.com/support`.

Piracy

Piracy of copyright material on the Internet is an ongoing problem across all media. At Packt, we take the protection of our copyright and licenses very seriously. If you come across any illegal copies of our works, in any form, on the Internet, please provide us with the location address or website name immediately so that we can pursue a remedy.

Please contact us at `copyright@packtpub.com` with a link to the suspected pirated material.

We appreciate your help in protecting our authors, and our ability to bring you valuable content.

Questions

You can contact us at `questions@packtpub.com` if you are having a problem with any aspect of the book, and we will do our best to address it.

1

Starting Out with Forensic Investigations and Big Data

Big Data forensics is a new type of forensics, just as Big Data is a new way of solving the challenges presented by large, complex data. Thanks to the growth in data and the increased value of storing more data and analyzing it faster—Big Data solutions have become more common and more prominently positioned within organizations. As such, the value of Big Data systems has grown, often storing data used to drive organizational strategy, identify sales, and many different modes of electronic communication. The forensic value of such data is obvious: if the data is useful to an organization, then the data is valuable to an investigation of that organization. The information in a Big Data system is not only inherently valuable, but the data is most likely organized and analyzed in such a way to identify how the organization treated the data.

Big Data forensics is the forensic collection and analysis of Big Data systems. Traditional computer forensics typically focuses on more common sources of data, such as mobile devices and laptops. Big Data forensics is not a replacement for traditional forensics. Instead, Big Data forensics augments the existing forensics body of knowledge to handle the massive, distributed systems that require different forensic tools and techniques.

Traditional forensic tools and methods are not always well-suited for Big Data. The tools and techniques used in traditional forensics are most commonly designed for the collection and analysis of unstructured data (for example, e-mail and document files). Forensics of such data typically hinges on metadata and involves the calculation of an MD5 or SHA-1 checksum. With Big Data systems, the large volume of data and how the data is stored do not lend themselves well to traditional forensics. As such, alternative methods for collecting and analyzing such data are required.

This chapter covers the basics of forensic investigations, Big Data, and how Big Data forensics is unique. Some of the topics that are discussed include the following:

- Goals of a forensic investigation
- Forensic investigation methodology
- Big Data – defined and described
- Key differences between traditional forensics and Big Data forensics

An overview of computer forensics

Computer forensics is a field that involves the identification, collection, analysis, and presentation of digital evidence. The goals of a forensic investigation include:

- Properly locating all relevant data
- Collecting the data in a sound manner
- Producing analysis that accurately describes the events
- Clearly presenting the findings

Forensics is a technical field. As such, much of the process requires a deep technical understanding and the use of technical tools and techniques. Depending on the nature of an investigation, forensics may also involve legal considerations, such as spoliation and how to present evidence in court.

 Unless otherwise stated, all references to forensics, investigations, and evidence in this book is in the context of Big Data forensics.

Computer forensics centers on evidence. Evidence is a proof of fact. Evidence may be presented in court to prove or disprove a claim or issue by logically establishing a fact. Many types of legal evidence exist, such as material objects, documents, and sworn testimony. Forensic evidence falls firmly in that legal set of categories and can be presented in court. In the broader sense, forensic evidence is the informational content of and about the data.

Forensic evidence comes in many forms, such as e-mails, databases, entire filesystems, and smartphone data. Evidence can be the information contained in the files, records, and other logical data containers. Evidence is not only the contents of the logical data containers, but also the associated metadata. Metadata is any information about the data that is stored by a filesystem, content management system, or other container. Metadata is useful for establishing information about the life of the data (for example, author and last modified date).

This metadata can be combined with the data to form a story about the who, what, why, when, where, and how of the data. Evidence can also take the form of deleted files, file fragments, and the contents of in-memory data.

For evidence to be court admissible or accepted by others, the data must be properly identified, collected, preserved, documented, handled, and analyzed. While the evidence itself is paramount, the process by which the data is identified, collected, and handled is also critical to demonstrate that the data was not altered in any way. The process should adhere to the best practices accepted by the court and backed by technical standards. The analysis and presentation must also adhere to best practices for both admissibility and audience comprehension. Finally, documentation of the entire process must be maintained and available for presentation to clearly demonstrate all the steps performed – from identification to collection to analysis.

The forensic process

The forensic process is an iterative process that involves four phases: identification, collection, analysis, and presentation. Each of the phases is performed sequentially. The forensic process can be iterative for the following reasons:

- Additional data sources are required
- Additional analyses need to be performed
- Further documentation of the identification process is needed
- Other situations, as required

The following figure shows the high-level forensic process discussed in this book:

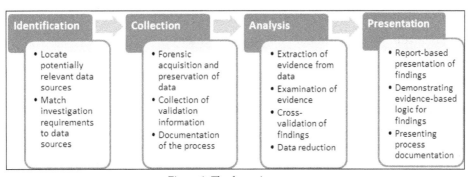

Figure 1: The forensic process

This book follows the forensic process of **Electronic Discovery Reference Model (EDRM)**, which is the industry standard and is a court-accepted best practice. The EDRM is developed and maintained by forensic and electronic discovery (e-discovery) professionals. For more information, visit EDRM's website at http://www.edrm.net/.

The sets of forensic steps and goals should be attempted to be applied for every investigation. No two investigations are the same. As such, practical realities may dictate which steps are performed and which goals can be met.

The four steps in the forensic process and the goals for each are covered in the following sections:

Identification

Identifying and fully collecting the data of interest in the early stages of an investigation is critical to any successful project. If data is not properly identified and, subsequently, is not collected, an embarrassing and difficult process of corrective efforts will be required — at a minimum — not to mention wasted time. At worst, improperly identifying and collecting data will result in working with an incorrect or incomplete set of data. In the latter case, court sanctions, a lost investigation, and ruined reputations can be expected.

The high-level approach taken in this book starts with:

- Examining the organization's system architecture
- Determining the kinds of data in each system
- Previewing the data
- Assessing which systems are to be collected

In addition, the identification phase should also include a process to triage the data sources by priority, ensuring the data sources are not subsequently used and/or modified. This approach results in documentation to back up the claim that all potentially important sources of data were examined. It also provides assurance that no major systems were overlooked. The main considerations for each source are as follows:

- Data quality

- Data completeness
- Supporting documentation
- Validating the collected data
- Previous systems where the data resided
- How the data enters and leaves the system
- The available formats for extraction
- How well the data meets the data requirements

The following figure illustrates this high-level identification process:

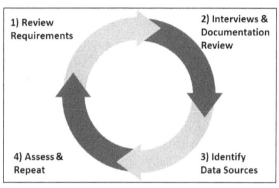

Figure 2: Data identification process

The primary goals for the identification stage of an investigation are as follows:

- Proper identification and documentation of potentially relevant sources of evidence
- Complete documentation of identified sources of information
- Timely assessment of potential sources of evidence from key stakeholders

Collection

The data collection phase involves the acquisition and preservation of evidence and validation information as well as properly documenting the process. For evidence to be court admissible and usable, it needs to be collected in a defensible manner that adheres to best practices. Collecting data alone, however, is not always sufficient in an investigation. The data should be accompanied by validation information (for example, log or query files) and documentation of the collection and preservation steps performed. Together, the collected data, validation information, and documentation allow for proper analysis that can be validated and defended.

The following figure highlights the collection phase process:

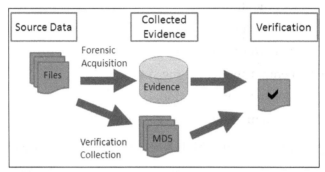

Figure 3: Data collection process

Data collection is a critical phase in a digital investigation. The data analysis phase can be rerun and corrected, if needed. However, improperly collecting data may result in serious issues later during analysis, if the error is detected at all. If the error goes undetected, the improper collection will result in poor data for the analysis. For example, if the collection was only a partial collection, the analysis results may understate the actual values. If the improper collection is detected during the analysis process, recollecting data may be impossible. This is the case when the data has been subsequently purged or is no longer available because the owner of the data will not permit access to the data again. In short, data collection is critical for later phases of the investigation, and there may not be opportunities to perform it again.

Data can be collected using several different methods. These methods are as follows:

- **Physical collection**: A physical acquisition of every bit, which may be done across specific containers, volumes, or devices. The collection is an exact replica of every bit of data and metadata. Slack space and deleted files can be recovered using this method.

- **Logical collection**: An acquisition of active data. The collection is a replica of the informational content and metadata, but is not a bit-by-bit collection.

- **Targeted collection**: A collection of specific containers, volumes, or devices.

Each of the methods is covered in this book. Validation information serves as a means for proving what was collected, who performed the collection, and how all relevant data was captured. Validation is also crucial to the collection phase and later stages of an investigation. Collecting the relevant data is the primary goal of any investigation, but the validation information is critical for ensuring that the relevant data was collected properly and not modified later. Obviously, without the data, the entire process is moot.

A closely-related goal is to collect the validation information along with the data. The primary forms of validation information are MD5/SHA-1 hash values, system and process logs, and control totals. Both MD5 and SHA-1 are hash algorithms that generate a unique value based on the contents of the file that serves as a fingerprint and can be used to authenticate evidence. If a file is modified, the MD5 or SHA-1 of the modified file will not match the original. In fact, generating two different files with the same value is virtually impossible. For this reason, forensic investigators rely on MD5 or SHA-1 to prove that the evidence was successfully collected and that the data analyzed matches the original source data. Control totals are another form of validation information, which are values computed from a structured data source — such as the number of rows or sum value of a numeric field. All collected data should be validated in some manner during the collection phase before moving into the analysis.

 Collect validation information simultaneously during or immediately after collecting evidence to ensure accurate and reliable validation.

The goals of the collection phase are as follows:

- Forensically sound collection of relevant sources of evidence utilizing technical best practices and adhering to legal standards
- Full, proper documentation of the collection process
- Collection of verification information (for example, MD5 or control totals)
- Validation of collected evidence
- Maintenance of chain of custody

Analysis

The analysis phase is the process by which collected and validated evidence is examined to gather and assemble the facts of an investigation. Many tools and techniques exist for converting the volumes of evidence into facts. In some investigations, the requirements clearly and directly point to the types of evidence and facts that are needed. These investigations may involve only a small amount of data or the issues are straightforward. For example, they only require a specific e-mail or only a small timeframe is in question. Other investigations, however, are large and complex. The requirements do not clearly identify a direct path of inquiry. The tools and techniques in the analysis phase are designed for both types of investigations and guide the inquiry.

The process for analyzing forensic evidence is dependent on the requirements of the investigation. Every case is different, so the analysis phase is both a science and an art. Most investigations are bounded by some known facts, such as a specific timeframe or the individuals involved. The analysis for such bounded investigations can begin by focusing on data from those time periods or involving those individuals. From there, the analysis can expand to include other evidence for corroboration or a new focus. Analysis can be an iterative process of investigating a subset of information. Analysis can also focus on one theory but then expand to either include new evidence or to form a new theory altogether. Regardless, the analysis should be completed within the practical confines of the investigation.

Two of the primary ways in which forensic analysis is judged are completeness and bias. Completeness, in forensics, is a relative term based on whether the relevant data has been reasonably considered and analyzed. Excluding relevant evidence or forms of analysis harms the credibility of the analysis. The key point is the reasonableness of including or excluding evidence and analysis. Bias is closely related to completeness. Bias is prejudice towards or against a particular thing. In the case of forensic analysis, bias is an inclination to favor a particular line of thinking without giving equal weight to other theories. Bias should be eliminated or minimized as much as possible when performing analysis to guarantee completeness and objective analysis. Both completeness and bias are covered in subsequent chapters.

Another key concept is data reduction. Forensic investigations can involve terabytes of data and millions of files and other data points. The practical realities of an investigation may not allow for a complete analysis of all data. Techniques exist for reducing the volume of data to a more manageable amount. This is performed using known facts and data interrelatedness to triage data by priority or eliminate data from the set of data to be analyzed.

Cross-validation is the use of multiple analyses or pieces of evidence to corroborate analysis. This is a key concept in forensics. While not always possible, cross-validation adds veracity to findings by further proving the likelihood that a finding is true. Cross-validation should be performed by independently testing two data sets or forms of analysis and confirming that the results are consistent.

The types of analysis performed depend on a number of factors. Forensic investigators have an arsenal of tools and techniques for analyzing evidence, and those tools and techniques are chosen based on the requirements of the investigation and the types of evidence. One example is timeline analysis, which is a technique used when chronology is important and chronological information exists and can be established. Timeline analysis is not important in all investigations, so it is not useful in every investigation.

In other cases, pattern analysis or anomaly detection may be required. While some investigations only require a single tool or technique, most investigations require a combination of tools and techniques. Later chapters include information about the various tools and techniques and how to select the proper ones. The following questions can help an investigator determine which tools and techniques to choose:

- What are the requirements of the investigation?
- What practical limitations exist?
- What information is available?
- What is already known about the evidence?

Documentation of findings and the analysis process must be carefully maintained throughout the process. Forensic evidence is complex. Analyzing forensic evidence can be even more complex. Without proper documentation, the findings are unclear and not defensible. An investigator can go down a path of analyzing data and related information—sometimes, linking hundreds of findings—and without documentation, detailing the full analysis is impossible. To avoid this, an investigator needs to carefully detail the evidence involved, the analysis performed, the analysis findings, and the interrelationships between multiple analyses.

The primary goals of the analysis phase are as follows:

- Unbiased and objective analysis
- Reduction of data complexity
- Cross-validation of findings
- Application of accepted standards

Presentation

The final phase in the forensic process is the presentation of findings. The findings can be presented in a number of different ways, such as a written expert report, graphical presentations, or testimony. Regardless of the format, the key to a successful presentation is to clearly demonstrate the findings and the process by which the findings were derived. The process and findings should be presented in a way that the audience can easily understand. Not every piece of information about the process phases or findings needs to be presented. Instead, the focus should be on the critical findings at a level of detail that is sufficiently thorough. Documentation, such as chain of custody forms, may not need to be included but should still be available should the need arise.

The goals of the presentation phase are as follows:

- Clear, compelling evidence
- Analysis that separates the signal from the noise
- Proper citation of source evidence
- Availability of chain of custody and validation documentation
- Post-investigation data management

Other investigation considerations

This book details the majority of the EDRM forensic process. However, investigators should be aware of several additional considerations not covered in detail in this book. Forensics is a large field with many technical, legal, and procedural considerations. Covering every topic would span multiple volumes. As such, this book does not attempt to cover all concepts. The following sections highlight several key concepts that a forensic investigator should consider—equipment, evidence management, investigator training, and the post-investigation process.

Equipment

Forensic investigations require specialized equipment for the collection and processing of evidence. Source data can reside on a host of different types of systems and devices. An investigator may need to collect several different types of systems. These include cell phones, mainframe computers, laptops with various operating systems, and database servers. These devices have different hardware and software connectors, different means of accessing, different configurations, and so on. In addition, an investigator must be careful not to alter or destroy evidence in the collection process. A best practice is to employ write-blocker software or physical devices to ensure that evidence is preserved in its original state. In some instances, specialized forensic equipment should be used to perform the collections, such as forensic devices that connect to smartphones for acquisitions. Big Data investigations rarely involve this specialized equipment to collect the data, but encrypted drives and other forensic devices may be used. Forensic investigators should be knowledgeable about the required equipment and come prepared to collect data with a forensic kit that contains the required equipment.

Evidence management

The management of forensic evidence is also critical to maintaining proper control and security of the evidence. Forensic evidence, once collected, requires careful handling, storage, and documentation. A standard practice in forensics is to create and maintain chain of custody of all evidence. Chain of custody documentation is a chronological description that details the collection, handling, transfer, analysis, and destruction of evidence. The chain of custody is established when a forensic investigator first acquires the data. The documentation details the collection process and then serves as a log of all individuals who take possession of the evidence, when that person had possession of the evidence, and details about what was done to the evidence. Chain of custody documentation should always reflect the full history and current status of the evidence. Chain of custody is further discussed in later chapters.

Only authorized individuals should have access to the evidence. Evidence integrity is critical for establishing and maintaining the veracity of findings. Allowing unauthorized — or undocumented — access to evidence can cast doubt on whether the evidence was altered. Even if the MD5 hash values are later found to match, allowing unauthorized access to the evidence can be enough to call the investigative process into question.

Security is important for preventing unauthorized access to both original evidence and analysis. Physical and digital security both play important roles in the overall security of evidence. The security of evidence should cover the premises, the evidence locker, any device that can access the analysis server, and network connections. Forensic investigators should be concerned with two types of security: physical security and digital security.

- Physical security is the collection of devices, structural design, processes, and other means for ensuring that unauthorized individuals cannot access, modify, destroy, or deny access to the data. Examples of physical security include locks, electronic fobs, and reinforced walls in the forensic lab.

- Digital security is the set of measures to protect the evidence on devices and on a network. Evidence can contain malware that could infect the analysis machine. A networked forensic machine that collects evidence remotely can potentially be penetrated. Examples of digital security include antivirus software, firewalls, and ensuring that forensic analysis machines are not connected to a network.

Investigator training and certification

Forensic investigators are often required to take forensic training and maintain current certifications in order to conduct investigations and testify to the results. While this is not always required, investigators can further prove that he has proper technical expertise by way of such training and certification. Forensic investigators are forensic experts, so that expertise should be documented and provable should anyone question their credentials. This can be achieved in part by way of training and certification.

The post-investigation process

After an investigation concludes, the evidence and analysis findings need to be properly archived or destroyed. Criminal and civil investigations require that evidence be maintained for a mandated period of time. The investigator should be aware of such retention rules and ensure that evidence is properly and securely archived and maintained for that period of time. In addition, documentation and analysis should be retained as well to guarantee that the results of the investigation are not lost and to prevent issues arising from questions about the evidence (for example, chain of custody).

What is Big Data?

Big Data describes the tools and techniques used to manage and process data that traditional means cannot easily accomplish. Many factors have led to the need for Big Data solutions. These include the recent proliferation of data storage, faster and easier data transfer, increased awareness of the value of data, and social media. Big Data solutions were needed to address the rapid, complex, and voluminous data sets that have been created in the past decade. Big Data can be structured data (for example, databases), unstructured data (such as e-mails), or a combination of both.

The four Vs of Big Data

A widely-accepted set of characteristics of Big Data is the four Vs of data. In 2001, Doug Laney of META Group produced a report on the needs of the changing requirements for managing the forms of voluminous data. In this report, he defined the three Vs of data: volume, velocity, and variety. These factors address the following:

- The large data sets
- The increased speed at which the data arrives, requires storage, and should be analyzed

- The multitude of forms the data, such as financial records, e-mails, and social media data

This definition has been expanded to include a fourth V for veracity — the trustworthiness of the data quality and the data's source.

 One way to identify whether a data set is Big Data is to consider the four Vs.

Volume is the most obvious characteristic of Big Data. The amount of data produced has grown exponentially over the past three decades, and that growth has been fueled by better and faster communications networks and cheaper storage. In the early 1980s, a gigabyte of storage costs over $200,000. A gigabyte of storage today costs approximately $0.06. This massive drop in storage costs and the highly networked nature of devices provides a means to create and store massive volumes of data. The computing industry now talks about the realities of exabytes (approximately, one billion gigabytes) and zettabytes (approximately, one trillion gigabytes) of data — possibly even yottabytes (over a thousand trillion gigabytes). Data volumes have obviously grown, and Big Data solutions are designed to handle the voluminous data sets through distributed storage and computing to scale out to the growing data volumes. The distributed solutions provide a means for storing and analyzing massive data volumes that could not feasibly be stored or computer by a single device.

Velocity is another characteristic of Big Data. The value of the information contained in data has placed an increased emphasis on quickly extracting information from data. The speed at which social media data, financial transactions, and other forms of data are being created can outpace traditional analysis tools. Analyzing real-time social media data requires specialized tools and techniques for quickly retrieving, storing, transforming, and analyzing the information. Tools and techniques designed to manage high-speed data also fall into the category of Big Data solutions.

Variety is the third V of Big Data. A multitude of different forms of data are being produced. The new emphasis is on extracting information from a host of different data sources. This means that traditional analysis is not always sufficient. Video files and their metadata, social media posts, e-mails, financial records, and telephonic recordings may all contain valuable information, and the data need to be analyzed in conjunction with one another. These different forms of data are not easily analyzed using traditional means.

Traditional data analysis focuses on transactional data or so-called structured data for analysis in a relational or hierarchical database. Structured data has a fixed composition and adheres to rules about what types of values it can contain. Structured data are often thought of in terms of records or rows, each with a set of one or more columns or fields. The rows and columns are bound by defined properties, such as the data type and field width limitations. The most common forms of structured data are:

- Database records
- Comma-Separated Value (CSV) files
- Spreadsheets

Traditional analysis is performed on structured data using databases, programs, or spreadsheets to load the data into a fixed format and run a set of commands or queries on the data. SQL has been the standard database language for data analysis over the past two decades — although many other languages and analysis packages exist.

Unstructured and semi-structured data do not have the same fixed data structure rules and do not lend themselves well to traditional analysis. Unstructured data is data that is stored in a format that is not expressly bound by the same data format and content rules as structured data. Several examples of unstructured data are:

- E-mails
- Video files
- Presentation documents

 According to VMWare's *2013 Predictions for Big Data*, over 80% of data produced will be unstructured, and the growth rate of unstructured data is 50-60% per year.

Semi-structured data is data that has rules for the data format and structure, but those rules are too loose for easy analysis using traditional means for analyzing structured data. XML is the most common form of semi-structured data. XML has a self-describing structure, but the structure of one XML file is not adhered to across all other XML files.

The variety of Big Data comes from the incorporation of a multitude of different types of data. Variety can mean incorporating structured, semi-structured, and unstructured data, but it can also mean simply incorporating various forms of structured data. Big Data solutions are designed to analyze whatever type of data is required. Regardless of the types of data are incorporated, the challenge for Big Data solutions is being able to collect, store, and analyze various forms of data in a single solution.

Veracity is the fourth V of Big Data. Veracity, in terms of data, indicates whether the informational content of data can be trusted. With so many new forms of data and the challenge of quickly analyzing a massive data set, how does one trust that the data is properly formatted, has correct and complete information, and is worth analyzing? Data quality is important for any analysis. If the data is lacking in some way, all the analyses will be lacking. Big Data solutions address this by devising techniques for quickly assessing the data quality and appropriately incorporating or excluding the data based on the data quality assessment results.

Big Data architecture and concepts

The architectures for Big Data solutions vary greatly, but several core concepts are shared by most solutions. Data is collected and ingested in Big Data solutions from a multitude of sources. Big Data solutions are designed to handle various types and formats of data, and the various types of data can be ingested and stored together. The data ingestion system brings the data in for transformation before the data is sent to the storage system. Distribution of storage is important for the storage of massive data sets. No single device can possibly store all the data or be expected to not experience failure as a device or on one of its disks. Similarly, computational distribution is critical for performing the analysis across large data sets with timeliness requirements. Typically, Big Data solutions enact a master/worker system—such as MapReduce— whereby one computational system acts as the master to distribute individual analyses for the worker computational systems to complete. The master coordinates and manages the computational tasks and ensures that the worker systems complete the tasks.

The following figure illustrates a high-level Big Data architecture:

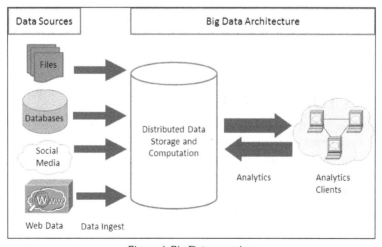

Figure 4: Big Data overview

Big Data solutions utilize different types of databases to conduct the analysis. Because Big Data can include structured, semi-structured, and/or unstructured data, the solutions need to be capable of performing the analysis across various types of files. Big Data solutions can utilize both relational and nonrelational database systems. NoSQL (Not only SQL) databases are one of the primary types of nonrelational databases used in Big Data solutions. NoSQL databases use different data structures and query languages to store and retrieve information. Key-value, graph, and document structures are used by NoSQL. These types of structures can provide a better and faster method for retrieving information about unstructured, semi-structured, and structured data.

Two additional important and related concepts for many Big Data solutions are text analytics and machine learning. Text analytics is the analysis of unstructured sets of textual data. This area has grown in importance with the surge in social media content and e-mail. Customer sentiment analysis, predictive analysis on buyer behavior, security monitoring, and economic indicator analysis are performed on text data by running algorithms across their data. Text analytics is largely made possible by machine learning. Machine learning is the use of algorithms and tools to learn from data. Machine algorithms make decisions or predictions from data inputs without the need for explicit algorithm instructions.

Video files and other nontraditional analysis input files can be analyzed in a couple ways:

- Using specialized data extraction tools during data ingestion
- Using specialized techniques during analysis

In some cases, only the unstructured data's metadata is important. In others, content from the data needs to be captured. For example, feature extraction and object recognition information can be captured and stored for later analysis. The needs of the Big Data system owner dictate the types of information captured and which tools are used to ingest, transform, and analyze the information.

Big Data forensics

The changes to the volumes of data and the advent of Big Data systems have changed the requirements of forensics when Big Data is involved. Traditional forensics relies on time-consuming and interruptive processes for collecting data. Techniques central to traditional forensic include removing hard drives from machines containing source evidence, calculating MD5/SHA-1 checksums, and performing physical collections that capture all metadata. However, practical limitations with Big Data systems prevent investigators from always applying these techniques. The differences between traditional forensics and forensics for Big Data are covered and explained in this section.

One goal of any type of forensic investigation is to reliably collect relevant evidence in a defensible manner. The evidence in a forensic investigation is the data stored in the system. This data can be the contents of a file, metadata, deleted files, in-memory data, hard drive slack space, and other forms. Forensic techniques are designed to capture all relevant information. In certain cases — especially when questions about potentially deleted information exist — the entire filesystem needs to be collected using a physical collection of every individual bit from the source system. In other cases, only the informational content of a source filesystem or application system are of value. This situation arises most commonly when only structured data systems — such as databases — are in question, and metadata or slack space are irrelevant or impractical to collect. Both types of collection are equally sound; however, the application of the type of collection depends on both practical considerations and the types of evidence required for collection.

Big Data forensics is the identification, collection, analysis, and presentation of the data in a Big Data system. The practical challenges of Big Data systems aside, the goal is to collect data from distributed filesystems, large-scale databases, and the associated applications. Many similarities exist between traditional forensics and Big Data forensics, but the differences are important to understand.

Every forensic investigation is different. When choosing how to proceed with collecting data, consider the investigation requirements and practical limitations.

Metadata preservation

Metadata is any information about a file, data container, or application data that describes its attributes. Metadata provides information about the file that may be valuable when questions arise about how the file was created, modified, or deleted. Metadata can describe who altered a file, when a file was revised, and which system or application generated the data. These are crucial facts when trying to understand the life cycle and story of an individual file.

Metadata is not always crucial to a Big Data investigation. Metadata is often altered or lost when data flows into and through a Big Data system. The ingestion engines and data feeds collect the data without preserving the metadata. The metadata would thus not provide information about who created the data, when the data was last altered in the upstream data source, and so on. Collecting information in these cases may not serve a purpose. Instead, upstream information about how the data was received can be collected as an alternative source of detail.

Investigations into Big Data systems can hinge on the information in the data and not the metadata. Like structured data systems, metadata does not serve a purpose when an investigation is solely based on the content of the data. Quantitative and qualitative questions can be answered by the data itself; metadata in that case would not be useful, so long as the collection was performed properly and no questions exist about who imported and/or altered the data in the Big Data system. The data within the systems is the only source of information.

 Collecting upstream information from application logs, source systems, and/or audit logs can be used in place of metadata collection.

Collection methods

Big Data systems are large, complex systems with business requirements. As such, they may not be able to be taken offline for a forensic investigation. In traditional forensics, systems can be taken offline, and a collection is performed by removing the hard drive to create a forensic copy of the data. In Big Data investigations, hundreds or thousands of storage hard drives may be involved, and data is lost when the Big Data system is brought offline. Also, the system may need to stay online due to business requirements. Big Data collections usually require logical and targeted collection methods by way of logical file forensic copies and query-based collection.

Collection verification

Traditional forensics relies on MD5 and SHA-1 to verify the integrity of the data collected, but it is not always feasible to use hashing algorithms to verify Big Data collections. Both MD5 and SHA-1 are disk-access intensive. Verifying collections by computing an MD5 or SHA-1 hash comprises a large percentage of the time dedicated to collecting and verifying source evidence. Spending the time to calculate the MD5 and SHA-1 for a Big Data collection may not be feasible when many terabytes of data are collected. The alternative is to rely on control totals, collection logs, and other descriptive information to verify the collection.

Summary

This book is an introduction to the key concepts and current technologies involved in Big Data forensics. Big Data is a paradigm shift in how data is stored and managed, and the same is true for forensic investigations of Big Data. A foundational understanding of computer forensics is important to understand the process and methods used in investigating digital information. Designed as a how-to guide, this book provides practical guidance on how to conduct investigations utilizing current technology and tools. Rather than rely on general principles or proprietary software, this books presents practical solutions utilizing freely-available software where possible. Several commercial software packages are also discussed to provide guidance and other ideas on how to tackle Big Data forensics investigations.

The field of forensics is large and continues to evolve. The field is new, and the technologies continue to change and develop. The constant growth in Big Data technologies leads to change in the tools and technologies for forensic investigations. Most of the tools presented in this book were developed in the past five years. Regardless of the tools used, this book is designed to provide readers with practical guidance on how to conduct investigations and select the appropriate tools.

This book focuses on performing forensics on Hadoop systems and Hadoop-based data. Hadoop is a framework for Big Data, and many software packages are built on top of Hadoop. This book covers the Hadoop filesystem and several of the key software packages that are built on top of Hadoop, such as Hive and HBase. A freely available Linux-based Hadoop virtual machine, LightHadoop, is used in this book to present examples of collecting and analyzing Hadoop data that can be followed by the reader.

Each of the stages of the forensic process is discussed in detail using practical Hadoop examples. *Chapter 2, Understanding Hadoop Internals and Architecture* details the Hadoop architecture and installing LightHadoop as a test environment. The remaining chapters cover each of the phases of the forensic process and the most common Hadoop packages that a forensic investigator will encounter.

2
Understanding Hadoop Internals and Architecture

Hadoop is currently the most widely adopted Big Data platform, with a diverse ecosystem of applications and data sources for forensic evidence. An Apache Foundation framework solution, Hadoop has been developed and tested in enterprise systems as a Big Data solution. Hadoop is virtually synonymous with Big Data and has become the de facto standard in the industry.

As a new Big Data solution, Hadoop has experienced a high adoption rate by many types of organizations and users. Developed by Yahoo! in the mid-2000s—and released to the Apache Foundation as one of the first major open source Big Data frameworks—Hadoop is designed to enable the distributed processing of large, complex data sets across a set of clustered computers. Hadoop's distributed architecture and open source ecosystem of software packages make it ideal for speed, scalability, and flexibility. Hadoop's adoption by large-scale technology companies is well publicized, and many other types of organizations and users have come to adopt Hadoop as well. These include scientific researchers, healthcare corporations, and data-driven marketing firms. Understanding how Hadoop works and how to perform forensics on Hadoop enables investigators to apply that same understanding to other Big Data solutions, such as PyTables.

Performing Big Data forensic investigations requires knowledge of Hadoop's internals and architecture. Just as knowing how the NTFS filesystem works is important for performing forensics in Windows, knowing the layers within a Hadoop solution is vital for properly identifying, collecting, and analyzing evidence in Hadoop. Moreover, Hadoop is rapidly changing—new software packages are being added and updates to Hadoop are being applied on a regular basis. Having a foundational knowledge of Hadoop's architecture and how it functions will enable an investigator to perform forensics on Hadoop as it continues to expand and evolve.

With its own filesystem, databases, and application layers, Hadoop can store data (that is, evidence) in various forms—and in different locations. Hadoop's multilayer architecture runs on top of the host operating system, which means evidence may need to be collected from the host operating system or from within the Hadoop ecosystem. Evidence can reside in each of the layers. This may require performing forensic collection and analysis in a manner specific to each layer.

This chapter explores how Hadoop works. The following topics are covered in detail: Hadoop's architecture, files, and data input/output (I/O). This is done to provide an understanding of the technical underpinnings of Hadoop. The key components of the Hadoop forensic evidence ecosystem are mapped out, and how to locate evidence within a Hadoop solution is covered. Finally, this chapter concludes with instructions on how to set up and run LightHadoop and Amazon Web Services. These are introduced as the Hadoop instances that serve as the basis for the examples used in this book. If you are interested in performing forensic investigations, you should follow the instructions on how to install LightHadoop and set up an Amazon Web Services instance at the end of this chapter. These systems are necessary to follow the examples presented throughout this book.

The Hadoop architecture

Hadoop is a reliable system for shared storage and analysis with a rich ecosystem of layered solutions and tools for Big Data. Hadoop is built on the concepts of distribution for storage and computing. It is a cross-platform, Java-based solution. Hadoop can run on a wide array of different operating systems, such as Linux and Windows, because it is built in Java, a platform-neutral language. Hadoop itself is a layer that sits on top of the host operating system. Hadoop's core functionalities are also built in Java and can be run as separate processes. With its own filesystem and set of core functionalities, Hadoop serves as its own abstract platform layer; it can be accessed and run almost entirely independent of the host operating system.

The following figure shows a high-level representation of the Hadoop layers:

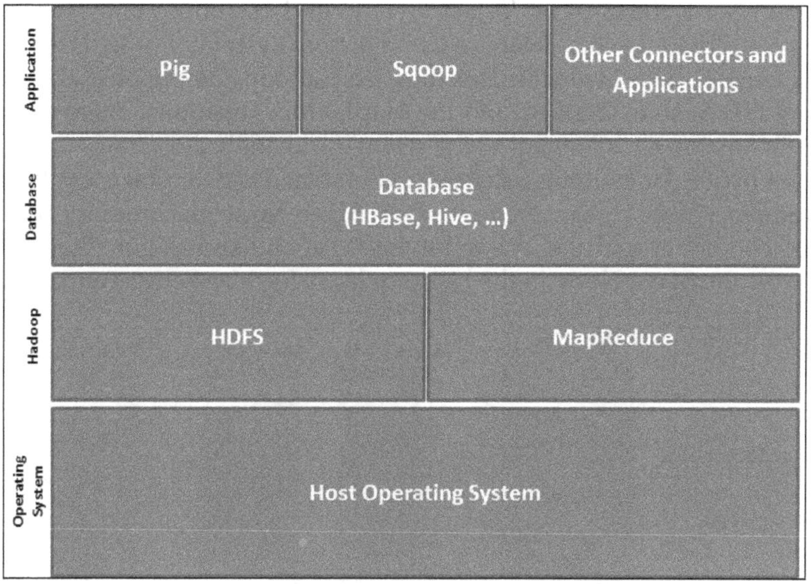

Figure 1: The Hadoop architecture layers

The Hadoop layers are an abstraction for how the various components are organized and the relationship between the other components. The following are the various Hadoop layers:

- **The Operating System layer**: The first layer is the Operating System on the host machine. Hadoop is installed on top of the operating system and runs the same regardless of the host operating system (for example, Windows or Linux).

- **The Hadoop layer**: This is the base installation of Hadoop, which includes the file system and MapReduce components.

- **The DBMS layer**: On top of Hadoop, the various Hadoop DBMS and related applications are installed. Typically, Hadoop installations include a data warehousing or database package, such as Hive or HBase.

- **The Application layer**: The Application layer is the top layer, which includes the tools that provide data management, analysis, and other capabilities. Some tools, such as Pig, can interact directly with the operating system and Hadoop layers. Other tools only interact with the database layer or other application-layer tools.

The components of Hadoop

The Hadoop layer is the most important layer in understanding how Hadoop works and how it is different from a database management system or other large-scale data processing engines. This layer contains the core Hadoop components, the **Hadoop Distributed File System** (HDFS), and the MapReduce functions. These elements form the key functions for managing the storage and analysis of data—and they are used in conjunction for running a distributed system. Distribution is controlled by a **Master Node** machine. This machine controls **Slave Node** machines for file storage and retrieval and data analysis. The following figure illustrates how the **Master Node** controls the **Slave Node** in the Hadoop layer for MapReduce and HDFS:

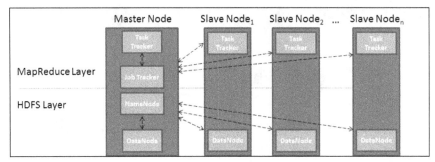

Figure 2: The Hadoop distributed process

Hadoop uses the HDFS to logically store data for use by Hadoop's applications. HDFS is designed to store data on commodity storage hardware in a distributed fashion. The **NameNode** file controls the tasks of storing and managing the data across each of the **DataNode**. When data is stored in Hadoop, the **NameNode** file automatically stores and replicates the data in multiple blocks (64 MB or 128 MB by default) across the various **DataNode**. This is done to ensure fault tolerance and high availability. HDFS is covered in more detail in the next section.

MapReduce is a key concept and framework for how Hadoop processes data. Using Hadoop's distributed processing model, MapReduce enables large jobs to be divided into Map() procedures and Reduce() procedures. Map() procedures are filtering and sorting operations, whereas Reduce() procedures are summary operations (for example, summation or counting). A single query can be divided into Map() and Reduce() procedures with a **Master Node** distributing the tasks to each of the **Slave Node**. The **SlaveNode** perform their discrete tasks and transmit the results back to the **Master Node** for analysis compilation and reporting.

The following figure is an example of how a MapReduce function works, in this case, for an aggregation of sales data:

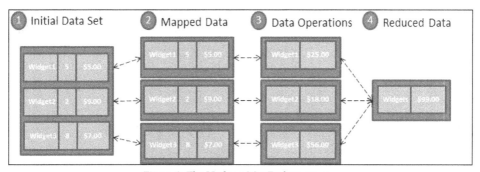

Figure 3: The Hadoop MapReduce process

The first step of MapReduce is to run a `Map()` function on the initial data. This creates data subsets that can be distributed to one or more nodes for processing. In this example, the data consists of information about widget sales quantity and price information, with each node receiving information about one widget. Each node that receives a record performs an operation on the record. In this case, the nodes calculate the total sales amounts. Finally, the `Reduce()` function computes the total sales amount for all widgets.

MapReduce programs can be written and executed in a number of different ways. First, programs can be written natively in Java using the `org.apache.hadoop.mapred` library. A MapReduce program is compiled using a Java compiler; it is then run in Hadoop using the Java runtime. Alternatively, additional Hadoop packages offer abstractions of MapReduce that can implement the `Map()` and `Reduce()` functions without using Java (for example, Pig).

For more information about programming in MapReduce, visit `http://hadoop.apache.org/docs/r1.2.1/mapred_tutorial.html`.

The layers above the Hadoop layer are the add-on functionality for process and resource management. These layers store, retrieve, convert, and analyze data. The following table provides examples of tools found in these layers:

Tool	Description
HBase	This is a column-based data warehouse for high-speed execution of operations over large data sets.
Hive	This is a data warehouse that offers SQL-like access to data in HDFS.

Tool	Description
Sqoop	This is a data transfer tool for moving to and from relational database systems.
Pig	This is the framework for executing MapReduce on HDFS data using its own scripting language.
Flume	This harvests, aggregates, and moves large amounts of log data in and out of Hadoop.

The Hadoop Distributed File System

HDFS is the filesystem primarily used by Hadoop. It is an abstracted filesystem layer that stores data in its own format to enable cross-platform functionality. The actual storage of the files resides in the host operating system's filesystem. However, the logical files are stored within Hadoop blocks; they are not necessarily directly accessible from the host operating system the way a file stored in the host operating system would be. HDFS serves the following purposes:

- The storage of data on a cluster
- The distribution of storage via NameNode and DataNode
- The division of files into blocks across DataNode
- The provision of access to the contents of the data blocks

HDFS is just one of over ten filesystems that can be implemented in Hadoop. While HDFS is the most popular Hadoop filesystem and the one presented in this book, investigators should be aware that a Hadoop cluster could use a different filesystem. Several examples of other Hadoop filesystems are Kosmos, Amazon S3, and the local filesystem.

Data is imported into HDFS and then stored in blocks for distributed storage. Files and data can be imported into HDFS in a number of ways, but all data stored in HDFS is split into a series of blocks. The blocks are split by size only. A file may contain record information, and the splits may occur within an individual record if that record spans a block size boundary. By default, blocks are 64 MB or 128 MB, but the size can be set to a different number by a system administrator. Hadoop is designed to work with terabytes and petabytes of data. The metadata about each block is stored centrally on a server, so Hadoop cannot afford to store the metadata about 4 KB blocks of data. Thus, Hadoop's block size is significantly larger than the blocks in a traditional filesystem.

After the data has been split, it is stored in a number of DataNode. By default, the replication level is set to three DataNode per block, but that setting can also be changed by a system administrator. Mapping information indicating where the data blocks are stored and other metadata are contained in NameNode, which is located in the Master Node. The following figure illustrates this process:

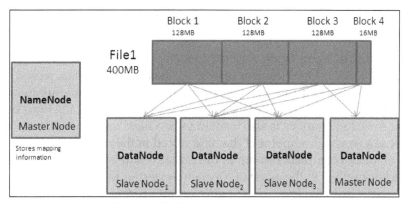

Figure 4: HDFS Data block distribution

 NameNode is a single point of failure. While DataNode information is stored in multiple locations, NameNode information only resides on a single machine—unless a secondary NameNode is set up for redundancy.

Files are stored logically in HDFS, and they can be accessed through HDFS just like a file in any other filesystem. Files may be stored in data blocks across a number of DataNode, but the files still retain their filenames and can be accessed in a number of ways. NameNode stores the information necessary to perform a lookup on a filename, identifies where the various blocks reside that comprise the file, and provides file-level security. When a file request is made in HDFS, Hadoop retrieves data blocks and provides access to the data as a file.

Once stored in HDFS, files can be accessed through a number of mechanisms. Files can be accessed via the Hadoop shell command line. The standard ways to locate and access files through the command line are the `ls` and `cp` commands, which are available through Hadoop. For example, the following commands can be executed to perform a folder listing and a file copy for HDFS data, respectively:

```
$ hdfs dfs -ls /user/hadoop/file1
$ hdfs dfs -cp /user/hadoop/file1 /user/hadoop/file2
```

Files can also be accessed through the HDFS web interface. The HDFS web interface provides information about the status of a Hadoop cluster. The interface enables browsing through directories and files in HDFS. By default, the web interface can be accessed at `http://namenode-name:50070/`.

These commands are possible because of the way information is stored in HDFS. Whether the Hadoop cluster is a single node or distributed across multiple nodes, the files are logically accessible in the same manner.

Information stored in NameNode is stored in memory, but it is also written to the filesystem for storage and disaster recovery. The in-memory data stored by NameNode is the active information used to locate data blocks and pull metadata. Because NameNode can have issues, or may need to be rebooted, the filesystem information stored in memory is also written to two files: `fsimage` and `edits`. The `fsimage` file is a recent checkpoint of the data stored in the memory of NameNode. The `fsimage` file is a complete backup of the contents and is sufficient to bring NameNode back online in the event of a system restart or failure. The `edits` file stores all changes from the last `fsimage` checkpoint process. This is similar to a database that utilizes a differential backup. NameNode does not utilize these files except for when NameNode is started, at which point, the contents of the files are brought into memory by NameNode. This is done by way of restoring the `fsimage` file data and then applying all updates from the `edits` file in the sequential order.

The `fsimage` file is similar in filesystem structure to a Windows **File Allocation Table (FAT)**. The file stores information about pointers to file locations; file locations are called inodes. Each inode has associated metadata about the file, including the number of blocks, permissions, modification and access times, and user and group ownership. The `fsimage` file can be useful in a forensic investigation when questions arise about metadata. The `fsimage` file is covered in more detail in later chapters.

The Hadoop configuration files

Hadoop contains standard system configuration files that store variables and default locations. Similar to an operating system, Hadoop uses a series of configuration files for storing and accessing system variables.

Configuration files are valuable in forensic investigations, especially in the data identification phase. These files identify where data is stored, the Hadoop applications that are used, and the various metadata about the data stores. Configuration files contain information that is useful in the following situations:

- The Hadoop system is offline and cannot be brought back online, so the Hadoop nodes need to be identified in order to collect data from each

- The system contains a large amount of data and specific folders (for example, log files) that need to be identified for a targeted collection

- The port information needs to be identified to reconstruct how the system operated

The following table is a list of Hadoop's standard configuration files:

Filename	Description
`hadoop-default.xml`	This contains the general default system variables and data locations
`hadoop-site.xml`	This contains the site-specific version of `hadoop-default.xml`
`mapred-default.xml`	This contains the MapReduce parameters
`job.xml`	This contains the job-specific configuration parameters

The `hadoop-default.xml` file is valuable because it contains the information about where data is stored, the temp directory location, log file locations, job history locations, and filesystem information. The `hadoop-site.xml` file contains configuration changes to the values in `hadoop-default.xml`. The `hadoop-default.xml` file is not supposed to be modified. Instead, administrators make modifications to the `hadoop-site.xml` file, which overrides the settings in `hadoop-default.xml`. Typically, administrators update the `hadoop-site.xml` file to set the JobTracker and NameNode parameters, such as the port information for job management and output, data path settings, and MapReduce folders. The other files are typically only valuable when information about the jobs that are run and the settings for each are potentially relevant.

The following is an excerpt from a sample `hadoop-site.xml` file:

```
<?xml version="1.0"?>
<?xml-stylesheet type="text/xsl" href="configuration.xsl"?>
<configuration>
  <property>
    <name>hadoop.tmp.dir</name>
    <value>/tmp/hadoop-${user.name}</value>
  </property>
  <property>
    <name>fs.default.name</name>
    <value>hdfs://localhost:8020</value>
  </property>
  <property>
    <name>mapred.job.tracker</name>
```

```
      <value>hdfs://localhost:54311</value>
   </property>
   <property>
     <name>dfs.replication</name>
     <value>8</value>
   </property>
   <property>
     <name>mapred.child.java.opts</name>
     <value>- Xmx200m </value>
   </property>
</configuration>
```

This configuration file contains the following information that may be of value to a forensic investigation:

- The HDFS temp directory used is `/tmp/hadoop-${user.name}`
- The NameNode file is located on the localhost on port 8020
- The MapReduce JobTracker is located on the localhost on port 54311
- The HDFS replication level is set to level 8

In addition to Hadoop configuration files, most Hadoop applications and data analysis packages have their own configuration files that determine where data is stored, permissions, and standard runtime parameters. These application configuration files are also useful for identifying and collecting forensic evidence.

Hadoop daemons

Hadoop daemons are the processes that provide the core Hadoop functionality, such as the NameNode and DataNode services. Hadoop's daemons are the processes that run and form the backbone of Hadoop's operations, similar to the daemons that provide operating system-level and other functionality within Linux and other Unix variants.

Hadoop runs several daemons in the host operating system's **Java Virtual Machine (JVM)**. The primary daemons are:

- NameNode
- DataNode
- SecondaryNameNode
- JobTracker
- TaskTracker

The daemons run as processes in the host operating system, so the status of the daemons can be monitored from the host operating system, not only within Hadoop. Because Hadoop is a Java-based system, the daemons are written in Java and the tool jps can be used to test whether there are active daemons. jps is the Java Virtual Machine Process Status Tool and it can be run from any host operating system with Java installed. If Hadoop is running, the jps output will contain the five daemons mentioned earlier. This is an excellent tool for investigators to use when working with a system suspected of running Hadoop. The following is an example of running jps and its output:

```
$ jps
```

The response from jps shows the process identifier (pid) and process name as follows:

- 1986 Jps
- 1359 ResourceManager
- 1223 RunJar
- 1353 NodeManager
- 1383 JobHistoryServer
- 1346 DataNode
- 1345 NameNode

Hadoop data analysis tools

Hadoop was designed to store and analyze large volumes of data. The ecosystem of tools for Hadoop analysis is large and complex. Depending on the type of analysis, many different tools can be used. The Apache Foundation set of tools has a number of standard options such as Hive, HBase, and Pig, but other open source and commercial solutions have been developed to meet different analysis requirements using Hadoop's HDFS and MapReduce features. For example, Cloudera's Impala database runs on Hadoop, but it is not part of the Apache Foundation suite of applications.

Understanding which data analysis tools are used in a Hadoop cluster is important for identifying and properly collecting data. Some data analysis tools store data in formatted files and may offer easier methods for data collection. Other tools may read data directly from files stored in HDFS, but the scripts used for the tool may serve as useful information when later analyzing the data. This section explores the three most common data analysis tools used in Hadoop—Hive, HBase, and Pig.

Hive

Hive is a data warehousing solution developed to store and manage large volumes of data. It offers an SQL-like language for analysis. Hive is a general purpose system that can be scaled to extremely large data sets. As a data warehousing system, data is imported into Hive data stores that can be accessed via an SQL-like query language called HiveQL.

The Hive service is the engine that manages the data storage and query operations. Hive queries are passed through the service, converted into jobs, and then executed with the results returned to the query interface. Hive stores two types of data: table data and metadata. Table data is stored in HDFS, and the metadata indicating where the partitions and data tables are stored is located in the Hive metastore. The metastore is a service and storage component that connects to a relational database (for example, MySQL or Oracle) for storage of the metadata. This enables Hive to retrieve data and table structure information. The following figure shows an overview of the Hive environment:

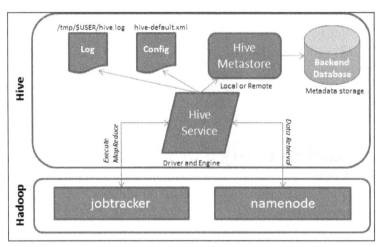

Figure 5: The Hive architecture

Depending on the data volume, Hive data is stored in the local HDFS filesystem. By default, data is stored in the `/user/hive/warehouse` directory. Hive can be configured to store data in other locations by way of modifying the `hive-default.xml` file's `hive.metastore.warehouse.dir` variable.

The following Hive query loads data to a new Hive table:

```
LOAD DATA LOCAL INPATH '/home/data/import.txt'
OVERWRITE INTO TABLE sampletable
```

This query imports the records from the `import.txt` file into a Hive table named `sampletable`. Since the default data location is `/user/hive/warehouse`, the data is stored in a new directory called `sampletable`. The metastore is also updated with metadata related to the new table and data location. The following Hadoop command shows the imported file:

```
$ hadoop fs -ls /user/hive/warehouse/sampletable/
```

The response from Hadoop is as follows:

```
import.txt
```

This example, however, only shows how Hive stores data when the local HDFS is used. Other options exist, so investigators should be aware that data can be stored in other locations. Hive table data can be stored in remote locations, such as cloud storage as well as on local nodes. Likewise, the metastore and its database can either be on the local machine or a remote machine. If the metastore is a required piece of an investigation, the location of the metastore should be identified.

Hive provides logging for critical events and errors. By default, Hive logs errors to `/tmp/$USER/hive.log`. The error log location can be specified for a different directory in the hive log configuration file `conf/hiv-log4j.properties`. The primary configuration file for Hive is the `hive-default.xml` file.

The alternative to searching all of these additional sources in an investigation is to extract data from Hive via queries. With the potential for multiple remote systems, a large metastore, and various system configuration and log files — a simpler solution to extract the data is required. This can be done by running HiveQL queries to retrieve the contents from all tables and store the results in flat files. This approach enables the investigator to retrieve the entire set of contents from Hive; it is useful when metadata or questions about data removal are not relevant.

HBase

HBase is currently the most popular NoSQL database for Hadoop. HBase is a column-oriented, distributed database that is built on top of HDFS. This database is commonly used for large-scale analysis across sparsely-populated datasets. HBase does not support SQL, and data is organized by columns instead of the familiar relational sets of tables.

HBase's data model is unique and requires understanding before data is collected by an investigator. HBase makes use of the following concepts:

- **Table**: HBase organizes data into tables, with each table having a unique name.

- **Row**: Data is stored in rows within each column, and the rows are identified by their unique row key.

- **Column Family**: The data within a row is organized by groupings of columns, called column families. Column families have a common prefix and are on the left-hand side of the colon in a column name. For example, the row columns location:city and location:street are both members of the location family, whereas name:first belongs to the name column family.

- **Column Qualifier**: The individual row columns are specified by the column qualifier. In the previous example, location:city is part of the location column family and its qualifier is city.

- **Cell**: The unique identification of a value within a row is a cell. Cells are identified by a combination of the table, row key, column family, and column qualifier.

The following figure shows a sample set of data within HBase. The table contains two column families: **name** and **location**. Each of the families has two qualifiers. A combination of the unique row key, column family, and column qualifier represents a cell. For example, the cell value for row key **00001** + name:**first** is **John**:

Row Key	Column Family - name		Column Family - location	
	first	last	city	street
00001	John	Doe	New York	Broadway
00002	Jane	Doe	New York	Sixth Ave
00003	Elizabeth	Doe	London	Baker St
00004	Brad	Doe	London	Baker St

Figure 6: HBase data

HBase stores all column family members together in HDFS. HBase is considered a column-oriented database, but the physical storage is actually performed by grouping columns and storing those together. Because of this storage methodology, column families are expected to have similar data size and content characteristics to enable faster sorting and analysis.

Tables are partitioned horizontally into sections of fixed-size chunks called regions. When a table is first created, the entire contents of the table are stored in a single region. As the number of rows reaches a certain size threshold, a new region is created for the additional rows. The new region is typically stored on a separate machine, enabling the data to scale without compromising the speed of storage and analysis.

HBase utilizes a set of servers and a database log file for running its distributed database. The region servers store the data contents and are the data analysis engines. Each region server has HFile data and a memstore. The region servers share a **write-ahead log (WAL)** that stores all changes to the data, primarily for disaster recovery. Each HBase instance has a master server, which is responsible for assigning regions to region servers, recovering from region server failure, and bootstrapping. Unlike the MapReduce process, master servers do not control operations for analysis. Large-scale HBase instances typically have a backup master server for failover purposes.

HBase also uses and depends on a tool called ZooKeeper to maintain the HBase cluster. ZooKeeper is a software package used for the maintenance of configuration information and performing synchronization across distributed servers. At a minimum, HBase uses a ZooKeeper leader server and a ZooKeeper follower server to assign tasks to HBase nodes and track progress. These servers also provide disaster recovery services.

The following figure highlights the configuration of an HBase and ZooKeeper environment:

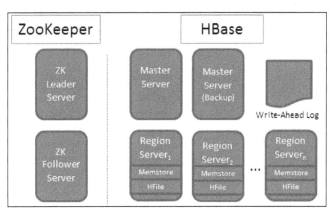

Figure 7: The HBase architecture

The data file format used by HBase is HFile. The files are written in 64 KB blocks by default. HFile blocks are not to be confused with HDFS blocks. HFiles are divided into four regions as follows:

- **Scanned Block Section**: The data content (that is, key and value pairs) and pointer information that is scanned; multiple data and leaf index blocks can be stored in this section.
- **Non-Scanned Block Section**: The meta information that is not scanned; multiple blocks can be stored in this section.

- **Load-on-Open Section**: The information loaded into memory when an HFile is opened by HBase.
- **Trailer Section**: The trailer information, such as offsets, compression codec information, and the number of block entry summary information.

The following file layout figure shows the structure of an HFile that is stored on a region server:

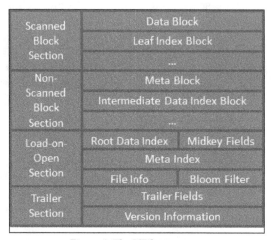

Figure 8: The HFile structure

Like Hive and other Hadoop applications, the HBase settings can be found in its configuration files. The two configuration files are `hbase-default.xml` and `hbase-site.xml`. By default, `hbase-site.xml` contains information about where HBase and ZooKeeper write data.

HBase data can be accessed in a number of ways. The following is a list of means by which HBase data can be accessed:

- **Java program**: HBase is a Java-based database that has its own object library that can be implemented in custom Java programs for querying
- **MapReduce**: HBase data can also be queried via Hadoop's MapReduce functions
- **Avro**: A Hadoop data serialization interface, called Avro, can be used
- **REST**: Data can be queried with responses formatted as JSON, XML, or other formats

Extracting data from HBase requires using one of these methods. This makes data collection more difficult, but the alternative is to identify all regional servers and use configuration files and knowledge of HFiles to carve out the relevant data. These and other HBase data collection and analysis issues are covered in later chapters.

Pig

Pig is a tool that creates an abstraction layer on top of MapReduce to enable simpler and faster analysis. Pig is a scripting language designed to facilitate query-like data operations that can be executed with just several lines of code. Native MapReduce applications written in Java are effective and powerful tools, but the time to develop and test the applications is time-consuming and complex. Pig solves this problem by offering a simpler development and testing process that takes advantage of the power of MapReduce, without the need to build large Java applications. Whereas Java programs may require 50-100 lines, Pig scripts often have ten lines of code or less. Pig is comprised of two elements as follows:

- An execution environment that runs Pig scripts against Hadoop data sets
- A scripting language, called Pig Latin

Pig is not a database or a data storage tool. Unlike HBase, Pig does not require data to be loaded into a data repository. Pig can read data directly from HDFS at script runtime, which makes Pig very flexible and useful for analyzing data across HDFS in real time.

 Pig scripts typically have a `.pig` extension. If the Pig scripts may be relevant or useful, investigators should collect the scripts to help understand the data and how that data was analyzed on the source system.

Managing files in Hadoop

Hadoop has its own file management concepts that come with many different mechanisms for data storage and retrieval. Hadoop is designed to manage large volumes of data distributed across many nodes built with commodity hardware. As such, Hadoop manages the distribution of large volumes of data using techniques designed to divide, compress, and share the data all while dealing with the possibilities of node failures and numerous processes accessing the same data simultaneously. Many of the filesystem concepts in Hadoop are exactly the same as in other systems, such as directory structures. However, other concepts, such as MapFiles and Hadoop Archive Files, are unique to Hadoop. This section covers many of the file management concepts that are unique to Hadoop.

File permissions

HDFS uses a standard file permission approach. The three types of permissions for files and directories are:

- **Read** (r): Read a file and list a directory's contents
- **Write** (w): Write to a file and create or delete files in a directory
- **Execute** (x): Access subdirectories (does not apply to files in HDFS)

Each file and directory has an associated owner, group, and mode. The owner and group are assigned based on who owns or created the file or directory, and the same is true for the group. The mode is the list of permissions for the owner, the members of the group, and all others (that is, a non-owner and non-group member for the file or directory). There are also superuser accounts in HDFS, and all superuser accounts can access any file or directory, regardless of permissions.

File permissions in HDFS are not as useful for determining the actual people and location of account logins as is the case with traditional operating systems. Client accounts in Hadoop run under process accounts. So rather than each individual having a login to the Hadoop instance, the clients access HDFS via an application that has its own account. For example, an HBase client has an associated account, HBase, by default and that account would be the one running analysis. While tools such as ZooKeeper provide **Access Control Lists (ACLs)** to manage such community accounts, one can see that having processes that act as user accounts can create difficulties for identifying which person or location performed specific actions.

> Some Hadoop packages contain access control mechanisms that enable more granular user access control. HBase, for example, has an Access Controller coprocessor that can be added to the hbase-site.xml configuration file to control which users can access individual tables or perform specific HBase actions. The ACL is stored in the HBase table _acl_.

Trash

Hadoop has a trash feature that stores deleted files for a specific amount of time. All Hadoop users have a .Trash folder, where deleted files are stored. When a file is deleted in Hadoop, a subdirectory is created under the user's $HOME folder using the original file path, and the file is stored there. All files stored in trash are permanently deleted when one of the following events happen:

- The periodic trash deletion process is run by Hadoop. This occurs after a fixed amount of time, as specified by a user-configured time.

- A user runs an expunge job. This can be performed from the Hadoop command line as follows:

```
%hadoop fs -expunge
```

 Files are only moved to the trash when deleted by a user from the Hadoop command line. Files deleted programmatically bypass the trash and are permanently deleted immediately.

Information about a Hadoop instance's trash configuration can be found in `core-default.xml` under the key `FS_TRASH_INTERVAL_KEY`. By default, `FS_TRASH_INTERVAL_KEY` is set to `0`, which means the trash feature is disabled and files are automatically deleted permanently. For example, if the key is set to `5`, then the trash feature is turned on, and trash is emptied every 5 minutes.

Log files

Log files are valuable sources of forensic evidence. They store information about where data was stored, where data inputs originated, jobs that have been run, the locations of other nodes, and other event-based information. As in any forensic investigation, the logs may not contain directly relevant evidence; however, the information in logs can be useful for identifying other locations and sources of evidence.

The following types of logs can be found on machines running a Hadoop cluster:

- **Hadoop daemon logs**: Stored in the host operating system, these `.log` files contain error and warning information. By default, these log files will have a `hadoop` prefix in the filename.

- **log4j**: These logs store information from the log4j process. The log4j application is an Apache logging interface that is used by many Hadoop applications. These logs are stored in the `/var/log/hadoop` directory.

- **Standard out and standard error**: Each Hadoop TaskTracker creates and maintains these error logs to store information written to standard out or standard error. These logs are stored in each TaskTracker node's `/var/log/hadoop/userlogs` directory.

- **Job configuration XML**: The Hadoop JobTracker creates these files within HDFS for tracking job summary details about the configuration and job run. These files can be found in the `/var/log/hadoop` and `/var/log/hadoop/history` directory.

- **Job statistics**: The Hadoop JobTracker creates these logs to store information about the number of job step attempts and the job runtime for each job.

Log file retention varies across implementation and administrator settings. Some logs, such as log4j, can grow very quickly and may only have a retention period of several hours. Even if logs are purged, a best practice for many types of logs is to archive them in an offline system for diagnostics and job performance tracking.

File compression and splitting

One method used by Hadoop for transferring data more efficiently is to compress data in transit. The benefit of compressing data is that the time to compress, transmit, and decompress data is often less than transmitting uncompressed data when the data volume is large. For this reason, Hadoop supports a number of compression algorithms and file formats. The following compression formats are supported by Hadoop:

- bzip2
- DEFLATE
- gzip
- LZO
- LZ4
- Snappy

 Files compressed with DEFLATE in Hadoop have a `.deflate` file extension.

While compressed files can be transmitted more easily, sending out one compressed file to multiple nodes is not always an efficient option. Hadoop's MapReduce is designed with a framework to enable sending out smaller jobs to multiple nodes. Each node does not need to receive the complete data set if it is only tasked with a subset of the data. Instead, the data should be split into subsets, with each node receiving only the subset it needs. For this reason, compression algorithms whose files can be split are preferred. DEFLATE does not support splitting, but formats such as bzip2, LZO, LZ4, and Snappy do.

A forensic investigator should be aware of split files that can be stored on node machines. These files may require forensic collection of the individual split data files on the various nodes to fully reconstruct the complete, original data container.

Hadoop SequenceFile

SequenceFile are Hadoop's persistent data structure for key-value pair data for MapReduce functions. These files are both the input and output format for MapReduce. They contain key-value pair values and have a defined structure. SequenceFile are a common file format in Hadoop, and they facilitate the splitting of data for each transfer during MapReduce jobs. There are three formats of SequenceFiles:

- **Uncompressed**: The plaintext data in individual records
- **Record-compressed**: Individual records compressed per segment
- **Blocked-compressed**: Multiple records compressed per segment

The three formats have a common file header format. The following table lists the fields found in the file header:

Field	Description
Version	This holds SEQ4 or SEQ6, depending on the SequenceFile version
keyClassName	This holds the name of the key class
valueClassName	This holds the name of the value class
Compression	This is used for key/pairs: 1 if compressed, 0 if uncompressed
blockCompression	This is used for key/pairs blocks: 1 if compressed, 0 if uncompressed
Compression Codec	This holds the compression codec name value
Metadata	This is user-defined metadata
Sync	This is a marker to denote the end of the header

The header segment defines the type of SequenceFile and the summary information for the file.

Both uncompressed and record-compressed SequenceFile have record and sync blocks. The only difference between the two is that the value within the record segment is compressed in the record-compressed format. The block-compressed format is comprised of alternating sync and block segments. Within the block segments, the keys and values are combined and compressed together.

The following figure illustrates the contents of each of the three SequenceFile formats:

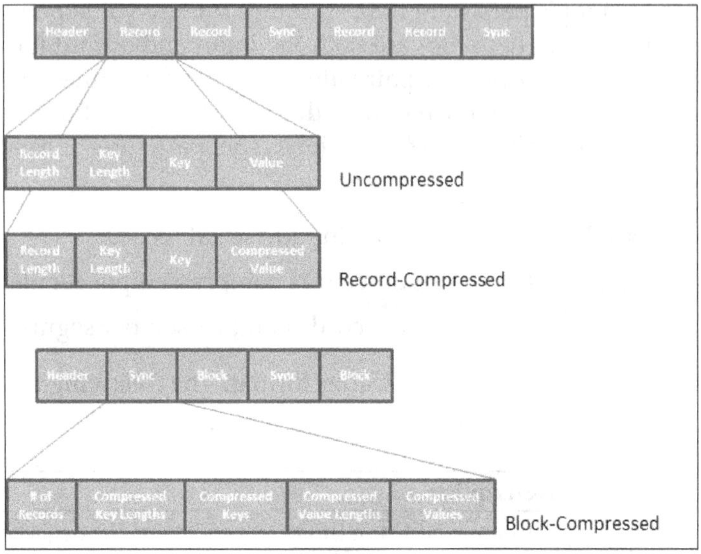

Figure 9: The SequenceFile structure

> Forensic investigations can require that investigators manually extract data using the file format as a reference or identify files by their structure. SequenceFile, for example, do not have a standard file extension, so investigators can only identify them by analyzing the file structure.

SequenceFile are the base data structure for several variants. MapFiles are a directory structure that have `/index` and `/data` directories. The key information is stored in `/index` and the key/pairs are stored in `/data`. SetFile and ArrayFile are MapFile variants that add functionality to the MapFile structure. Finally, BloomFiles are extensions of MapFiles that have a `/bloom` directory for storing bloom filter information. All of these types of MapFile and MapFile variants can be readily identified by the presence of these directories.

The Hadoop archive files

HDFS is designed to work with large data sets as evidenced by the large block sizes of 64 MB to 128 MB. The NameNode file stores namespace information for identifying files and blocks. As the number of files increases, the NameNode's file lookup speed is reduced. The number of files NameNode manages is also limited by the amount of physical memory, because all file information managed by NameNode is stored in memory. One method in HDFS for solving this problem is storing multiple files in a single container file, called **Hadoop Archive** (**HAR**) files.

HAR files are multiple small files stored in a single, uncompressed container file. HDFS has an interface that enables the individual files within a HAR file to be accessed in parallel. Similar to the TAR container file format that is common in UNIX, multiple files are combined into a single archive. Unlike TAR, however, HAR files are designed such that individual files can be accessed from inside the container. HAR files can be accessed by virtually all Hadoop components and applications, such as MapReduce, the Hadoop command line, and Pig.

While HAR files offer several advantages for Hadoop, they also have limitations. The advantage of HAR files is the capability to access multiple small files in parallel, which reduces the NameNode file management load. In addition, HAR files work well in MapReduce jobs because the individual files can be accessed in parallel. HAR files also have their disadvantages. For example, because they are permanent structures, they cannot be modified after they are created. This means new HAR files have to be created any time new files should be added to a HAR file. Accessing a file within a HAR file also requires an index lookup process, which adds an extra step to the process.

The HAR file format has several elements. The following three elements comprise the HAR format:

- `_masterindex`: The file hashes and offsets
- `index`: The file statuses
- `part-[1-n]`: The actual file data content

The file data is stored in multiple part files based on block allocation, and the content location is stored in the `_masterindex` element. The `index` element stores the file statuses and original directory structure.

Individual files from within a HAR file can be accessed via a `har://` prefix. The following command copies a file called `testFile`, originally stored in a directory called `testDir`, from a HAR file stored on NameNode called `foo` to the local filesystem:

```
% hadoop fs -get har://namenode/foo.har#testDir/testFile
localdir
```

HAR files are unique to Hadoop. When forensically analyzing HAR data, investigators should export the data from Hadoop to a local filesystem for analysis.

Data serialization

Hadoop supports several data serialization frameworks. Data serialization is a framework for storing data in a common format for transmission to other applications or systems. For Hadoop, data serialization is primarily used for transmitting data for MapReduce-related tasks. The three most common data serialization frameworks in Hadoop are:

- Apache Avro
- Apache Thrift
- Google Protocol Buffers

Data serialization frameworks are designed to transmit data that is read and stored in memory, but the data files used for storage and transmission can be relevant forensic evidence. The frameworks are fairly similar in overall structure and forensic artifacts. The forensic artifacts for all three would be the data schema file that defines the data structure and the text- or binary-encoded data files that store the data contents.

Avro is currently the most common data serialization framework in use for Hadoop. An .avro container file is the artifact created when data is serialized. The .avro file includes a schema file that is a plaintext definition of the data structure; it also includes either a binary or text data content file. For the data format, Avro supports both its own binary encoding and JSON text-based encoding. Avro files can be extracted either directly through Avro or through Avro's Java methods.

The following figure illustrates the Avro container file format:

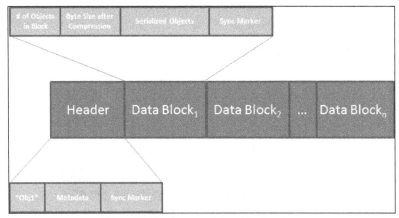

Figure 10: The Avro container file structure

Packaged jobs and JAR files

MapReduce jobs can be executed natively in Java, and those jobs can be compiled into **Java Archive (JAR)** files for reuse. Hadoop developers and analysts have many options for how to create and run data import, management, and analysis jobs. While tools such as Pig are extremely popular, some developers still prefer to develop in Java. Forensic investigators may encounter JAR files or Java source code (`.java`) files in their collection process.

JAR files are archive container files. The source code, class files, corresponding data files, and compiler instructions can all be stored in the same JAR file, which then can be subsequently transferred and unpacked for execution. The compression and single container file make JAR a popular option for storing the applications. While a forensic investigator does not need to know how to create or execute a JAR file, they may need to extract the contents in order to review the Java class and source code information. To preview the contents of a JAR file named `jarTestFile`, the following can be run for the Java command line:

```
$ jar tf jarTestFile
```

To extract the full set of contents from `jarTestFile`, the JAR extract command can be run from the following Java command line:

```
$ jar xf jarTestFile
```

The Hadoop forensic evidence ecosystem

Forensics is based on evidence. For digital investigations, evidence is data. For Hadoop, the evidence is the information stored on disk and in memory. Not all information stored in Hadoop is relevant; it depends on the nature of the investigation. Evidence that is relevant in one investigation may not be relevant in another. This section summarizes the various sources of evidence and the overall ecosystem of Hadoop forensic evidence.

Standard Hadoop processes or system-generated diagnostic information may not be relevant to a forensic investigation. For example, a Hadoop cluster installed without any customizations that only stores and analyses web log data may not require a collection of all files and process data. Instead, a targeted collection of the web log data can be performed without losing evidence. In other investigations, collecting the log and configuration files may be necessary.

Forensic data in Hadoop falls into three categories:

- **Supporting information**: This is the data that helps identify evidence or provides context about the Hadoop cluster's operations or configurations.

- **Record evidence**: This is any data that is analyzed in Hadoop, whether that is HBase data, text files for MapReduce jobs, or Pig output.

- **User and application evidence**: This is the third form of forensic data of interest. This evidence includes the log and configuration files, analysis scripts, MapReduce logic, metadata, and other forms of customization and logic that act on the data. This form of evidence is useful in investigations when questions arise about how the data was analyzed or generated.

The following figure lists the most common form of data for each type of forensic evidence:

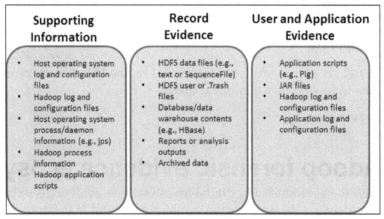

Figure 11: Types of forensic evidence

The difficulty in facing a forensic investigator working with a Big Data system such as Hadoop is the volume of data as well as data being stored across multiple nodes. An investigator cannot simply image a single hard drive and expect to have all data from that system. Instead, forensic investigators working in Hadoop need to first identify the relevant data, and only then can the actual evidence be collected. Some forms of data such as log and configuration files are valuable for identifying where evidence is stored and whether data archives exist. This type of evidence is categorized as supporting information. It is valuable in both the early and late stages of an investigation for identifying information and piecing together how the Hadoop cluster operated.

Record evidence is the most common form of evidence for Hadoop investigations. In nonBig Data investigations, the files and e-mails from employees can be the most valuable form of evidence; however, most organizations' employees do not interact much with Hadoop. Rather, Hadoop is managed and operated by IT and data analysis staff. The value of Hadoop is the data stored and analyzed in Hadoop. That data is the transactional and unstructured data stored in Hadoop for analysis as well as the outputs from the analyses. These structured and unstructured data are forms of record evidence. The challenging aspect of Hadoop investigations is identifying all potentially relevant sources of record evidence as record evidence can exist in multiple forms and in multiple applications within Hadoop.

User and application evidence is any type of evidence that shows how the system operates or the logic used to run analysis as they directly relate to the record evidence. In some investigations, questions arise about what was done to data or how operations were performed. While these questions can sometimes be answered by analyzing the record evidence, user and application evidence provides a simpler and more powerful way to answer such questions. User and application evidence ranges from the scripts used to import and analyze data to the configuration and log files within Hadoop.

Running Hadoop

Hadoop can be run from a number of different platforms. Hadoop can be installed and run from a single desktop, from a distributed network of systems, or as a cloud-based service. Investigators should be aware of the differences and versed in the various architectures. Hadoop runs in the same manner on all three setups; however, collecting evidence may require different steps depending on how the data is stored. For instance, a cloud-based Hadoop server may require a different collection because of the lack of physical access to the servers.

This section details how to set up and run Hadoop using a free virtual machine instance (LightHadoop) and a cloud-based service (Amazon Web Services). Both LightHadoop and Amazon Web Services are used in the examples throughout this book. They serve as testbed environments to highlight how Big Data forensics is performed against different setups.

LightHadoop

Many of the examples in this book are intended to be hands-on exercises using LightHadoop. LightHadoop is a freely distributed CentOS Hadoop virtual machine instance. This Hadoop distribution differs from larger ones such as Cloudera. LightHadoop requires less hardware and fewer storage resources. This makes LightHadoop ideal for learning Hadoop on a single machine and enables one to create many virtual machines for testing purposes without requiring large storage volumes or multiple nodes. Due to the small **virtual machine** (**VM**) size, LightHadoop does not include all of the major Hadoop-related Apache packages. However, it does include the main ones required for learning about Hadoop and running a **database management system** (**DBMS**). The following Apache packages are currently included in LightHadoop:

- Hadoop
- Hive
- Pig
- Sqoop

Oracle VM VirtualBox is the virtual machine software that runs LightHadoop. It is an open source, freely distributed virtualization software. It can be run in the following operating systems: Windows, Mac OS X, Solaris, and numerous Linux builds.

The following steps explain how to install and set up VirtualBox with LightHadoop. This environment is discussed throughout the book to demonstrate how to conduct forensics against a live Hadoop environment:

1. The Oracle VM VirtualBox installation file can be downloaded for free at `www.oracle.com/technetwork/server-storage/virtualbox/downloads/index.html`.

2. After downloading and installing Oracle VM VirtualBox, download the latest LightHadoop VM from `www.lighthadoop.com/downloads/`. Download the Pseudo-Distributed Mode VM version of LightHadoop.

3. Next, load LightHadoop by following these steps:

    1. Run Oracle VM VirtualBox.

    2. Select **File** | **Import Appliance**. Select the location of the **LightHadoop.ova** file, and click **Next**.

3. Review the default settings, and click **Import**.

4. Start the VM and log into LightHadoop. Enter the username as `root` and the password as `lighthadoop`.

LightHadoop can run either as a distributed system or as a single machine. This book uses the Pseudo-Distributed Mode VM version of LightHadoop (that is, single machine) for ease of installation. The same forensic principles apply to both the single machine and distributed system versions.

Amazon Web Services

This book includes a number of examples for performing forensics against cloud-based Hadoop setups. The cloud-based examples utilize **Amazon Web Services** (**AWS**), a cloud-based service that enables one to set up Hadoop solutions and run them in a cloud environment. More organizations are moving their data storage and processing operations to cloud-based environments, and Hadoop is no exception. Forensic investigators should have a strong understanding of the differences between cloud computing and traditional server environments when performing investigations.

AWS enables users to initialize and run storage and computing solutions from a web-based control panel. One of AWS's solutions, **Elastic MapReduce** (**EMR**), is a Hadoop-based environment that can be set up with various Hadoop applications. EMR is the environment used in this book for cloud-based Big Data forensics and HBase collections.

To set up EMR, follow these steps:

1. Create an AWS account at `aws.amazon.com/account`.

2. Create a key pair for **Secure Shell** (**SSH**) login using the following steps:

   1. Navigate to the AWS Console, and click **EC2 Virtual Servers** in the cloud.

   2. Click **Key Pairs**.

   3. Click **Create Key Pair**, and name the key pair.

   4. Copy the key pair PEM created in the previous step to a location where one can load it into the SSH program.

3. Navigate to the **AWS** Console, and click **EMR Managed Hadoop Framework** under the **Analytics** section.

4.   In the EMR console, click **Create cluster** and follow these steps:

1.   Name the cluster and set the S3 folder name. S3 is the storage folder and must be uniquely named across AWS. The following screenshot shows an example:

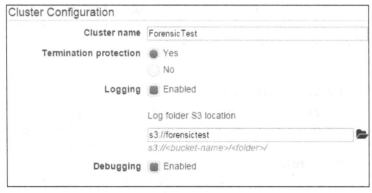

Figure 12: The EMR setup – Part 1

2.   Select the default software configurations, and add HBase as an additional application. The following screenshot shows an example configuration:

Figure 13: The EMR setup – Part 2

3.   Under **Security and Access**, select the EC2 key pair just created.

4.   Leave all other items with their default settings, and click **Create cluster**.

5.   After a few minutes, the cluster will be created. This can be accessed from the EMR **Cluster List** menu once the cluster's status is **Running**.

AWS charges per minute of runtime, whether or not an instance is being accessed. Ensure that all AWS instances are terminated after use to avoid unwanted charges.

The cluster can be accessed from an SSH terminal program such as PuTTY. To access the cluster using PuTTY, follow these steps:

1. Convert the `.pem` key file created previously into a `.ppk` file.

2. Locate the instance's master public **Domain Name System** (**DNS**) in the EMR Cluster List. The following screenshot illustrates an example of configuration:

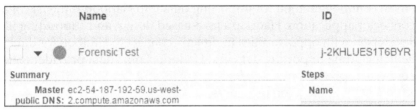

Figure 14: The EMR setup – Part 3

3. Using PuTTY, provide the location of the .ppk key file, and enter the host name as `ec2-user@<Master Public DNS value>`.

4. Connect with those parameters, and the EMR instance will load the Linux session.

Loading Hadoop data

Hadoop offers a number of mechanisms for loading data. The following are the most common methods for importing data into HDFS:

- Copy files from the local filesystem to HDFS

- Use a data transfer tool, such as Sqoop

- Use a Hadoop connector application

- Use a third-party data manager, such as Cloudera or Hortonworks

HDFS has built-in commands that can be used to copy data from the local filesystem. The two commands are as follows:

- hadoop fs -put <local file> <HDFS target location>

- hadoop fs -copyFromLocal <local file> <HDFS target location>

Both the -put and -copyFromLocal commands achieve the same results. The only difference is that -put enables one to copy nonlocal files to HDFS.

Sqoop is an Apache Foundation tool designed to transfer bulk data sets between Hadoop and structured databases. Sqoop can either directly import data into HDFS, or it can import data indirectly by way of a Hive store that is stored in HDFS. Sqoop has the ability to connect to a number of different data sources, such as MySQL and Oracle databases. Sqoop connects to the data source and then efficiently imports the data either directly into HDFS or into HDFS via Hive.

The third most common method for importing data into Hadoop is the use of a Hadoop connector application. Hadoop's Java-based design and supporting libraries provide developers with opportunities to directly connect to Hadoop for data management, including importing data into Hadoop. Some data providers offer Hadoop connector applications. Google, MongoDB, and Oracle are three examples of Hadoop connector application providers.

The fourth method is to use a Hadoop data or file manager. Several major Hadoop distributions offer their own file and data managers that can be used to import and export data from Hadoop. Currently, the most popular Hadoop packages that offer this are Hortonworks and Cloudera.

Methods for exporting or extracting data from HDFS are covered in the subsequent chapters.

Importing sample data for testing

The sample data used in this book is a subset of the New York Stock Exchange ticker data from 2000–2001, which is a freely available data set. The data is available at `https://s3.amazonaws.com/hw-sandbox/tutorial1/NYSE-2000-2001.tsv.gz`. This data contains over 800,000 records, which makes the data large enough to demonstrate concepts, yet manageable enough to learn forensics.

To load the data into AWS, use the following steps:

1. Upload the file to the `/home/ec2-user` folder using an SFTP utility (for example, WinSCP).
2. Log in to the EMR instance via PuTTY.
3. Run the following HDFS -put command:
   ```
   hadoop fs -put /home/ec2-user/NYSE-2000-2001.tsv /tmp
   ```

4. Confirm that the file is now stored in HDFS:

```
hadoop fs -ls /tmp
```

This returns the following output:

```
-rw-r--r--   1 ec2-user supergroup   44005963 2015-01-26 22:23
/tmp/NYSE-2000-2001.tsv
```

To load the data into LightHadoop, access the file from the local filesystem via the mounted drive inside of VirtualBox. Repeat steps 3 and 4 running the HDFS -put command and verifying the file was copied with the HDFS -ls command.

The data is now loaded into HDFS. It can be accessed by Hadoop MapReduce and analysis tools. In subsequent chapters, the data from this exercise is loaded into analysis tools to demonstrate how to extract data from those tools.

Summary

This chapter covered many primary Hadoop concepts that a forensic investigator needs to understand. Successful forensic investigations involve properly identifying and collecting data, which requires the investigator to know how to locate the sources of information in Hadoop as well as understand data structures and the methods for extracting that information. Forensic investigations also involve analyzing the data that has been collected, which in turn requires knowing how to extract information from the Hadoop file structures.

The next chapter discusses how to identify evidence. This process involves standard investigative skills such as conducting interviews as well as applying technical knowledge about Hadoop to identify relevant evidence.

3

Identifying Big Data Evidence

Identifying and fully collecting relevant evidence in the early stages of an investigation is critical to success. Improperly collecting evidence will, at a minimum, result in an embarrassing and difficult process of corrective efforts as well as wasted time. At worst, an improper collection will result in working with the incorrect set of data. In the latter case, court sanctions, lost cases, and ruined reputations can be expected. This chapter provides the guidance to ensure all relevant data is identified, so these situations do not occur.

Identifying evidence

Identifying evidence is a complex process. It involves surveying a set of possible sources of evidence and determining which sources warrant collection. Data in any organization's systems is rarely well organized or documented. Investigators will need to take a set of investigation requirements and determine which data needs to be collected. This requires the following steps:

- Properly reviewing system and data documentation
- Interviewing staff
- Locating backup and noncentralized data repositories
- Previewing data

The process of identifying Big Data evidence is made difficult by the large volume of data, distributed filesystem, the numerous types of data, and the potential for large-scale redundancy in evidence.

Big Data solutions are also unique since evidence can reside in different layers within it. Within Hadoop, evidence can take on multiple forms, as described in *Chapter 2, Understanding Hadoop Internals and Architecture*. To properly identify the evidence in Hadoop, multiple layers are examined. While all the data may reside in the **Hadoop Distributed File System** (**HDFS**), the form may differ in a Hadoop application (for example, HBase), or the data may be more easily extracted to a viable format through HDFS using an application (such as Pig or Sqoop).

Identifying Big Data evidence can also be complicated by redundancies caused by:

- Systems that input to, or receive output from, Big Data systems
- Archived systems that may have previously stored the evidence in the Big Data system

The primary goal of identifying evidence is to capture all relevant evidence while minimizing redundant information. For example, a database may push all sales information into a Hadoop system. The sales database and the sales data in Hadoop may be an exact match, or there may be discrepancies caused by one or both systems updating the data after the push. If the information is identical, collecting both would be redundant, resulting in wasted time and resources. A forensic investigator needs to understand the correct source from which the evidence should be collected or if both sources should be captured.

Outsiders looking at a company's data needs may assume that identifying information is as simple as asking several individuals where the data resides. In reality, the process is much more complicated for a number of possible reasons:

- The organization may be an adverse party and cannot be trusted to provide reliable information about the data
- The organization is large and no single person knows where all data is stored and what the contents of the data are
- The organization is divided into business units with no two business units knowing what data the other one stores
- The data is stored with a third-party data hosting provider
- The IT staff may know where data and systems reside, but only the business users know the type of content the data stores

For example, one might assume a pharmaceutical sales company would have an internal system structured with the following attributes:

- A division where the data is collected from a sales database
- An HR department database containing employee compensation, performance, and retention information
- A database of customer demographic information
- An accounting department database to assess what costs are associated with each sale

In such a system, that data is then clearly unified and compelling analyses are created to drive sales. In reality, an investigator will probably find that the Big Data sales system is actually comprised of a larger set of data that originates inside and outside the organization. There may be a collection of spreadsheets on sales employee's desktops and laptops, along with some of the older versions on backup tapes and file server shared folders. There may be a new Salesforce database implemented two years ago that is incomplete and is actually the replacement for a previous database, which was custom developed and used by 75 percent of employees. A Hadoop instance running HBase for analysis receives a filtered set of data from social media feeds, the Salesforce database, and sales reports. All of these data sources may be managed by different teams, so identifying how to collect this information requires a series of steps to isolate the relevant information.

The problem for large, or even midsize companies is much more difficult than the pharmaceutical sales company example. Simply creating a map of every data source and the contents of those systems could require weeks of in-depth interviews with key business owners and staff. Several departments may have their own databases and Big Data solutions that may or may not be housed in a centralized repository. Backups for these systems could be located anywhere. Data retention policies will vary by department and most likely by system. Data warehouses and other aggregators may contain important information that will not show themselves through normal interviews with staff. These data warehouses and aggregators may have previously generated reports that could serve as valuable reference points for future analysis; however, all data may not be available online, and some data may be inaccessible. In such cases, the company's data will most likely reside in off-site servers maintained by an outsourcing vendor, or worse, in a cloud-based solution.

Big Data evidence can be intertwined with non-Big Data evidence. E-mail, document files, and other evidence can be extremely valuable for performing an investigation. The process for identifying Big Data evidence is very similar to the process for identifying other evidence, so the identification process described in this book can be carried out in conjunction with identifying other evidence. For investigators, an important factor to keep in mind is whether Big Data evidence should be collected (that is, determining whether it is relevant or if the same evidence can be collected more easily from other nonBig Data systems). Investigators must also consider whether evidence needs to be collected to meet the requirements of an investigation.

The approach presented in this book starts with this high-level approach:

- Examining requirements
- Examining the organization's system architecture
- Determining the kinds of data in each system
- Assessing which systems to collect

This approach results in the documentation to back up the claim that all potentially important sources of data were examined and provides assurance that no major systems were overlooked.

The main considerations for each source of data include the following:

- The quality of the data
- The completeness of the data
- The supporting documentation
- Validating the collected data
- The previous systems where the data resided
- How the data enters and leaves the system
- The available formats for extraction
- How well the data meets the data requirements

Locating sources of data

Finding the sources of data to collect is an iterative process. This process includes gathering data requirements, identifying which systems are available, determining which systems contain data that match the requirements, and assessing whether the data in those relevant systems is viable for collection. This top-down approach is represented in detail in the following figure:

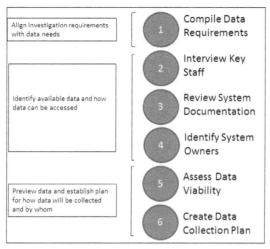

Figure 1: The identification process

Compiling data requirements

The first step is to compile the list of data requirements. For a litigation-related collection, these data requirements are determined based on the merits of the case. In the meet and confer process, the requirements are often quite broad. For a business crisis, all stakeholders should agree on the date range of events, all possible business units involved, and the facts in question. From this, a list of high-level information that could answer the questions should be derived. For example, in an investigation for a financial restatement, the main stakeholders would be accounting, finance, and IT. The time period would be two years before the restatement through the end of the reporting period. The possible high-level information that would be required includes previous financial statements, journal entries, general ledger data, a list of employees involved in the initial financial statement, and a list of file locations for those employees from IT.

The most important aspect of the requirements phase is to be fully inclusive. Being overly inclusive when gathering the requirements is a much easier issue to manage than not being inclusive enough. Paring down overly inclusive requirements is simply a matter of not collecting or analyzing the unnecessary data. If the requirements are not inclusive enough, systems may be ignored and/or large swaths of data could go uncollected. Collecting data a second time or starting over with interviews of key stakeholders is much more expensive and time consuming than simply ignoring parts of the data that have already been collected or omitting certain data ahead of the collection phase. There is a difference between an overly inclusive and a fully inclusive approach. The overly inclusive occurs when little thought is given to the value of the information, whereas the fully inclusive meets all the requirements and even captures the "this might be useful" information as well.

The initial sets of facts that need to be analyzed are typically identified by legal counsel or the business group that identified an issue. A problem requiring Big Data analysis does not originate out of a vacuum, it occurs in a business or legal setting with established rules for addressing the problem. The business and/or legal issues at hand are best identified and framed by a person qualified to address and seek the remedy to a problem. Those people must be heavily involved in the process of distilling issues into facts. They should, however, work with someone well versed in Big Data analysis to understand how those facts will later be proven or disproven by data. A Big Data analyst can provide insights into how data can be used to form the analysis and what the final analysis will consist of, as well as ground the facts in realistic terms about the types of facts the data can prove.

Gathering data requirements begins with fully expanding the issue into the facts that need to be analyzed. Issues can take several forms, but for any issue, the merits of allegation must be distilled into discrete facts that can be proven or disproven. For example, a defendant may be a former employee of the plaintiff and stand accused of stealing sensitive trade secret documents from the plaintiff and implementing a copycat version of the product in 2012. Converting that issue into facts is a process of identifying the manner by which the allegation can be proven or disproven. This issue, while seemingly narrow, can expand into a larger set of sub-issues. First, what are the trade secret documents? What access did the defendant have to the trade secret documents? Could someone else be involved? In what ways are the products similar and different? For all of these questions, what are the specific dates of the alleged activity?

The next step is compiling the Big Data collection requirements based on the facts that have been identified. The facts are converted into data requests that will later be made more specific with the inclusion of system-based information. Taking the preceding example, one requirement would be to identify all trade secret documents stored in the plaintiff's system during the time of the defendant's employment. Another requirement would be to collect all system access records that could show which documents the defendant accessed. Requirements in the early stages should state the desired goal of the data collection without being too specific about the type of system expected to contain the data. Keep in mind that different organizations may store information in different types of systems.

Several standard topics and requirements arise in investigations involving Big Data. The following topics should be addressed at some level in the requirements:

- **Dates in question**: Identify key date ranges as well as surrounding dates in order to test for normal behavior.

- **Persons of interest**: Identify key people by name or behavior and consider including similar, but not "in question" people in order to test for normal behavior.

- **Systems of interest**: Identify the types of systems suspected of containing key information. Also, consider upstream and downstream systems that may validate or refute the targeted system's data.

Reviewing the system architecture

The system architecture review phase involves meeting with company and department heads and reviewing documentation about the available systems. The goal of this phase is to have a high-level understanding of the sources and types of data available along with the key personnel and business owners. The first step is to meet with the appropriate high-level employees to either get the necessary high-level information or to identify the appropriate person with whom to speak. Some examples of the first people to interview include:

- CIO/CTO

- The CFO

- The IT/Financial Audit manager

- The Information Systems manager

- The HR manager

- The Subject Matter manager (for example, head of engineering or pharmaceutical development)

The interviews for the high-level personnel are typically brief. It is important to stress the importance of the interview to the interviewee and also to ask the same list of questions to each. While one interviewee may have told the investigator about a particular system, he may have a limited view or knowledge of the system. As such, asking the same question to multiple interviewees can result in a more complete and accurate answer. Several of the important topics to cover in the interview include:

- Which systems definitely contain data pertaining to the requirements?

- What is the size of each of those systems (number of records, size on disk, and so on)?

- Who are the IT and business owners of each system?

- What other systems might contain information pertaining to the requirements?

- Who else might know of systems that pertain to the requirements?

- Are there any known data quality or completeness issues related to the system?

Collecting documentation is critical throughout the data location process, but it is especially critical in the early stages to help identify sources of data that might have slipped the attention of the interviewees. Ask each interviewee to provide all requested documentation. If they are unable to provide any, ask them who would be able to, or have them request the documentation from their team. The following types of documentation can be extremely helpful:

- System architecture diagrams
- Database listings
- Database diagrams
- IT budgets (to identify Big Data hardware expenditures)
- Software versions, specifications, and implementation details

To conclude the system architecture review phase, fully document all interviews that were conducted, being sure to note who was interviewed, when, by whom, and what was covered. Also, be sure to note action items and any additional details of note. Next, compile the list of additional points of contact and schedule interviews with them. Finally, review all documentation, and create an initial spreadsheet about each system mentioned, including all details pertaining to them.

Interviewing staff and reviewing the documentation

The staff interview and documentation review process has the following goals:

- To clearly define the scope of what needs to be collected
- To identify data limitations
- To construct a collection plan that will either be carried out by internal staff or external analysts

The process consists of using the initial scope created in the system architecture review phase, fleshing out the details by speaking to lower-level staff, and examining the data. In addition, it is critical to fully document any data gaps, such as missing backups, purged data, or data made inaccessible by the software. Finally, create a plan detailing every step of the collection, including means for logging the process and collecting control numbers and error messages. This can be accomplished by fully reviewing all documentation and working closely with the IT personnel responsible for the data.

Staff are typically the ones who best understand the details of the available data and business processes. They work with the data, in the processes, and execute the procedures. Key staff members have already been identified or previously interviewed before the staff interview process, so the C-suite staff most likely do not need to be interviewed again. The staff interview process focuses on the day-to-day operations personnel. Examples of the staff that should be interviewed include:

- Manager-level staff
- The top technical and IT staff, including database administrators and programmers
- The HR personnel (for employee information and identifying additional staff for interviews)
- The subject matter experts for the matter in question (for example, financial analysts, accountants, and engineers)

The focus of the interviews is to identify relevant data sources, possible approaches to acquire the data, and any limitations or caveats that apply to the data. Most of the relevant systems have already been identified. Follow up with the interviewees about these systems to find out more information about the systems. Determine what the standard business process is for the system, such as how data gets created and imported into the systems, how data in the system is used, and data or reports generated from the systems. Business-side interviewees are critical for understanding how the systems are used, so ask key questions about the processes that exist.

Technical staff, such as database administrators, are the best source of information for understanding the data life cycle and how to potentially extract data from the source systems. Retention policies are an important issue to cover in technical interviews. Does the source system have a data purge policy that automatically removes data of a certain age from the system? If so, does an archive version of the data exist in a different system or on backup media? Likewise, ask if any retired or archived systems that may contain relevant information are available. In addition, not all systems provide a method for quick and easy data extraction. Discuss with the technical interviewee what the possible approaches are for extracting the data. Big Data systems have a number of methods for data extraction, though some may impact business operations more than others. Communicate the time requirements, and establish conservative time estimates for how long extracting the data will take.

All available documentation should be requested in every interview. Documentation provides additional information about systems, and it can serve as a road map for understanding business processes, system interrelationships, and the details of how data are stored in the systems. Ideally, interviews are only conducted once, so requesting the documentation during or before the interview will reduce the need for a follow-up interview.

Investigators will want to request the following documentation in the staff interviews:

- The business and subject matter experts
    - ○ Policy and procedure documents
    - ○ Business process guides and manuals
    - ○ Application manuals
    - ○ Sample reports
    - ○ Organization chart
- The technical and IT Staff
    - ○ Data dictionaries
    - ○ Entity-relationship diagrams
    - ○ Schema documentation
    - ○ Descriptions of coded values stored in the database
    - ○ System architecture diagrams
    - ○ System manuals
    - ○ Data retention policies
    - ○ Summary of user access rights and security rules
    - ○ Application listings

No interview can be truly complete and answer all questions that may ever arise. The focus of the interview, however, is to get a deep enough understanding of the systems and available data to firmly establish which sources of data are relevant, how the data can be extracted, and which business rules were in place to create and make use of the data. Focusing on those critical questions will streamline the process. Some interviews can only be performed once, especially in cases of a hostile client or a company that will be terminating that person's employment. Conducting the interview with the mindset of having only one shot at it makes for a more complete and informative interview. If there is the opportunity for a future follow-up interview, remember to collect that person's e-mail and phone information, and express that a future interview may be required.

The following figure is a sample questionnaire with initial questions for interviewing a database administrator:

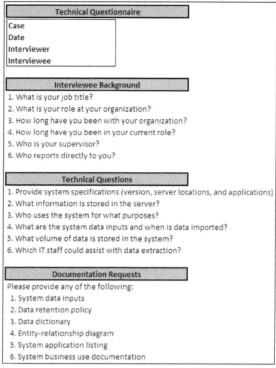

Figure 2: A sample questionnaire

Assessing data viability

Assessing the viability of data serves several purposes such as the following:

- It allows the investigator to identify which data sources are potentially relevant
- It yields information that can corroborate the interview and documentation review information
- It highlights data limitations or gaps
- It provides the investigator with information to create a better data collection plan

Up until this point in the investigation, the investigator has only gathered information about the data. Previewing and assessing samples of the data gives the investigator the chance to actually see what information is contained in the data and determine which data sources can meet the requirements of the investigation.

Assessing the viability and relevance of data in a Big Data forensic investigation is different from that of a traditional digital forensic investigation. In a traditional digital forensic investigation, the data is typically not previewed out of fear of altering the data or metadata. With Big Data, however, the data can be previewed in some situations where metadata is not relevant or available. This factor opens up the opportunity for a forensic investigator to preview data when identifying which data should be collected.

There are several methods for previewing data. The first is to review a data extract or the results of a query, or collect sample text files that are stored in Hadoop. This method allows the investigator to determine the types of information available and how the information is represented in the data. In highly complex systems consisting of thousands of data sources, this may not be feasible or it might require a significant investment of time and effort.

 Querying Hadoop databases such as HBase and Hive are covered in the later chapters.

The second method is to review reports or canned query output that were derived from the data. Some Big Data solutions are designed with reporting applications connected to the Big Data system. These reports are a powerful tool, enabling an investigator to quickly gain an understanding of the contents of the system without requiring much up-front effort to gain access to the systems.

Data retention policies and data purge schedules should be reviewed and considered in this step as well. Given the large volume of data involved, many organizations routinely purge data after a certain period of time.

Data purging can mean the archival of data to near-line or offline storage, or it can mean the destruction of old data without backup. When data is archived, the investigator should also determine whether any of the data in near-line or offline backup media needs to be collected or whether the live system data is sufficient. Regardless, the investigator should determine what the next purge cycle is and whether that necessitates an expedited collection to prevent loss of critical information. Additionally, the investigator should determine whether the organization should implement a litigation hold, which halts data purging during the investigation. When data is purged without backup, the investigator must determine:

- How the purge affects the investigation
- When the data needs to be collected
- Whether supplemental data sources must be collected to account for the lost data (for example, reports previously created from the purged data or other systems that created or received the purged data)

The following figure is a high-level depiction of the various sources of information and methods for assessing the data in the identification phase:

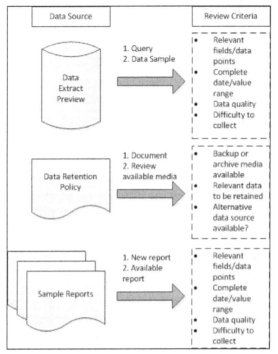

Figure 3: The data assessment process

Identifying data sources in noncooperative situations

Not all investigations involve a cooperative organization with staff who can be interviewed. Most investigations have one or several of the following types of staff:

- **Cooperative**: Willing to be interviewed and unlikely to attempt to hide or destroy evidence or attempt to deceive the investigator

- **Hostile/Adverse**: Somewhat willing or unwilling to be interviewed and likely to attempt to hide or destroy evidence or attempt to deceive the investigator

- **Unavailable**: Staff knowledgeable of the evidence but unavailable to be interviewed (for example, the company went bankrupt or potential interviewees are in police custody)

Identifying evidence when the staff members are either unavailable , hostile, or adverse is more difficult. Each of these cases requires a specific approach. First, working with hostile or adverse staff poses problems with the identification of evidence and the availability and veracity of the data. Hostile staff members are more likely to cause problems with the identification of data by giving incomplete or dishonest answers to questions or by hindering access to systems. Hostile staff members may feel encumbered, annoyed, or somehow inconvenienced by the investigation and will act accordingly. They should still be interviewed because they may provide useful information that can be validated.

Strategies for dealing with hostile staff include the following:

- Conducting a standard investigation with interviews of other staff and review of documentation
- Expressing to the interviewee the importance of the investigation and all the ramifications that may exist for their noncompliance
- Verifying the interviewee's answers with those of other interviewees
- Cross-validating data from systems owned or accessed by the interviewee with other data sources

Adverse staff members are also likely to be difficult and may not be trustworthy. In addition, they may carry out actions that could affect the investigation. Adverse staff members may be subjects of the investigation, or they may be negatively affected by the outcome of the investigation. For example, in the Bernard Madoff Ponzi scheme investigation, key programmers and IT personnel were both parties to the litigation as well as some of the only staff with information pertaining to key programs and data. Adverse staff members should be interviewed, but their answers require careful scrutiny and verification. In addition, they may carry out actions to alter or destroy the data or create new data to stymie the investigator.

Strategies for dealing with adverse staff include the following:

- Expediting the collection of potentially relevant data and/or freezing all adverse staff's access to the data
- Conducting a standard investigation by interviewing other staff members and reviewing the documentation (if possible)
- Expressing to the interviewee the importance of the investigation and all the ramifications that may exist for their noncompliance

- Verifying the interviewee's answers with those of other interviewees
- Cross-validating data from systems owned or accessed by the interviewee with other data sources

The third scenario is where no or limited staff members are available for interviews. This can arise in situations such as:

- Bankruptcy
- All staff members are subject to the investigation and refuse to cooperate
- No staff members knowledgeable about the data or systems are available

This scenario requires placing more of an emphasis on the review of documentation and the previewing of system data. This scenario also requires much more time for the investigator. The time saved by having someone knowledgeable identify the systems is replaced with reviewing even more documentation and determining the type of data available in each system. For Big Data, this is not overly problematic, because there are typically only several Hadoop instances. However, identifying all of the underlying data and Hadoop applications requires significant effort.

Strategies for handling situations where staff members are not available include the following:

- Collecting and reviewing key system-related documentation
- Identifying the location (physical or logical) of systems and data sources
- Performing a detailed review of data in the identified systems

Data collection requirements

Detailing the data collection is a process that involves assimilating all information from the client interviews and gathered documentation to form a precise plan and set of requirements for collecting all relevant data. The requirements should be in clear, plain language that can be understood by anyone. Complex requirements in highly technical or legal language can result in a misunderstanding between the investigator and the data collector. Be sure to state the relevant facts about the types of data that need to be collected, and explicitly spell out all supporting documentation requests and considerations.

The data collection stage involves identifying data source information as well as working with both structured and unstructured data. The following sections cover these topics in detail.

Data source identification

Based on the facts and issues identified in the initial stages, list all systems that could potentially contain relevant information. The system documentation and interview information will provide a wealth of necessary, semi-useful, and extraneous data. Obviously, the investigator will need to include the necessary data sources in the data collection requirements. However, the question of whether to include the semi-useful and extraneous data sources is centered on the data size and the time limitations of the investigation. There may be the potential for additional analysis that was not deemed essential during the initial stages.

When a system contains semi-useful data, several questions should be answered as follows:

- Does the necessary data source contain information that can address all facts? If not, does the semi-useful data source address any of the remaining facts?
- Is the effort required to collect the semi-useful data minimal, and is the data volume manageable?
- Does the semi-useful data source serve as a bridge between the necessary data sources, or does it serve to fill a gap or address a data weakness in the necessary data?

If the answer to any of these questions is yes, then the investigator should consider including the semi-useful data in the data collection. The reasons for this include:

- The semi-useful data is actually necessary
- The data collection impact is minimal, and it doesn't hurt to include the data
- The semi-useful data serve a secondary role in enabling the analysis to be performed with the necessary data

 Plan for data gaps and anomalies. Assume that the system(s) will have data issues. Collecting data from multiple systems can allow for validating data across systems and can cover gaps in data.

The investigator should carefully consider any data that is deemed non-relevant during the data collection phase. The risk of not collecting data during the initial stages is that there will not be a second chance to collect it. The data may be deleted or modified later, and another opportunity to collect the data may not exist. The timing of performing a second data collection may hamper analysis at a later stage.

Consider the following when determining whether a data source is unnecessary:

- What information does the data contain?
- Is the data completely redundant to another data source that will be collected?
- Will the data still exist in its current form at a later date?

Even if the data source is unnecessary, the investigator should document the answers to those questions. Ignoring a data source can require justification at a later stage. Documenting the reasons when the information is first made available will help the investigator provide a clear answer should any questions be asked at a later stage.

Regardless of the type of data source, document the following about each data source:

- The official name of the data source
- The data source owner(s)
- The description of the type of information the data source contains
- The type of data source (for example, HBase database)
- The data volume: size on disk and number of records
- The method for data extraction
- The effort required for extraction: man-hours, system impact, and total time
- The associated costs for extraction

Structured and unstructured data

Chapter 1, Starting Out with Forensic Investigations and Big Data, covered the concepts of structured and unstructured data. However, the line between the two can become extremely blurred when collecting Big Data. Both structured and unstructured data can be stored in a Big Data system. The investigator needs to understand the difference between these forms and whether data should be collected in a structured or unstructured format. Structured data offers the advantage of easier analysis, but collecting unstructured data in its original form can be faster and may contain more content.

Big Data systems can include data in numerous forms. Unstructured text files can be imported, stored, and queried in Hadoop. This unstructured data can then be transformed into a structured form or otherwise combined with other data sources. The investigator should be aware of the various structures of the data that is to be identified and collected.

Some forms of unstructured and semi-structured data fall under the umbrella of a structured data analysis in later stages. For example, users at a company may maintain a set of delimited or markup files for accounting purposes. These files, while technically considered unstructured, contain structured data. Ignoring these files would not be prudent simply because they were stored in an unstructured file format. Instead, the spreadsheets should be collected and later transformed into a structured format for analysis. The following table shows the format of the data contained in a delimited file:

CustNum	Name	Addr1	City	State	Zip	Notes
1000011	John Doe	123 Main St	Centreville	VA	55555	Paid on time
1000012	Jane Doe	123 Main St	Centreville	VA	55555	Delinquent; follow-up required
1000013	Joe Doe	456 Center Rd	Anytown	GA	55554	N/A
1000014	Jill Doe	456 Center Rd	Anytown	GA	55554	Call 5551230002

Unstructured data do not have the same rules and composition restrictions that structured data have. This lack of rigidity and structure allows data to be stored and presented in varied ways. Some of the most common forms of unstructured data include:

- E-mail
- Presentation documents
- Video and audio files
- Textual documents (for example, MS Word documents and PDF files)
- Graphics files
- Executable binary files (for example, Windows .EXE files)

Some forms of these files may contain structured information, despite being unstructured or semi-structured files. Client interviews should allow the investigator to determine whether these files should be collected and whether an option exists for collecting the data in a structured or unstructured form. For example, unstructured text files can be stored in an HDFS, but this data can be collected in a structured form via Hive or Sqoop. The investigator also needs to consider how to validate collected data, which is easier if the entire unstructured file is collected.

The next three chapters provide information on how to choose the proper method for collecting both structured and unstructured data.

Data collection types

Two primary categories of data collections can be made. First, the data collection can be performed by the investigator. In this situation, the investigator performs the forensic collection by accessing the source systems and collects the data for offline analysis. Alternatively, in some cases, such as civil litigation, the investigator can request the system owner or third-party to collect the data. In such cases, the investigator may oversee, advise, or simply be a passive participant in the collection process.

The requirements of the investigation dictate which option is chosen. Investigator-led collections have the advantage of being correctly performed and verifiable. The investigator knows what data needs to be collected and performs the collection using best practices. Because the investigator is unbiased, the collection is less likely to be questioned. An organization-led or third-party collection has the advantages of potentially being cheaper and less disruptive to the organization. The disadvantages are the collection may not be performed correctly, data may be accidentally or intentionally altered, and the collection may not be performed as quickly. The individual investigation requirements such as investigation issues, time considerations, and cost factors are the ultimate arbiter that determines who should perform the collection.

In-house or third-party collection

Having an internal organization collect its own data or relying on a third-party to perform the collection is contingent on carefully specified requirements. Criminal and civil cases involving forensics routinely involve data collected by someone other than the investigator. Under certain circumstances and after carefully documenting requirements, someone other than the investigator can successfully perform a data collection. The key is to properly identify the data sources, the specific data points, and any filters that are required. Also, the investigator must make it clear to the party collecting the data that the evidence cannot be modified. The investigator may need to train the party performing the collection on best practices. From there, a detailed data collection request can be delivered to the party conducting the data collection.

The types of data to request

Multiple types of data requests can be made. Some investigations are simple and only involve a single data source, such as a single Hive database. Data requests for investigations with a single data source (for example, one database) are much faster and simpler than investigations whose data span multiple systems. Each of the data sources identified can be categorized to simplify the way in which the requests are written.

The main types of requests are:

- Loose files (for example, XML or JSON files)
- Entire databases
- Specific database tables
- Specific types of records from multiple database tables
- Specific records from a single database table

Evaluate each of the data sources deeply to identify the type of data request each is. Documenting this level of detail allows the data collector to better identify collection options.

A data request involving loose files will need to address the following:

- Filenames, folder names, and/or file share locations
- File types (for example, text files or spreadsheets)
- File versions
- Date ranges for file creation or last update

Requesting the collection of an entire database server is straightforward; the investigator just needs to state the name of the server and the format of the extracted data.

Requesting specific objects from a database is a more complex request. It is performed when only specific information is needed from the data source and when the volume of data of the entire data source is too great to extract everything at once. Databases can store terabytes to petabytes of data in tens of thousands of objects. Extracting all the information can be an overly burdensome request that would negatively affect business operations or would take too much time. As such, targeted data collections can be performed instead to limit the impact to the data source and business operations, as well as reduce the amount of time to perform the extraction and transfer the data. The request for the individual objects from a database should explicitly state which objects are needed and spell out any filtering criteria that need to be applied.

The data collection request

The data collection request document is a formal document that clearly presents all collection request details and the parties responsible. The keys to a successful data collection request document are:

- Clear, plain requirements

- Specifics (for example, system name and output format)
- Accountability
- Stating deadlines
- Standardized requests

One example of a poor data collection request would consist of an e-mail to a database administrator requesting "all records in 2008 related to sales". The database administrator, in this example, would be left to make a judgment call about the nature of the request. The "2008" portion of the request may result in the DBA providing all sales records that were fulfilled in 2008, rather than all possible orders, including cancellations. In addition, the DBA may not properly capture all types of records that would relate to sales, such as inventory records and customer communications. Moreover, the DBA may provide the extract in a cumbersome data format and assume that he has three weeks to complete the request. Any of these miscommunications can result in a failed investigation.

Instead, the request should be very specific, assign a deadline, and be in a standardized request format. The specifics of the request depend on the type of system being collected; however, several types of details are typically presented:

- The exact servers, databases, and tables from which to exact the data. If backup media are involved, clearly explain which backup media to use.
- The fields to collect.
- The types of date and user restriction criteria. For example, all records with a "date ordered" between 2008 and 2010, or all records with a "last updated by" a Miami office user.
- Look up or code definition tables that provide detail on embedded code meanings.

Clearly identifying people responsible for each task and assigning their deadline is critical. Most investigations are time sensitive, so having clearly defined deadlines can help eliminate surprises and help set expectations so the analysis can be performed on time. Communicating with only the person responsible for the task may not be sufficient; consider including their boss and/or general counsel to ensure others are aware of the deadline and can help push the request along. While seemingly insignificant, specifying the output format can also avoid unwanted surprises when the data is delivered. The investigator's analysis tool may not support the data in the format provided, which would require an entirely new data extraction to be performed. The person providing the data may supply the data in a proprietary database format, whereas the investigator may need the data in a pipe-delimited text file with double quote text qualifiers. Establishing the desired format up front is critical to avoiding such problems.

The language of the request should be understandable to anyone involved. A DBA and a lawyer should both have a complete understanding of the request. Including legal language in a data request is a simple way to confuse IT staff, while including highly technical language will confound an attorney. Stating a precise technical request such as "left join table 1 to table 2 on non-null values in field X" will make sense to someone well versed in databases, but that language is meaningless to outsiders. Instead, make the requests in plain English so that anyone can understand what needs to be collected. Avoid using jargons such as "left join." In this example, the investigator would want to rephrase the request to say "include all records from table 1 and also provide any matches between table 1 and 2 on records that match in the field X when that field is populated in both tables. Include records from table 1 when no matches exist in table 2." While wordier, the language is precise and its meaning is not dependent on legal or technical translation.

Collecting the correct documentation about the collection is critical for later verifying that the collection was performed correctly. The collection will need to be verified, so information about how the collection was performed as well as when, and by whom, is needed to ensure the collection was performed correctly and completely. Control totals and information about how much data was collected is also later used to verify that all data was correctly collected and loaded into an analysis platform.

Specify all required documentation related to the data collection in the request. Requesting documentation that pertains to what was collected and the method used to collect it will be important when verifying the data collection. It will also serve later to prove that the data was properly and completely collected.

The first form of collection documentation includes the query files used to extract the data or the log files that show what was collected. The queries are the logic run that determine what types of records were pulled. A review of the query files will show how the extraction was performed. The result is then cross-validated with the requirements to prove that the correct logic was applied. Log files, likewise, are used when the extraction was performed without a query. The log files are generally created through database backups or automated extraction programs. These logs will show when the data was extracted, by whom, how many objects and records were extracted, and if any filter criteria were applied.

Control totals and hash values are an important component of collection documentation and should be included in the request. Hash values are typically the MD5 or SHA-1 computed values for a file or data container. These are collected when information is collected either from the host operating system or HDFS. Control totals are computed and collected when data is collected from other means most often from databases via queries. No best practice rules exist that precisely outline what needs to be collected, but at a minimum, the number of records, tables or schemas, and/or databases should be collected. In addition, collecting computed values is useful for proving that key fields or records were not altered. For example, standard methods for validating that a collection was performed properly include computing the summed value of a key numeric column or computing the list of distinct names and the number of records per name.

Screenshots and server logs are also useful forms of documentation. The screenshots can show the steps taken to perform the collection. Screenshots can also be taken to gather control totals from system monitor applications or other utilities. Screenshots are valuable when collecting control totals or logs is difficult or infeasible. Server logs can also contain valuable control total information that can be more easily collected than control totals. If server logs contain the necessary information and are easily obtained, an investigator should consider requesting these in lieu of control totals.

Several other key requirements should be specified to avoid confusion or delays in the collection:

- Specify the output format of data (for example, CSV)
- Request column headers and field definitions
- Note any data limitation requirements (for example, do not include **personally identifiable information** (**PII**), such as SSN)
- Specify how to transfer data (for example, encrypted hard drive or **Secure File Transfer Protocol** (**SFTP**))
- Provide a standardized data collection form for the collector to fill out

The following figure shows a sample data collection request document that can be adjusted to the requirements of the request being made:

Data Collection Request	
Date Request Deadline Requester	Background:
To: Name Company Division Address Line 1 Address Line 2 Email	Deliver To: Name Company Division Address Line 1 Address Line 2 Email

Request 1	
System Name	
System Owner	
System Type	
Collection Method	
Database(s)	
Table(s)/Schema(s)	
Data Volume	
Field(s)	
Filter Criteria	
Date Ranges	
Documentation to Provide	
Additional Detail Required	

Figure 5: The data collection request form

An investigator-led collection

In the identification phase, an investigator-led collection is virtually identical to a collection performed in-house or by a third party. An investigator who intends to perform the collection should also draft a collection plan that specifies the same information as a data request document. This document should clearly outline the following:

- What information needs to be collected

- The steps that will be taken to collect the information
- How the collection process will be documented

Depending on the nature of the investigation, an investigator may want to share the collection plan with the owners of the systems to ensure that all systems will be made available. This will also help minimize any potential disruption to the organization.

The next three chapters detail the steps necessary for an investigator to perform the data collection. The remaining chapters cover the analysis and presentation phases, which apply to both an investigator-led collection and collections performed by other parties.

The chain of custody documentation

The chain of custody documentation needs to be established as soon as evidence is collected. If a collection is being performed by in-house staff or a third-party, chain of custody forms should be filled out by the person performing the collection and anyone who takes possession of the evidence. The chain of custody documentation is a chronological history that shows who had possession of the evidence. This is important in both criminal and civil investigations to prove who had access to the evidence and who could have potentially altered the evidence. Every time the evidence is exchanged between two people, the chain of custody documentation should be updated to document when the transfer occurred and who was involved. The following figure is a sample chain of custody document:

Date/Time	Released by	Received by	Purpose
	Name	Name	☐ Analysis ☐ Create Image ☐ Lock Up/Storage
	Signature	Signature	☐ Transfer ☐ Release to Client ☐
	Name	Name	☐ Analysis ☐ Create Image ☐ Lock Up/Storage
	Signature	Signature	☐ Transfer ☐ Release to Client ☐
	Name	Name	☐ Analysis ☐ Create Image ☐ Lock Up/Storage
	Signature	Signature	☐ Transfer ☐ Release to Client ☐
	Name	Name	☐ Analysis ☐ Create Image ☐ Lock Up/Storage
	Signature	Signature	☐ Transfer ☐ Release to Client ☐

Figure 6: The chain of custody form

Summary

The data identification phase is an iterative process of locating sources of information about potentially relevant data. Part art and part science, data identification requires making use of available sources of information. Data identification first establishes the full set of data sources, who owns those data sources, and what the data sources contain. From there, an investigator can home in on exactly what information is available in each data source and determine what information from each data source needs to be collected. Big Data systems are voluminous and collecting petabytes of data is rarely a viable option, so an investigator needs to exert caution when determining what data to collect. However, that caution has to be tempered with the need to completely collect relevant data the first time because that data may not be available after the collection process is finished.

The next two chapters explain how to collect the forensic evidence identified by the steps in this chapter. The next chapter covers forensic collection of the HDFS layer, which involves both traditional and Big Data-specific forensic techniques to collect bit- and file-level evidence.

4
Collecting Hadoop Distributed File System Data

The **Hadoop Distributed File System (HDFS)** is the primary source of evidence in a Hadoop forensic investigation. Whether Hadoop data is used in Hive, HBase, or a custom Java application, the data is stored in HDFS. This means the forensic evidence can be collected from HDFS. Investigators can take two collection approaches: collect HDFS data from the host operating system or directly from Hadoop.

The advantage of collecting from HDFS is investigators can collect much more data than they can from a data analysis layer or application layer. Some potentially relevant data can only be collected through HDFS. This includes metadata, configuration files, user files that were not imported into an application, custom scripts, and other information. In some forensic investigations, this otherwise ancillary data can be crucial for determining how the system operated and how the system was used.

Collecting evidence from HDFS can be more time- and effort-intensive than collecting the evidence from a Hadoop application. HDFS evidence is the raw data, and that data can be voluminous and distributed across a number of nodes. Collecting data from HDFS in a Hadoop cluster with over 100 nodes can require going to each node and collecting all of the individual data with that data later being pieced together for analysis. Both the collection and analysis of the data can require much more time and effort than a collection involving querying the relevant data out of Hive, for example.

As a distributed system, collecting HDFS data may require collecting data from each node. Both the NameNode and DataNodes contain potentially relevant information. Collecting HDFS data can involve collecting from each node separately for certain collection approaches. Depending on the collection method and Hadoop architecture, this can be difficult. With cloud-based storage and geographically disparate systems, the collection can require extra time to complete or it may be altogether impossible if the evidence cannot be located. A distributed architecture can require multiple different collection approaches or at least a more complex and time-consuming process.

HDFS data can be collected in several different ways as follows:

1. Take a complete forensic image of the host operating system and all attached Hadoop storage for all nodes.

2. Mount HDFS to the host operating system and image the mounted drives for all nodes.

3. Make a logical copy of all HDFS files and directories.

4. Take a targeted collection of only the relevant files.

Throughout this chapter, references are made to the various Hadoop layers and different techniques for collecting data from HDFS. Conceptually, all Hadoop data should be thought of as residing in disk storage accessible from the host operating system. That data can be collected in numerous ways from each layer. Each collection method has its pros and cons, and an investigator must weigh these in accordance with the circumstances and requirements of the investigation.

This chapter covers the techniques used for collecting HDFS evidence. The greatest challenge to collecting HDFS evidence is collecting them from multiple nodes. So in this chapter, we'll spend time on how to handle this situation. We also cover the following topics:

- Collecting HDFS data from the host operating system using HDFS mounting tools

- Collecting HDFS data through the Hadoop command line

- Capturing metadata

- Using Sqoop to collect HDFS data

- Collecting HDFS evidence from remote storage (such as Amazon's S3 storage)

Forensically collecting a cluster system

Collecting Hadoop data requires acquiring data across multiple cluster nodes. Hadoop's cluster design is structured, so data is distributed across multiple nodes. With the potential for node failure, that data is also redundantly stored across nodes. For a forensic investigator, this means data collection involves collecting data from most or all of the nodes.

In traditional forensic investigations, a single machine or server array is acquired. An investigator can pull the hard drive and perform a physical acquisition of the hard drive. The investigator may not be permitted to turn off the server and pull the server's hard drives. However, the investigator can access the server and collect the server data and any data on attached storage devices.

For Hadoop, or any cluster system, this is rarely the case. A Hadoop cluster may have a series of connected nodes, or its nodes could be geographically distributed. Regardless, multiple nodes are connected through Hadoop, and these nodes may not be connected in a way that is accessible through the host operating system. The volume of data stored by Hadoop can make the full collection of all nodes infeasible, and the data stored in HDFS is obscured by the Hadoop layer. These factors require an investigator to approach Hadoop collections differently from non-cluster server collections.

Several options exist for collecting Hadoop cluster data:

- Collect data from the host operating system individually for each node
- Collect data from HDFS using a Hadoop client
- Collect data from Hadoop applications (for example, HBase)

The first option, and the most difficult and time-consuming, is collecting data from the host operating system individually for each node. This method requires the investigator to collect the HDFS data stored on each node from the host operating system. This can either be achieved by imaging the Hadoop partitions or by performing a targeted collection of the HDFS data containers from the host operating system. The drawback to this method is that every node in the cluster must be identified and collected. For example, if a cluster has 50 nodes, all 50 nodes must be collected. This method is useful and sometimes required when the Hadoop cluster is offline, such as when there is a concern the Hadoop cluster data may be modified or lost if it is left or brought online. This method also preserves metadata and enables investigators to use forensic tools such as dd for the collection.

Data can be lost when Hadoop is taken offline. This topic is covered in the discussion on `fsimage` and `edits` files in the section *Hadoop offline image and edits viewers*. The second option is collecting HDFS data by connecting to the cluster from a Hadoop client. This method has a great advantage. An investigator can perform the collection from a single machine while preserving the metadata. The process involves collecting evidence through the Hadoop command line. If the NameNode and all DataNodes are online and accessible, this method enables the investigator to capture all online data and its metadata without having to collect from each individual DataNode. This method is only viable when the NameNode and all of the required DataNodes are online.

The third option is collecting data from Hadoop applications. Rather than collect data from the host operating system or directly from HDFS, collecting from applications often meets the requirements of an investigation. Big Data investigations typically hinge on the contents of the data in the system applications, and not on the metadata. This method involves collecting data through the applications, usually via queries or data extracts. The drawback is that metadata, deleted data, and other forensic artifacts are not collected. This, however, is not always an issue with Big Data investigations. In fact, collecting data from applications is the preferred method for many types of investigations in which the contents of the system are the prime evidence.

A hybrid approach can also be applied. An investigator need not be limited to only one option. If the primary data of interest can be accessed from an application, but Hadoop log data is also of value, the investigator can use two methods—one to forensically collect from the application and one to forensically collect the log data. Typically, an investigator only uses one method. However, best practice supports a hybrid approach when practical factors dictate that an investigator use multiple approaches to meet the requirements of the investigation.

For a host operating system collection, acquire means a forensic acquisition or targeted collection. For a Hadoop client collection, acquire means to perform a file-based targeted collection. For a Hadoop application collection, acquire means using a query-based acquisition method. Note that the use of **Acquire** in the illustration means something different in each method. The following figure illustrates the differences between these three methods:

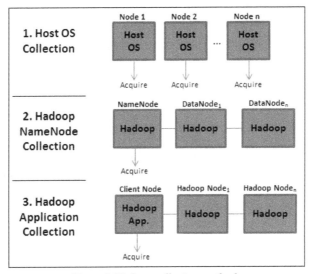

Figure 1: Hadoop collection methods

Another consideration with Hadoop collections is non-HDFS storage. Hadoop can work with data outside of HDFS by importing input data, analyzing the data, and then deleting the input data. In addition to inputs, Hadoop output can be stored outside of HDFS. Hadoop applications can generate analysis that gets transferred outside of HDFS for further analysis or data storage. HDFS data can also be archived outside of HDFS for data retention purposes.

Investigators need to be mindful of these possibilities and ensure that data outside of HDFS is properly identified so they can make the correct determination about collecting the data. Failing to collect the HDFS inputs and outputs can result in an incomplete collection, and subsequently, the analysis will be incomplete as well.

 Instances of non-HDFS data input and output data storage can be located during the identification phase by analyzing scripts and interviewing personnel.

Physical versus remote collections

Hadoop data collection can either be performed directly on the Hadoop cluster or via remote access. Physical collections are any form of data acquisition in which the investigator is physically interacting with the cluster, typically by pulling the cluster's hard drives and imaging them. Alternatively, collections can also be performed remotely. In such cases, the investigator accesses the cluster through a network connection and acquires the data through a terminal over the network connection.

Hadoop can be run in many different designs and configurations. The Hadoop cluster can be run on physical devices with Hadoop being installed on the host operating system. Hadoop clusters can also be set up using a series of virtual machines. With the increased use of cloud computing, Hadoop also can be run as a **Platform as a Service (PaaS)** with the actual servers running Hadoop being masked by the abstraction of the cloud service. Additionally, Hadoop can be designed and run as a combination of these configurations.

The different Hadoop designs have their own issues for forensic collections. Hadoop clusters installed on the host operating system are the most straightforward of the designs for an investigator to collect. With this design, the investigator has the option to pull the hard drives and collect the data in one of three ways: through the host operating system, through the Hadoop command line, or by running an application-based acquisition. With virtual machines, the collection and analysis phases are more difficult if the investigator wishes to pull the hard drives. In such situations, the investigator needs to acquire the entire set of drives that contain the virtual machines and then carve out the relevant data from each of the virtual machines. This can require the investigator to install the same virtual machine host software to access the virtual machine data. Finally, cloud or PaaS acquisitions limit the investigator's ability to physically access the machine. In this situation, the investigator is typically limited to command-line or application-based acquisitions. Even in these cases, the cloud or PaaS service provider may have applied security limitations that prevent software from being loaded or certain system files from being accessed.

Non-local or offline storage is also a major consideration in Hadoop investigations. The massive data volumes stored in Hadoop make on-site, physical storage of all data infeasible for some organizations. Some organizations choose to store parts of Hadoop data offline. This data can either be HDFS or non-HDFS data. In either case, the information can be relevant for an investigation. Even if all HDFS data is stored on-site and is physically accessible, other data can be stored off-site, either within that organization's systems or with a third-party provider.

HDFS collections through the host operating system

The host operating system is where many traditional forensic investigations begin and end. The forensic evidence resides in disk storage accessible by the host operating system, which stores metadata about the evidence that cannot be accessed from other layers. The same cannot necessarily be said for Hadoop, but there are methods for collecting HDFS data from the host operating system.

Currently, HDFS is not natively recognized by any of the modern operating systems, so HDFS cannot be natively accessed by the host operating system as a filesystem. HDFS is stored in the host operating system's filesystem, but this information resides in the allocated space that cannot be read from the host operating system. This means an investigator cannot easily perform a forensic collection of HDFS data through the host operating system. There are three primary methods for collecting Hadoop evidence from the host operating system:

- Imaging the host operating system
- Mounting HDFS and imaging the mounted HDFS drive
- Performing a targeted file collection

Imaging the host operating system is useful for collecting all evidence from the host operating system and HDFS. This method captures Hadoop configuration files stored in the host operating system and the entire contents of HDFS. The significant downside to this method is the difficulty in analyzing the collected evidence. To extract the data during analysis, the investigator has to carve the HDFS data from the image for analysis.

Mounting HDFS is a much simpler method for collecting all HDFS data. This method makes all the HDFS data available for collection without having to later carve out the evidence. Mounting HDFS enables an investigator to target the HDFS data without needing to collect the host operating system data. There are several drawbacks to this method, however. Investigators may need to install a mounting tool on the host operating system, a mounted HDFS partition has a slower response speed, metadata is not accessible, and mounting software offerings tend to have bugs.

Performing a targeted file collection involves collecting Hadoop data stores from the host operating system. This method enables the investigator to work in the host operating system and collect the HDFS data. Performing a targeted collection offers an easy method for collecting HDFS data, but it also requires more effort in the analysis phase to access the collected data.

Next, the three methods for collecting Hadoop evidence from the host operating system are examined.

Imaging the host operating system

Host operating system collections take a complete copy of one or more disk volumes from the host operating system. The copies, called images, are exact bit-by-bit replicas of the source disk volume and are stored in a data file for later analysis. Typically, forensic investigators also compute a checksum using MD5 or SHA-1 to verify the image is an exact copy. The following figure illustrates the forensic copy process:

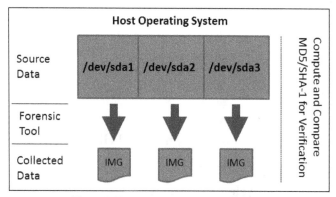

Figure 2: Host operating system collection

Host operating system collections can be performed by imaging an entire disk volume. If possible, the investigator should attempt to perform this type of collection with the source filesystem mounted in the read-only mode. This can be achieved by booting the system with a copy of Linux designed for forensic collections that automatically mounts all drives as read-only. This is not always possible, especially with Big Data systems. When the system cannot be acquired in the read-only mode, the investigator should note this in his documentation.

 One of the most popular bootable freeware Linux forensic distributions is Helix. For more information about Helix, visit www.e-fense.com/products.php.

Imaging the host operating system collections works best when the investigator has physical access to the machine and the ability to run administrator-level commands. The investigator needs to be able to access certain parts of the host operating system that are only accessible with administrator-level access. The primary cause of failure for this method is performing it against cloud storage, or a PaaS or SaaS solution. In those setups, key components are not accessible, thus blocking the investigator from imaging the entire filesystem.

Imaging the host operating system to collect HDFS data requires identifying the disk volume and disk location of the Hadoop data. The host operating system stores HDFS data in a configurable location within the host filesystem. The configuration file that stores the information is `hdfs-site.xml`, which is typically located in the `/etc/hadoop` directory on Linux and Unix systems. The value of the DataNode is stored in the variable `dfs.data.dir`. The default value for `dfs.data.dir` in LightHadoop is `/var/hadoop/datanode`.

The `/var/hadoop/datanode` directory contains a lock file and a current directory. Within the current directory, a text file called VERSION stores useful information about the storage ID, cluster ID, and DataNode ID. This information is very important if the Hadoop service is turned off or otherwise inaccessible because the investigator must use this information to piece together the cluster. The subdirectory (or subdirectories) in the DataNode directory contain the actual data HDFS contents. This information is ultimately what gets collected for HDFS forensic analysis.

Many different forensic tools exist for imaging a hard drive. Commercial tools, such as EnCase and Forensic Toolkit (FTK), provide graphical and command-line interfaces for forensically acquiring the entire contents of a disk. These tools offer robust capabilities for acquisitions. The following are several examples of their features:

- Metadata gathering
- Automatic MD5 or SHA-1 computations
- Generation of acquisition documentation
- Error correction

A freely-available tool used in this book for forensic collections is **dd**. The dd tool is an imaging utility found in Linux and Unix variants. As one of the oldest forensic utilities, dd has limited features compared to newer commercial forensic tools. dd creates exact bit-by-bit copies of an input data source, offers an error-skipping option, and enables users to configure the block size of an image. The following is the syntax for running dd:

```
dd if=/dev/sda1 of=./disk1.img bs=65536 conv=noerror,sync
```

This command specifies the following:

- The source data to image is `/dev/sda1`
- The image output file is stored as `disk1.img` in the current directory
- The block size is `65536` bytes
- If an error is encountered, continue creating the image file
- If an error is encountered, null fill that block in the image file

Specifying the block size offers some advantages. For example, data can be collected faster by specifying a larger block size. However, if there is an error, a larger block size means the entire block will be zero-filled. By contrast, a smaller block size would only fill the smaller block with zeros. The advantage of using 512 KB blocks instead of 64 KB blocks is the increased speed. However, if an error is encountered, the entire 512 KB block would be zero-filled, whereas only 64 KB would be zero-filled if the smaller block size were used.

dd has several advantages over commercial software packages. It is a standard Linux and Unix utility, so it is part of those operating system's builds. It is a free utility that does not require significant training time to use. Because dd acquires entire disk volumes, it is well-suited for complete acquisitions.

An investigator must take several steps to prepare the source system before running dd:

1. Connect a wiped target drive that will store the collected image to the source system.
2. Identify the disk volume(s) or file(s) that need to be acquired.
3. Perform the collection and compute the MD5 checksum of the source data.

The first step is to connect a wiped drive to the source system for the collection. The drive should be large enough to collect all of the source system evidence. Otherwise, the investigator will need to divide the collection into data subsets, so the evidence is collected on multiple drives with each drive storing an image that fits on the drive. The investigator should also organize the drive with directories that correspond to each source system. The directories can either be created at this stage or immediately before the collection begins.

The second step is to identify the disk volume(s) or file(s) that need to be acquired. The `fdisk` command provides the listing of disk volumes. The following is the command for `fdisk`:

```
fdisk -l
```

The following figure illustrates the output for this command:

```
Disk /dev/sda: 21.5 GB, 21474836480 bytes
255 heads, 63 sectors/track, 2610 cylinders
Units = cylinders of 16065 * 512 = 8225280 bytes
Sector size (logical/physical): 512 bytes / 512 bytes
I/O size (minimum/optimal): 512 bytes / 512 bytes
Disk identifier: 0x00028801

   Device Boot      Start         End      Blocks   Id  System
/dev/sda1   *           1          64      512000   83  Linux
Partition 1 does not end on cylinder boundary.
/dev/sda2              64        2611    20458496   8e  Linux LVM
```

Figure 3: The fdisk output

This command lists the full set of partitions, along with the system description, number of blocks, sector size, and total disk size. From this, the investigator can identify which volume(s) should be acquired, and he can determine the best method for collecting the data so that the collected evidence will fit on the target drive(s). In addition, the investigator should identify which volume is the target drive to which the image will be written.

Finally, the command to collect the data and compute the MD5 hash value can be constructed. The investigator can now start the forensic collection using dd. The following command collects the /dev/sda1 volume, stores it in a file called sda1.img on the target drive volume, and uses a piped command to compute the MD5 hash value of the source data:

```
dd if=/dev/sda1 of=/dev/sdb1/disk1.img bs=65536 conv=noerror,sync |
md5sum /dev/sda1 > /dev/sdb1/md5.txt
```

This command returns the following information about the amount of data copied into the image file, as illustrated in the following figure:

```
8000+0 records in
8000+0 records out
524288000 bytes (524 MB) copied, 25.12 s, 20.9 MB/s
```

Figure 4: The dd and md5sum output

This piped command creates three outputs. First, the command generates a dd image file called /dev/sdb1/disk1.img. This file contains the complete image of /dev/sda1. The second output is written to stdout, which is the information about the amount of data read from the input and written to the image file, as shown in preceding figure. The investigator should document this information. The third output is a text file containing the MD5 value of /dev/sda1. Both the dd image file and MD5 file should be stored on the target device.

The MD5 hash value is the bit-level unique fingerprint of the data. If the source data is not mounted in read-only mode, the MD5 hash value can change. So if an investigator does not mount the volume in the read-only mode, the MD5 hash values taken in this step may not match the ones in the acquired image.

In cases where capturing an MD5 or SHA-1 hash value is not feasible, the investigator should capture other information to show that the collection was performed properly. For example, acquisition logs and file size information are useful for documenting the process to prove the data was not modified.

When collecting multiple volumes or files, run dd separately for each to create separate image files. dd does enable the concatenation of multiple inputs, but identifying where one volume ends and the next begins requires additional effort in the analysis phase.

The final step of this process is to run md5sum on the image file, document the result, and compare it to the computed MD5 hash value of the source volume. If an MD5 is not being captured, this step can be skipped. MD5 may not be collected in situations where the data volume is too large to run MD5 in a timely manner, or if other prohibitive factors exist. Otherwise, the investigator should validate that the MD5 hash values from the source system and the acquired image file match. If they do not, the investigator must reacquire the data. The following figure shows a comparison of the MD5 of the source volume and the acquired image file:

```
[root@lighthadoop ~]# less md5.txt
f672fb3c803b05bd8c13cf6e194b00de  /dev/sda1
[root@lighthadoop ~]# md5sum test.img
f672fb3c803b05bd8c13cf6e194b00de  test.img
```

Figure 5: MD5 comparisons

Documentation can now be completed. Investigators should include the following forms:

- The chain of custody form
- The acquisition form

These forms should document the following:

- What was collected
- When the collection took place
- Who performed the collection
- Who took possession of the acquired data
- Detailed information about the target drive onto which the acquired source data was copied, including the make, model, and serial number
- What was acquired, including hard drive and system serial numbers, and descriptions of the system
- Validation information (for example, MD5)

Imaging a mounted HDFS partition

Investigators can also collect HDFS data from the host operating system by mounting HDFS using a mounting tool. This approach involves running a mounting tool and modifying the host operating system's filesystem table so it can access HDFS as if it were a local filesystem. The advantage of this approach is that the HDFS directory structure and files are directly accessible from the host operating system. This makes the collection process more seamless and similar to a live collection of a server.

Several tools are currently available for locally mounting HDFS. The primary package is FUSE, which is an Apache project that is part of the MountableHDFS set of projects. FUSE is a cross-platform tool that can mount HDFS, and it offers access to basic operations (such as cp, ls, and more). However, all standard file and directory operations are not available with FUSE. For a forensic investigator, FUSE's lack of access to file permissions or file ownership makes it less than an ideal tool.

 For more information about FUSE, visit the **MountableHDFS** page at `https://wiki.apache.org/hadoop/MountableHDFS`.

Other mounting tools are available, such as:

- FUSE variants (HDFS-FUSE and FUSE-J both extend FUSE's capabilities for HDFS)
- WebDAV (enables access to HDFS through a WebDAV interface)
- Hadoofus

However, all of these tools' current implementations have issues that make them less desirable choices for HDFS forensic collections. First, mounting software packages do not provide access to file permissions, owner information, and other metadata. This defeats the purpose of collecting HDFS directly from the filesystem instead of through software queries (for example, HBase). Mounting software packages have not been designed with forensic collections in mind; rather, they are intended to offer a means to access the files. Second, the process of using mounting software is a slow one. The software either needs to be prebuilt in the host operating system or acquisition operating system, or it will need to be built on the host operating system. The mounting software itself is slower than acquiring the data directly through the host operating system or the Hadoop command line. Third, every one of these tools currently on the market has bugs. These bugs primarily relate to large-scale systems and the mounting software packages' need for static writes. The presence of known bugs makes the evidence obtained through mounting software packages less defensible and subject to scrutiny.

As discussed in later sections, the Hadoop command line provides all the advantages of mounting. Mounting HDFS provides the investigator with access to the HDFS files, but so does accessing files through the Hadoop command line. Because mounting HDFS requires Hadoop to be running, mounting HDFS only adds an extra layer; it does not provide any additional data or metadata that cannot be accessed already through the Hadoop command line.

Given the current state of available tools, using mounting software for forensic collections is not recommended. Potentially, a forensic-grade mounting software may become available in the future. Such a software package would need to eliminate the bugs and provide access to HDFS metadata. Until that time, the use of mounting software for HDFS collections is not advisable, except in extenuating circumstances.

Targeted collection from a Hadoop client

The third method for collecting HDFS data from the host operating system is a targeted collection. The HDFS data is stored in defined locations within the host operating system. This data can be collected on a per-node basis through logical file copies. Every node needs to be collected to ensure the HDFS files can be reconstructed in the analysis phase.

The same process is conducted for both targeted collections and imaging collections, except for a couple of differences. With imaging collections, entire disk volumes are collected and hashed. Targeted collections involve the copying of individual files and directories. In both methods, the investigator collects the data, documents the process, and computes MD5/SHA-1 hash values. However, there are differences. In targeted collections, MD5/SHA-1 is computed on the files but not the volumes, the collection process requires multiple copies rather than a single image file, and certain metadata is not preserved. Also, investigators typically perform the targeted collection using scripts rather than manually typing the commands at runtime.

The first step for performing the targeted collection is to identify the location where the host operating system stores the HDFS files. For Linux, Unix, OS X, and other Unix variants, this can be found in the `hdfs-site.xml` file. While typically stored in the `/etc/hadoop` directory, it can be stored in other locations, so the investigator first needs to find this location before beginning. In Windows, this information is typically located in the Windows Hadoop installation directory `c:\hadoop`. To find the directory location from the command line, run the following command:

```
cd %HADOOP_NODE_INSTALL_ROOT%
```

Most production Hadoop environments do not run in a Windows environment; the Windows Hadoop distribution is development-only. Unlike the Linux Hadoop distribution, the Windows Hadoop distribution has not been tested for production deployment.

After identifying the location of the `hdfs-site.xml` file, find the `dfs.name.dir` and `dfs.data.dir` variables and navigate to those directories. The following figure illustrates the contents of `hdfs-site.xml` that contain `dfs.name.dir` and `dfs.data.dir`:

```
<property>
        <name>dfs.permissions</name>
        <value>true</value>
</property>
<property>
        <name>dfs.name.dir</name>
        <value>/var/hadoop/namenode</value>
</property>
<property>
        <name>dfs.data.dir</name>
        <value>/var/hadoop/datanode</value>
</property>
```

Figure 6: The dfs.data.dir variable in hdfs-site.xml

HDFS data is stored in the `/var/hadoop/datanode` directory in this example, and the NameNode's filesystem metadata is stored in the `/var/hadoop/namenode` directory. The DataNode directory contains the HDFS distributed data blocks, and the NameNode directory contains the `fsimage` and `edits` files that store the HDFS filesystem metadata that is read into memory when Hadoop is brought online.

The DataNode directory tree structure is illustrated in the following figure:

```
── current
│   ── BP-1468292389-127.0.0.1-1410576020288
│   │   ── current
│   │   │   ── dfsUsed
│   │   │   ── finalized
│   │   │   │   ── blk_1073741825
│   │   │   │   ── blk_1073741825_1001.meta
│   │   │   │   ── blk_1073741826
│   │   │   │   ── blk_1073741826_1002.meta
│   │   │   ── rbw
│   │   │   ── VERSION
│   │   ── dncp_block_verification.log.curr
│   │   ── dncp_block_verification.log.prev
│   │   ── tmp
│   ── VERSION
── in_use.lock
```

Figure 7: The DataNode tree structure

The investigator should collect the entire DataNode tree structure. The structure is comprised of the following directories and files:

- BP-<integer>-<IP Address>-<creation time>: This directory is the block pool that collects the blocks of data belonging to that DataNode.

- finalized/rbw: The actual data blocks are stored in these directories. The finalized directory stores the blocks that have been completely written to disk. The rbw directory stands for replica being written and stores the blocks that are currently being written to HDFS.

- VERSION: This text file stores property information. Each DataNode has a DataNode-wide VERSION file and also VERSION files for each block pool.

- blk_<block ID>: The binary data blocks content files.

- blk_<block ID>.meta: The binary data blocks metadata files.

- dncp_block_verification: This file tracks the times in which the block was last verified via checksum.

- in_use.lock: This is a lock file used by the DataNode process to prevent multiple DataNode processes from modifying the directory.

The investigator should also collect the entire NameNode tree structure. The NameNode tree structure is illustrated in following figure:

```
─ current
    ├─ edits_0000000000000000001-0000000000000000013
    ├─ edits_0000000000000000014-0000000000000000014
    ├─ edits_0000000000000000015-0000000000000000015
    ├─ edits_0000000000000000016-0000000000000000016
    ├─ edits_inprogress_0000000000000000017
    ├─ fsimage_0000000000000000015
    ├─ fsimage_0000000000000000015.md5
    ├─ fsimage_0000000000000000016
    ├─ fsimage_0000000000000000016.md5
    ├─ seen_txid
    └─ VERSION
─ in_use.lock
```

Figure 8: The NameNode tree structure

The NameNode tree structure is comprised of the following directories and files:

- edits_<start transaction ID>-<end transaction ID>: This binary log file lists each filesystem change since the most recent fsimage file was generated.

- fsimage_<end transaction ID>: This binary file stores the complete metadata image up through the end transaction ID.

- fsimage_<end transaction ID>.md5: This text file contains the MD5 hash value for the corresponding fsimage file.

- `in_use.lock`: This lock file is used by the NameNode process to prevent multiple NameNode processes from modifying the directory.

In addition to the HDFS contents, the following potentially relevant data can be collected:

Directory	File	Description
`/etc/hadoop Files`	`core-site.xml`	This has default Hadoop settings
	`hadoop-env.sh`	This configures Hadoop environment variables
	`hadoop-policy.xml`	This has Hadoop security settings
	`httpfs-log4j.properties`	This has Hadoop log4j settings
	`hdfs-site.xml`	This has HDFS-related configuration settings
	`core-site.xml`	This has default Hadoop settings
`/lib/hadoop/logs`	`hadoop-env.sh`	This configures Hadoop environment variables
	`hadoop-policy.xml`	This has Hadoop security settings
	`httpfs-log4j.properties`	This has Hadoop log4j settings
	`hdfs-site.xml`	This has HDFS-related configuration settings
	`log4j.properties`	This has Hadoop log4j settings
`/tmp/root`	`hive.log`	This has the Current Hive log
	`hive.log.<DATE>`	This has the Archived Hive log

Other Hadoop configuration and log files may be of interest, and the actual directory locations vary across Hadoop setups.

After identifying the HDFS file location(s), the next step is to prepare the script to collect the files and compute the MD5 hash values. The following sample script performs the cp and md5sum commands across a folder location:

```
#!/bin/sh
#File and error counter variables
fileCount = 0
failCount = 0
echo "Collection script: basename $0" >
/dev/sdb1/collection_log.txt
echo "Collection start: $(date)" >> /dev/sdb1/collection_log.txt
# First file copy
cp /tmp/root/hive.log /dev/sdb1/ | md5sum /tmp/root/hive.log >
/dev/sdb1/md5.txt
if [ $? -ne 0 ]
then
echo "/tmp/root/hive.log not acquired" >>
/dev/sdb1/collection_log.txt
failCount=$((failCount+1))
else
fileCount=$((fileCount+1))
fi
# Second file copy
cp /etc/hadoop/core-site.xml /dev/sdb1/ | md5sum /etc/hadoop/core-
site.xml >> /dev/sdb1/md5.txt
if [ $? -ne 0 ]
then
echo "/etc/hadoop/core-site.xml not acquired" >>
/dev/sdb1/collection_log.txt
failCount=$((failCount+1))
else
fileCount=$((fileCount+1))
fi
# [Additional file copy commands omitted]
echo "Total files copied: $(fileCount)" >>
/dev/sdb1/collection_log.txt
echo "Total failed copies: $(failCount)" >>
/dev/sdb1/collection_log.txt
echo "Collection end: $(date)" >> /dev/sdb1/collection_log.txt
```

After running the script, the final steps are to validate the MD5 hash values and prepare the documentation. Next, md5sum should be run across all collected files and compared to the values previously collected. Each collected file's MD5 hash value should be validated before moving to the next step. If any mismatches exist, the nonvalidated files should be recollected. Several methods are available for performing the comparison:

- Spreadsheet comparisons
- Database comparisons
- Script comparisons

After validating the collection, the investigator should complete the chain of custody and acquisition forms, and all scripts used in the process should be copied and retained for the investigator's records.

Because each HDFS node stores blocks of data and not actual HDFS files, the DataNode collection has to be performed on every node. The process for collecting from each DataNode involves the same steps as described in the following:

1. Identify the location of the DataNode data storage directory on each directory.
2. Generate a separate collection script for each DataNode.
3. Collect and validate all DataNode files.

The final step is to complete the acquisition log and chain of custody documentation. In addition, the investigator should retain copies of the collecting scripts used in the collection.

The Hadoop shell command collection

Collecting HDFS data from within the Hadoop layer solves many of the problems that affect host operating system collections. First, the collection only has to be performed from a single machine. By accessing Hadoop through a Hadoop client's command line, all HDFS files are available, so the collection does not involve collecting data from each node individually. Second, the collected data does not require any piecing together or file carving in the analysis phase. The data that is collected is already pieced together as the logical Hadoop files, so no carving or data reconstruction is required.

The following is a list of limitations of collecting HDFS data from the Hadoop shell command line:

- This method is only possible when Hadoop is online and its command line is accessible

- Forensic tools such as dd and md5sum cannot easily be used during the collection of the data

- Deleted data and data in memory that has not been written to disk may not be available

- Hadoop does not store the same type of metadata that is available through a normal operating system data collection

The advantages of collecting HDFS from the Hadoop shell often outweigh the disadvantages. The contents of the data stored in HDFS are typically the primary evidence, and slack space data, metadata, and other forensic artifacts are not the crucial element. The investigator needs to ensure the requirements of the investigation enable the collection to be performed at the Hadoop layer.

Hadoop shell command collection utilizes Hadoop's shell functionality and file management tools to collect HDFS files. The Hadoop shell commands, hadoop and hdfc, are run from the host operating system to locate and copy the files in HDFS to a target drive. These tools provide access to the actual files and not the data blocks. This has the advantage of not requiring any piecing together of files later by the investigator. The following figure illustrates the process by which a Hadoop client sends a file copy command to Hadoop and how the cluster's files are sent to a forensic target drive for acquisition:

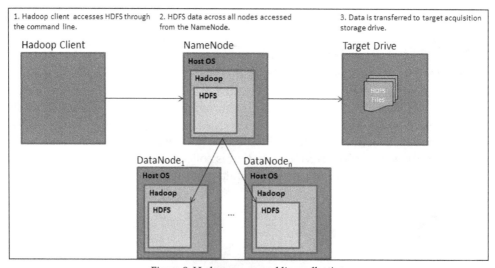

Figure 9: Hadoop command line collection

Information about the configuration and status of the Hadoop cluster can be collected via a Hadoop tool called the Hadoop Offline Image Viewer. This tool dumps the contents of the `fsimage` file into a readable file suitable for analysis. This tool is covered later in this section.

 The Hadoop shell commands and Hadoop Offline Image Viewer work with HDFS and any other filesystem compatible with Hadoop.

Collecting HDFS files

Collecting HDFS files using Hadoop shell commands is a multistep process. The first step is to locate all potentially relevant files that should be collected. This identification can either be done during the data identification phase or on the Hadoop cluster using Hadoop shell commands during the collection phase. The second step is the collection of the files from the target drive using the Hadoop shell get command. The final steps are to compute the MD5 hash values for the collected files and complete the acquisition documentation.

Locating files in HDFS is performed by running a file listing command. The investigator runs the file listing command and pipes the results into a text file that is then used to generate a file copy script. The following is the shell command used to list all files in HDFS:

```
hdfs dfs -lsr /
```

This command runs a recursive directory listing starting in the root directory. The output is a complete listing of every file stored in the Hadoop cluster. The file listing includes the standard metadata information: permissions, owner, group, file size, creation date, filename, and directory information.

Because Hadoop clusters are typically voluminous, the investigator needs to assess the file sizes of all files and how to collect them. Single hard drives are usually too small to store the entire contents of a Hadoop cluster, so the investigator needs to determine how to divide the files into sets that can fit on a collection of drives. For example, if the investigator only has a set of 5 TB hard drives for the collection, but there is over 200 TB of data, a plan needs to be constructed to identify which files to collect and store on each individual drive. Several methods exist for determining how to best divide files across each drive. The best-fit allocation and first-fit allocation algorithms work well for this. However, a simple method is to identify the largest files and allocate those to a drive first, then fill the rest of the drive, and repeat this process until all files have been allocated to a drive.

The collection of files is best scripted inside of a host operating system script. The following Hadoop file copy command copies the Hadoop file /home/hadoopFile.txt to the target drive location /dev/sdb1/hadoopFile.txt. The command also copies the file even if it has a Hadoop CRC error:

```
hdfs dfs -get -ignorecrc /home/hadoopFile.txt
/dev/sdb1/hadoopFile.txt
```

Next, the get command is scripted for every file and an MD5 hash value is computed and stored for each copied file. The following script runs the collection and documents the results:

```
#!/bin/sh
#File and error counter variables
fileCount = 0
failCount = 0
echo "Collection script: basename $0" >
/dev/sdb1/collection_log.txt
echo "Collection start: $(date)" >> /dev/sdb1/collection_log.txt
# First file copy
hdfs dfs -get -ignorecrc /home/hadoopFile.txt
/dev/sdb1/hadoopFile.txt
if [ $? -ne 0 ]
then
  echo "/tmp/root/hive.log not acquired" >>
/dev/sdb1/collection_log.txt
  failCount=$((failCount+1))
else
  fileCount=$((fileCount+1))
  md5sum /dev/sdb1/hadoopFile.txt > /dev/sdb1/md5.txt
fi
# [Additional file copy commands omitted]
echo "Total files copied: $(fileCount)" >>
/dev/sdb1/collection_log.txt
echo "Total failed copies: $(failCount)" >>
/dev/sdb1/collection_log.txt
echo "Collection end: $(date)" >> /dev/sdb1/collection_log.txt
```

This script does the following:

- Generates the collection log collection_log.txt
- Copies the HDFS file /home/hadoopFile.txt to the target drive /dev/sdb1
- Computes the MD5 hash value and stores it in the target drive as md5.txt

The MD5 computation has to be performed on the target file after collection because no MD5 tool exists within Hadoop. Hadoop does have an MD5 API function, but no Hadoop tool exists, so the MD5 should be calculated on the collected data as part of a script. This collection technique provides an MD5 that can be shown and verified in later stages and compensates for Hadoop's lack of built-in MD5 functionality.

This process of computing the MD5 after the copy completes is not unusual, and Hadoop's file import and export commands do not modify the file. To prove this, the following sets of commands can be run on any file to demonstrate that the MD5 is not affected by either the Hadoop import or export commands:

```
hdfs dfs -put ./testFile.txt /home/hadoopFile.txt

hdfs dfs -get /home/hadoopFile.txt ./testFile_copy.txt

md5sum testFile.txt

md5sum testFile_copy.txt
```

The MD5 hash values for the original file and copied file that passed through Hadoop will match, proving that the get command followed by md5sum is a suitable and valid forensic approach.

 Hadoop maintains checksums of the local filesystem (for example, HDFS). The process it uses consists of calculating a CRC32 for every 512 bytes on each data node. When the checksum is requested by the filesystem, the CRC32s are concatenated and an MD5 hash value is generated from that string. While Hadoop does utilize a form of MD5 in its filesystem, the method itself is not forensically sound.

After the script runs, the collection log is reviewed to check for errors. If file copy errors are found, those files should be investigated and recollected. After the errors have been accounted for, the chain of custody and acquisition forms should be completed.

HDFS targeted data collection

Another technique forensic investigators use in Big Data collections is to target specific files. Targeted collections can be performed in two ways:

- By collecting a predefined set of files
- By previewing files to determine which files contain potentially relevant data

The investigator can determine which files to collect during the identification phase or through instruction from one of the other parties in the investigation. From the list of files, a collection script can be developed to collect the files in the same manner as the full Hadoop shell command collection.

Alternatively, a subset of files can be collected. Most Hadoop clusters have data feeds with related file names. These files contain the same data points and information and have a consistent structure. Rather than collecting all files, the collection can be focused on only the relevant subset of files. For example, a Hadoop cluster may contain tens of thousands of files, but the files are comprised of only three types, all with the same file prefix. The investigation may only hinge on one of those three types of files, so rather than expending time, effort, and disk space on collecting all three, the investigator can collect just the one relevant file type.

Identifying which types of files are relevant requires collecting a complete file listing, determining which categories of files are available, previewing the files, and assessing which files should be collected. The complete file listing is acquired first to identify the universe of available files. The second step is to establish the types of file categories by way of interviews and previewing sample files. Previewing the files is an effective method for establishing the categories and identifying the relevant files if a consistent filename or directory structure convention is followed. If the files are named using different conventions and/or files are stored across directories without consistency, previewing files may fail to fully identify all relevant files. After the categories of relevant files are identified, the investigator should combine that information with the file listing to create a list of files to collect.

[Completely collecting all potentially relevant files is the goal of the collection phase. If questions arise about whether or not a file should be collected, it is best to err on the side of caution and collect the file.]

After the files have been identified, the collection process is the same. The files are collected by way of a script and validated and documented in the same way as they would be in a full Hadoop shell command collection.

Hadoop Offline Image and Edits Viewers

Hadoop provides a built-in method to dump the contents of fsimage into a readable file. The fsimage file is Hadoop's point-in-time snapshot of the filesystem's metadata. The Hadoop Offline Image Viewer extracts the contents of the fsimage file and makes it available in several different formats. The first format is an HTTP server that reads the fsimage contents and presents those as a WebHDFS API that can be accessed through HTTP REST requests. The second format, and the one of most value to investigators, is an XML file that is generated and can be analyzed offline. The third format is the File Distribution tool output, which gives aggregated information about the number of files within certain file size ranges.

The Hadoop Offline Image Viewer works well in tandem with a Hadoop shell command collection by supplementing the HDFS file collection with the metadata generated by the Hadoop Offline Image Viewer. The Hadoop Offline Image Viewer provides the following information in the XML output file:

- **NameNode**: This provides level information, such as the namespace ID, last inode ID, and last transaction ID

- **Inode**: This provides level information, such as path, ID, last modified and access times, permissions, and replication factors

The metadata generated in the Hadoop Offline Image Viewer XML file can be used as supplemental data to the files collected via Hadoop shell commands. The Hadoop shell get command does not provide complete metadata, so the XML file can fill that void because the metadata captured accurately reflects the files.

The following command generates a Hadoop Offline Image Viewer XML file:

```
hdfs oiv -i fsimage_0000000000000000015 -o fsimage_output.xml -p XML
```

The following figure illustrates the output generated by this command:

```
<?xml version="1.0"?>
<fsimage><NameSection>
<genstampV1>1000</genstampV1><genstampV2>1000</genstampV2><genstampV1Limit>0</ge
nstampV1Limit><lastAllocatedBlockId>1073741824</lastAllocatedBlockId><txid>16</t
xid></NameSection>
<INodeSection><lastInodeId>16396</lastInodeId><inode><id>16385</id><type>DIRECTO
RY</type><name></name><mtime>1410576045628</mtime><permission>root:supergroup:rw
xr-xr-x</permission><nsquota>9223372036854775807</nsquota><dsquota>-1</dsquota><
/inode>
<inode><id>16386</id><type>DIRECTORY</type><name>user</name><mtime>1410576042341
</mtime><permission>root:supergroup:rwxr-xr-x</permission><nsquota>-1</nsquota><
dsquota>-1</dsquota></inode>
<inode><id>16387</id><type>DIRECTORY</type><name>root</name><mtime>1410576049575
</mtime><permission>root:supergroup:rwxr-xr-x</permission><nsquota>-1</nsquota><
dsquota>-1</dsquota></inode>
```

Figure 10: The Hadoop Offline Image Viewer output

The Hadoop Offline Image Viewer metadata collection should be run immediately after the file collection in order to accurately capture the metadata with as few metadata modifications as possible.

Hadoop also has an Offline Edits Viewer to export the contents of the edits file. This utility is useful for extracting information about updates to the filesystem since the last fsimage file update. The edits file contains transaction-level updates to the filesystem, such as file updates. If the investigation requires information about the history of file updates, examining the edits file (or files) is a great resource of such information.

The following command generates a Hadoop Offline Edits Viewer XML file:

```
hdfs oev -i edits_0000000000000000017 -o edits_output.xml -p XML
```

The following figure illustrates the output generated by this command, which includes the file name, inode, and timestamps for the file:

```
<?xml version="1.0" encoding="UTF-8"?>
<EDITS>
  <EDITS_VERSION>-55</EDITS_VERSION>
  <RECORD>
    <OPCODE>OP_START_LOG_SEGMENT</OPCODE>
    <DATA>
      <TXID>17</TXID>
    </DATA>
  </RECORD>
  <RECORD>
    <OPCODE>OP_ADD</OPCODE>
    <DATA>
      <TXID>18</TXID>
      <LENGTH>0</LENGTH>
      <INODEID>16397</INODEID>
      <PATH>/wiki_page_hits.txt._COPYING_</PATH>
      <REPLICATION>1</REPLICATION>
      <MTIME>1424185543359</MTIME>
      <ATIME>1424185543359</ATIME>
      <BLOCKSIZE>134217728</BLOCKSIZE>
      <CLIENT_NAME>DFSClient_NONMAPREDUCE_-198239203_1</CLIENT_NAME>
      <CLIENT_MACHINE>127.0.0.1</CLIENT_MACHINE>
      <PERMISSION_STATUS>
        <USERNAME>root</USERNAME>
```

The following screenshot shows additional information from the Offline Edits Viewer output, including the file's group, file permissions mode, and block ID:

```
      <GROUPNAME>supergroup</GROUPNAME>
      <MODE>420</MODE>
    </PERMISSION_STATUS>
    <RPC_CLIENTID>a3114baf-6a33-4a7d-820d-5e0d8f18d775</RPC_CLIENTID>
    <RPC_CALLID>3</RPC_CALLID>
  </DATA>
</RECORD>
<RECORD>
  <OPCODE>OP_ALLOCATE_BLOCK_ID</OPCODE>
  <DATA>
    <TXID>19</TXID>
    <BLOCK_ID>1073741825</BLOCK_ID>
  </DATA>
</RECORD>
<RECORD>
  <OPCODE>OP_SET_GENSTAMP_V2</OPCODE>
  <DATA>
    <TXID>20</TXID>
    <GENSTAMPV2>1001</GENSTAMPV2>
  </DATA>
</RECORD>
```

Figure 11: The Hadoop Offline Edits Viewer output

In a forensic investigation, the combination of the `fsimage` and `edits` files provides a wealth of information about who created and modified files, the permissions, and storage locations. As long as `fsimage` and `edits` files are available for a specific period of time, these files tell the story of all filesystem changes. Hadoop has a configurable setting that determines how long and how many versions of both files are retained. If this information is potentially relevant, the Offline Image and Edits Viewer extractions should be performed for all available versions.

The following analyses can be performed later using the output from these utilities:

- Chronological file history analysis
- File deletion, modification, and overwrite identification
- File age analysis

Collection via Sqoop

Sqoop is an Apache Foundation package designed to transfer bulk data from HDFS to relational databases. As a data migration tool, Sqoop is used to transfer data to and from HDFS. The primary purpose for Sqoop is to serve as a utility for transferring data between data warehouses and Hadoop clusters. It can also be used as a forensic tool when HDFS data can be exported as relational data.

Sqoop reads data from HDFS and transfers the data to a relational database. It reads entire directories of files and then parses them based on specified delimiters and qualifiers. Sqoop imports the parsed data into databases using a series of `INSERT` commands. It then tracks errors and exceptions and reports on any such failed inserts.

Sqoop imports data into the following databases:

- HSQLDB
- MySQL
- Oracle
- PostgreSQL

Other databases are supported via Sqoop connectors, including MS SQL Server.

To export HDFS data to a relational database using Sqoop, the investigator runs Sqoop from a machine that can access both HDFS and the **relational database management system** (**RDBMS**). The investigator also needs to create the table(s) in the relational database that match the structure of the data being imported from HDFS. This requires a priori knowledge of the structure of the files. If data that does not match the structure resides in the data being collected from HDFS, then the Sqoop data collection will fail.

The following figure illustrates the use of Sqoop for collecting HDFS data:

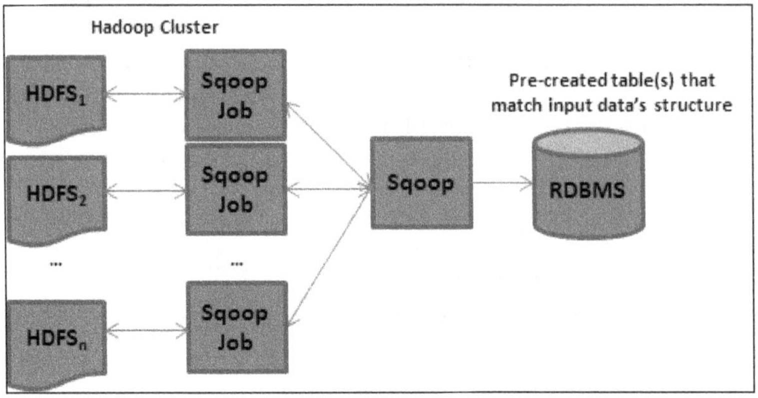

Figure 12: The Sqoop collection process

Sqoop is a useful tool when the structure of the data is already known and a relational database can be connected to the Hadoop client. Sqoop efficiently transfers data to a relational database, which eliminates any data preparation steps. With Hadoop clusters' large data sets, directly importing the data to a database rather than collecting it and storing it on individual hard drives saves quite a bit of effort. However, there are difficulties with Sqoop. Investigators must know the structure in advance and have the capability to connect to a database. Because investigators often collect data on the premises, ensuring there is a Hadoop client that can connect to the cluster, and to a database for later analysis, can be problematic. The other issue is that Sqoop will fail on any files or records that do not adhere to the predefined data structure. This is a problem in forensic investigations because archived data stored in a different format or data anomalies cannot be captured using this method.

The following code collects all data from the HDFS directory analysis and imports it into a localhost MySQL server in the forensic database's analysis table:

```
sqoop export --connect jdbc:mysql://127.0.0.1/forensic --table
analysis \ --export-dir /results/analysis
```

Sqoop returns information about the number of records exported to MySQL:

```
15/02/20 09:54:18 INFO manager.SqlManager: Migrated 150301 records
from `analysis` to `analysis`
```

Other HDFS collection approaches

Two other collection approaches require consideration when collecting HDFS data: custom-developed Java programs and third-party collections. The first, using custom-developed Java programs, collects HDFS data utilizing the Hadoop Java API and standard Java methods. Two of the drawbacks to collecting HDFS data through shell commands are that the **Java Virtual Machine (JVM)** has to start and finish for every copy command, considerably slowing down the copy process, and MD5 computations can only be performed after the file has been copied. Hadoop's Java API provides methods for calculating the MD5 of files inside HDFS, and the program can perform all copies inside a single JVM session. The drawback is that custom-developed Java solutions require significant testing and some Hadoop Java API methods are still under development. For this reason, the investigator should carefully develop and test any program used to perform the collection to avoid unintended behavior or errors.

Another method for collecting HDFS data is where the system owner or a third party performs the file collection. This approach is typically performed in non-criminal investigations and ones in which accessing the system is either difficult or prohibitive. The system owner usually IT staff or another party with forensic expertise performs the collection. Then a copy of the collected data (or the original data) is transferred to the investigator.

The investigator should carefully consider whether having an outside party conducting the collection is acceptable. In some situations, the investigator cannot perform the collection. In other situations, having an outside party perform the collection is not required, but it may be the most cost-effective or otherwise prudent approach. The investigator should consider the following when deciding whether the collection should be performed by another party:

- Does the other party understand the requirements of the investigation (for example, methods and documentation protocols), and do they know which data to collect?

- What are the benefits of having the other party perform the collection (for example, cost, timeliness, and business continuity)?

- Who assumes liability for the collection if mistakes are made?

- Have the requirements been clearly communicated in writing?

- What is the chain of custody protocol for the collection?
- Is the other party better or equally well-equipped to perform the collection?
- What are the risks of having the other party perform the collection?

If the risks are controlled and the requirements can be met, having another party perform the collection is an acceptable method. The investigator should ensure all documentation is created and transferred as well as communicating the proper process for data collection and transfer protocols.

Summary

This chapter covered several methods investigators can use to collect data from HDFS. Investigators can collect HDFS data from the host operating system by imaging or collecting logical files. They can also collect HDFS data via the Hadoop shell, a data transfer tool such as Sqoop, or using other methods, such as a custom-developed Java application, or relying on an outside party to perform the collection. Each method has its own advantages and disadvantages. The pros and cons for each are covered in the following tables:

Methods	Pros	Cons
Host operating system collection	This has a complete forensic collection	This requires collection across each node and manual re-piecing of data blocks for analysis
	This follows standard forensic process	This is a time-consuming and cumbersome process
	This captures the system as is, including slack space and deleted files	This requires extra disk space for extraneous collected data
Hadoop shell command collection	This collects Hadoop files	This requires collection across each node and manual re-piecing of data blocks for analysis
	This uses native application for collection	The load time for JVM to run Hadoop commands is slow
	This can be performed on a single node or client	This requires scripting to perform on a large set of files

Methods	Pros	Cons
Sqoop	This collects data into a database repository	In this data must have a known structure and cannot have anomalies
	Sqoop is already available in most Hadoop environments	This requires connection to a database system
Custom java application	This collects data in native Java language	This requires careful testing and verification
	This can perform MD5 on Hadoop files before they're copied	It's subject to outside scrutiny
Other party collection	This can offer cost and time savings	There's a risk of incomplete or incorrect collection
	This is a workable solution when an investigator cannot perform the collection	This requires detailed communication and review

The next chapter will cover an alternative method for collecting Hadoop data—application-based collections.

5
Collecting Hadoop Application Data

Hadoop evidence can be forensically collected from more than just the filesystem. Evidence can also be collected from Hadoop applications. Hadoop data is formatted for use by its applications, and these applications provide means for more easily extracting relevant data. The process of collecting evidence from Hadoop applications instead of from HDFS offers many advantages, but the approach is very different. Some forensic artifacts, such as metadata, cannot be captured from a Hadoop application collection. However, collecting data from an application avoids some of the time-consuming and challenging tasks involved in forensically imaging HDFS or collecting data from each node individually.

Any Hadoop software outside of the Hadoop layer is considered an application. Two of the most common application packages are Hive and HBase. Both packages operate in ways similar to a database, and their data can be collected through the software itself. Hadoop applications that do not directly analyze or store data are not applicable to this process because they offer no way to collect data. Applications that fall into this category include ZooKeeper and YARN.

The process for collecting evidence from the applications differs from filesystem collections in a number of ways. First, collecting data from applications involves extracting the informational content not creating a bit-by-bit replica of the source system. This means the evidence gathered is the information accessible by the application and is not every bit of disk space. Therefore, it does not represent every form of metadata and slack space in the source system. Second, the investigator need only use a single system client to access all data in the cluster's application collection, so the investigator does not need to collect evidence from each node independently. Third, the person who performs the application collection only needs to know how to query the application as well as the steps to document and properly secure the collected data in order to perform the collection.

Collecting Hadoop data through its applications has a number of advantages that make it the preferred choice for most investigations. The following is a list of the advantages of collecting data through applications:

- One only needs to access Hadoop from a single client
- Data is limited to relevant information accessed by the applications
- Even if data is replicated across nodes, only a single copy is collected
- An application collection is less intrusive to the system and causes less business interruption
- A subset of the data can be targeted

This approach is best when the contents of the system are the only relevant evidence. For investigations in which metadata, logs, and other data outside of the applications is relevant, the investigator should employ a filesystem collection, either in lieu of the application collection or as a supplement to the application collection.

This chapter covers the process for application collections and how to perform sample collections from Hive and HBase. Each of the collection methods are discussed along with how to determine the best method for a particular investigation. Examples of how to perform the collection are given for Hive and HBase.

Application collection approaches

Hadoop data is stored in a unique structure. Unlike most relational database systems, which loads and stores data in a proprietary format, Hadoop applications typically store data in sets of flat files similar to a hierarchical database. Files are imported into the application, and the application stores those files in a separate file structure and generates the metadata about that data.

Application-based collections have advantages over filesystem-based collections of the application's underlying files. While the file-based storage of files in Hadoop applications enables logical copies of the flat files, these files may not be structured in a format that can be quickly analyzed or the collection may require sampling of files to identify the relevant files. Collecting data from the applications has the following advantages:

- The investigator can collect the data in a format that is quickly and readily analyzable
- The data can be collected more easily by third parties
- The collection can be performed from a single client machine

Data in Hadoop can potentially be accessed by more than one application, so the investigator should be aware of which application is best suited for the application-based collection and whether that application can access all relevant data.

The method of collecting data from applications depends on which application stores or accesses the data and the means it provides for exporting data. Every application is different. Some applications only offer query-based means to access the data, some require scripts to be written, and others have multiple querying mechanisms available. Like filesystem collections, several application collection methods are available to the investigator. These methods are similar to those used for database collections and include the following:

- **Backup-based collection**: This collects a newly-created or archived application backup

- **Query-based collection**: This collects all data or a subset of the data via queries

- **Script-based collection**: This collects all data or a subset of the data via scripts or another application (for example, via Pig)

- **Software-based collection**: This collects data through an application that connects to the source application

Each application collection method is largely the same as the one used for collecting relational and other database system types. Backup-based collections are a very common method when a full copy of a database is required. This method offers the advantage of quickly collecting every component of a database with minimal effort. In Big Data collections, there are some differences in the collection process based on the application. For instance, some applications do not have built-in backup mechanisms. Query- and script-based collections are commonly employed in three instances: 1) when backup methods are not available, 2) when queries or scripts are the easiest collection method, or 3) when only a subset of data is required. Software-based collections are common for commercial database packages such as Oracle and SQL Server, but are not yet a common solution for Big Data collections.

Practical considerations also dictate how the collections are performed. If metadata and filesystem-level detail is required, application collection is not ideal, or requires a supplemental data collection method. However, if only the contents of the stored data are relevant, application data collections are typically faster, easier, and produce evidence in a format that is more readily analyzed. Once the decision is made to employ an application collection, choosing which method to use is based on other practical considerations.

These include the following:

- Whether the application has a backup mechanism
- Whether all or only a subset of the data from the application is relevant
- How quickly the application produces full record data sets from queries and scripts
- Whether the volume of data is small enough to extract through queries and scripts

The following table lists the advantages and disadvantages of each method:

Methods	Advantages	Disadvantages
Backup-based collection	This is a complete data collection	This may contain extraneous data
	This has no upfront decision making	This is not always available
	This has minimal impact to organization	This is potentially a slow collection process
Query-based collection	This has ability to limit data scope	This may not capture all relevant data and requires upfront review of data and data structure
	This contains queries that can be scheduled to run during off-hours	This has a high impact to source system
	This is potentially a fast collection process	This is potentially difficult to verify
Script-based collection	This has ability to limit data scope	This may not capture all relevant data and requires upfront review of data and data structure
	In this scripts can be scheduled to run during off-hours	This has a high impact to source system
	This is potentially a fast collection process	This is potentially difficult to verify
Software-based collection	This can collect data automatically to desired output format	This is not always an available option for source system software
	This is a simple and fast option	This can be disruptive to organization's systems

Unlike backup-based collection, query- and script-based collections offer a great deal of flexibility in relation to what is collected. Both methods enable an investigator to collect all or a subset of the data. For a Big Data investigation, this is very important and valuable. In some cases, all of the data is required. In many other cases, however, the volume of data and the facts of the investigation make collecting only a subset of the data the best solution. Big Data systems can store petabytes of information, and much of that data volume might be accessed by an application, if only a subset is required, that can save a tremendous amount of time, disk space, and cluster availability for normal use. A subset can be collected in one or more of the following ways:

- Limiting the number of data sets
- Limiting the number of data points or fields
- Limiting the number of records based on filter criteria

The investigator already knows which information is relevant from his findings in the identification phase. This information is then translated into queries or scripts that are used to perform the collection.

Backups

Backups are unique in Hadoop. Unlike a standard database system, Hadoop applications store data across a vast multi-node cluster, with the amount of data potentially measuring in the petabytes. When compared to the single database backup or dump files in MS SQL Server or Oracle, this massive scale makes backups in Hadoop seem impossible. However, methods do exist for most applications. Because Hadoop is an enterprise system that requires backups for disaster recovery, Hadoop applications offer backups that are familiar to most database administrators as well as unique backup options. The range of Hadoop application backup methods include:

- Snapshots that can be restored using the Hadoop application
- Replication to another cluster
- Full export to Hadoop SequenceFiles
- Table copies to text files

Each method has varying degrees of speed and system impact depending on the application. For example, dumping the application contents to text files is fast, but it is highly system-resource intensive. The use of SequenceFiles and snapshots tend to be slower but have less impact to the source system.

Investigators need to consider the output format of backups before beginning any application backup collection. Unless the backup output is a set of text files, the backups may require some form of data loading and/or conversion before the files can be analyzed. Exporting application data to SequenceFiles requires conversion of the SequenceFiles to a format that can be extracted. If the output is a snapshot, the snapshot requires loading through that application (for example, HBase snapshots must later be loaded in HBase) before analysis can be performed.

Query extractions

Query extractions use the application's native query language to access and collect the application data. Applications designed for data analysis have their own query language, and queries can be written in that language to access and collect a subset or all of the data to text files. The following methods are available with query-based collections:

- Collection of all available data
- Collection of the relevant subset of data
- Sampling of data for statistical analysis

Querying the data enables the investigator to retrieve all or some of the data and output the results to text files or another application. The benefits of query extractions are the ease of access to the data and the capability to custom-select which fields are captured and apply any data filters. Query extractions require the investigator to access the data structure and perform some initial analysis before the data can be collected. This analysis can be done at the time of collection or during the identification phase.

Script extractions

Script extractions are very similar to query extractions. Rather than use the application's native query language, a scripting tool is used to access and collect the data. Whether a script is written in Pig, Java, or another language, the investigator can write scripts or programs that access the data and output the results to a desired format and location. Like query extractions, script extractions give the investigator the ability to customize which fields are collected and to apply filters to the data if only a subset of the data is relevant.

In addition to being a replacement for querying, scripting languages can be used to access unstructured data in Hadoop that is not accessible by other querying languages. Some Hadoop clusters are designed to analyze unstructured data, and applications may not provide a means for querying the data. This type of unstructured data is analyzed through MapReduce functions. An investigator can collect the data with a custom script extraction utilizing the same means used in a query extraction.

Software extractions

While a useful and common technique in standard database collections, software extractions are not common in forensic Big Data investigations. Software utilities such as commercial products that connect to databases and **Open Database Connectivity** (**ODBC**) drivers are valuable to investigators because they can easily connect to database systems and provide a reliable means for many different types of application collections. At this time, these types of software are not yet common for Hadoop applications and are not yet regularly employed by forensic investigators.

Validating application collections

Collecting application data requires a different form of information for validation. Validating a collection involves proving the following:

- The collection was performed correctly and completely
- The collected data is a replica of the source system's data

Unlike file-based collection methods, record-based collections compiled through an application are not typically validated with hash values. Hash values are useful for proving that data was not modified and that the collection was performed correctly. Supplemental information (for example, collection logs) is used to prove that the collection was performed completely. The use of hash values, however, is not always appropriate for application collections. There are several reasons why hash values are not used to validate application collections:

- It is not necessary to calculate hash values because of the absence of metadata or other artifacts that are collected
- Large data volumes make computing hash values infeasible in some cases
- It is faster to use non-hash methods
- Computing a hash value of the output does not prove that the contents remained unchanged during the collection process

All four points relate to the nature of the data that was collected. First, collecting records from applications does not yield metadata, so if the record is collected, the contents of the information is all that is needed. Second, Big Data is voluminous, and validating the collection through hash values can be infeasible if MD5/SHA-1 cannot be run on the source system. Also, it is possible the data is simply too large to compute a hash value in a reasonable amount of time. Third, alternative methods for validating a collection can be faster with pre-existing validation information or more quickly producible forms of validation information. Finally, hash values only work when the hash value is computed on the data source at the time of collection. Collecting records from an application rather than collecting the source files themselves, and then computing the hash values of the output files does not meet the forensic requirement for computing a hash value. That is, the hash value of the acquired data and not the source data, only proves that the acquired data was not modified between the time it was collected and when the hash was later confirmed. This does not necessarily prove that the source data remains unchanged.

Record-based data collected from Hadoop applications can be validated in other forensically-acceptable manners. The following methods for collection are used as means to prove what was intended to be collected was in fact, collected and not modified after collection:

- Control totals
- System logs
- Extraction queries and scripts
- Process documentation

The use of control totals is the primary means for validating a collection. Control totals are values from the source system that can be compared to the collected data. Control totals can take forms such as:

- Number of records
- Number of unique values
- Numeric aggregate total of a particular field or key value

The idea of a control total is to show that the data is complete and that the values in the selected fields were accurately acquired. The control totals are collected at the time of data collection. The control totals are either immediately compared to the collected data or later during a subsequent data validation step. The comparison is typically performed in an analysis database.

System logs, extraction queries and scripts, and process documentation can be used in lieu of or in addition to control totals. These forms of validation information can serve to prove that the collection method was correct and complete. Each shows the method used to collect the data, and they can also be used to show how much data was collected and whether the collection was complete. Whenever a query or script is used, it should be retained for validation purposes. Likewise, if an application can generate logs or output reports, that information should be collected and retained as well. Finally, as with any form of forensic collection, the investigator should maintain a log of all steps performed and the results. He should also transcribe those results into an acquisition form to further demonstrate that the steps performed were done so correctly.

Collecting Hive evidence

Hive is a platform for analyzing data. It uses a familiar SQL querying language, so there is no need to write Java code for MapReduce functions. Hive operates such as a database and stores all metadata in a database, so accessing the database via queries should be familiar to people who have experience working with relational databases. Hive has several important components that are critical to understand for investigations:

- **Hive Data Storage**: The type and location of data stored and accessed by Hive, which includes HDFS, Amazon S3, and other locations
- **Metastore**: The database that contains Hive data metadata (not in HDFS)
- **HiveQL**: The Hive query language, which is a SQL-like language
- **Databases and Tables**: The logical containers of Hive data
- **Hive Shell**: The shell interpreter for HiveQL
- **Hive Clients**: The mechanisms for connecting a Hive server, such as Hive Thrift clients, **Java Database Connectivity (JDBC)** clients, and ODBC clients

Hive stores record-based data in files. When data is loaded to Hive, Hive creates links to or copies of the data to a configurable location. Hive internally stores the data in databases and tables. The metastore stores metadata about the data, such as table structure, in a relational database. The data can be accessed via the Hive shell with the use of HiveQL commands, or Hive clients can be used to access the data. Hive clients are scripts or programs that utilize Hive's drivers to access the data. The following are the three types of Hive clients:

- **Thrift Client**: This is a remote client library that is compatible with a number of program languages, such as C++, Java, PHP, Python, and Ruby

- **JDBC Client**: This is a Java Database Connectivity library that allows for JDBC calls to Hive

- **ODBC Client**: This is an Open Database Connectivity library that allows for ODBC calls to Hive

Hive internally organizes data in database and table structures. A Hive server can have one or more databases. Tables of data are created within each database. When tables are created, the database is specified, and new databases can be created through Hive commands. If a table is created without a database name explicitly stated, the table is created in the default database. Similarly, a table specified in a query without a database name is automatically interpreted as belonging to the default database.

HiveQL is the query language for Hive. HiveQL's syntax is very similar to ANSI SQL and other SQL variants. The familiar SELECT, FROM, and WHERE clauses are foundational to HiveQL queries. The powerful aspect of Hive is that the standard SQL queries are converted into MapReduce jobs, which harnesses the power of MapReduce's distributed processing via SQL queries. In the Hive shell, queries can either be loaded from query files or entered interactively in the shell. Both modes enable output to be directed to files and error messages to be logged.

A Hive application collection differs from collecting Hive data through HDFS. With a Hive application collection, the data is collected either as a backup from HDFS with the Hive metastore, or the Hive service is used to interface with the data for collection. The following figure illustrates the process for performing a backup collection of Hive.

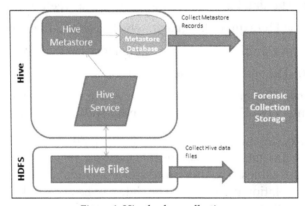

Figure 1: Hive backup collection

Alternatively — and most commonly — the Hive service is used as the means for accessing and collecting Hive data. The Hive service can be accessed through Hive queries, scripts, or Hive connectors.

The following figure illustrates how the data flows through this collection process:

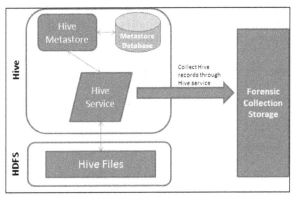

Figure 2: Hive service collection

Loading Hive data

Hive collections are performed against data stored in Hive itself. To follow along with the Hive data collection steps covered in this section, perform the following steps in either LightHadoop or Amazon S3:

1. Load data to HDFS.
2. Create Hive table.
3. Load data to Hive table.
4. Confirm the data load.

The first step for loading Hive data is to bring data into HDFS. While methods exist for directly loading data to Hive without this intermediate step, this method is simplest. The sample data used for this exercise is the subset of NYSE trades from 2000-2001 from *Chapter 2, Understanding Hadoop Internals and Architecture*. The first step is to copy the data into HDFS from the local system's /home/ec2-user directory:

```
hadoop fs -put /home/ec2-user/NYSE-2000-2001.tsv /tmp
```

The second step is to create the Hive table that will store the NYSE data. First, enter the following command to access the Hive shell:

```
hive
```

This brings up the Hive shell command line interface:

```
hive>
```

Next, run the following Hive command to create the table:

```
CREATE TABLE 'NYSE' (exchange1 string, stockSymbol string, dateVal
date, stockPriceOpen float, stockPriceHigh float, stockPriceLow
float, stockPriceClose float, stockVolume float, stockPriceAdjClose
float)
ROW FORMAT DELIMITED FIELDS TERMINATED BY '\t';
```

This command produces the following output:

```
OK
Time taken: 0.152 seconds
```

Next, load the data to the NYSE table using the following command:

```
LOAD DATA INPATH '/hdfs/tmp/NYSE-2000-2001.tsv' INTO TABLE NYSE;
```

Finally, confirm the data load by examining the total number of records loaded using the following command:

```
SELECT COUNT(*) from NYSE;
```

This creates a MapReduce job that generates the following output:

```
[...]
812990
Time taken: 68.492 seconds, Fetched: 1 row(s)
```

The data can now be viewed using queries, such as this one that returns the first 10 records:

```
SELECT * from NYSE LIMIT 10;
```

Identifying Hive evidence

Hive evidence can be identified through HiveQL commands. The following commands can be used to get a full listing of all databases and tables as well as the table's formats:

Command	Description
SHOW DATABASES;	This lists all available databases
SHOW TABLES;	This lists all tables in current database
USE databaseName;	This makes databaseName the current database
DESCRIBE (FORMATTED|EXTENDED) table;	This lists the formatting details about the table

Identifying all tables and their formats requires iterating through every database and generating a list of tables and each table's formats. This process can be performed either manually or through an automated HiveQL script file. These commands do not provide information about database and table metadata, such as number of records and last modified date, but they do give a full listing of all available online Hive data.

Deleted Hive data can also be recovered in some instances. When data is deleted from Hive, the metadata is removed from the database, but the files in HDFS or other storage are moved to the .Trash directory. In cases of a misconfigured .Trash file, Hive cannot move files to the .Trash, so the files remain in their original folders. However, the metadata records in the Hive metastore are erased. If there are questions about whether data has been deleted, the raw files should be collected, even if the metadata is no longer available.

Hive backup collection

Hive does not have a natural backup mechanism. Most Hive environments are configured to replicate the metastore and data files to a replication cluster. This limitation means that true database backups of the entire Hive environment are not possible; however, the replication process can be performed in order to collect all evidence. To replicate Hive, the following steps are performed:

- Forensically, copy all Hive data files based on the file location information found in the Hive configuration file
- Perform a full database backup of the metastore database

The metastore can be hosted in a number of different types of databases, such as SQL Server and MySQL. A full backup of that database should be collected, but the same considerations apply when collecting the metastore database. Namely, a current copy should be collected and the output should be in a format that the investigator can access and read during the analysis phase.

If the Hive environment has an embedded metastore, a slightly different process should be taken. By default, Hive is installed to run a local Derby database that is intended for testing purposes. Most production Hive environments are configured to run with a standalone database, but an investigator may encounter a Hive metastore configured to run Derby. Derby database viewing and extraction can be performed through the Apache SQuirreL SQL Client. SQuirreL is a Java-based package that interfaces with Derby through JDBC calls. If an investigator encounters a Derby metastore, SQuirreL and custom-developed Java packages are the best methods for extracting the metastore contents.

The metastore backend can be identified in the Hive configuration file
`hive-site.xml`, which can be found in the `$HIVE_HOME/conf` directory. The
`javax.jdo.option.ConnectionURL` property will list the connection URL for
the metastore, and from this, the investigator can identify the type of metastore
database backend being used by Hive.

Depending on the Hadoop installation, third-party backup tools may be available
that can generate Hive backups. One commercial product, Cloudera Manager, offers
a backup and disaster recovery tool that can generate Hive backups. As with all
backups, the investigator should be prepared and able to extract the backup file to
a usable format, which may require having a copy of Cloudera Manager or
whatever backup tool was used to generate the backup file.

Hive query collection

Hive's query language, HiveQL, is a powerful tool that is suitable for performing
forensic collections. HiveQL offers the flexibility and granular querying capabilities
necessary for performing query-based collections. Entire tables can be collected in
the same format in which they are stored in Hive, or subsets of data can be collected
by specifying which fields to collect and applying any necessary filter criteria. The
queries can be run either from the Hive shell or in batches via HiveQL query files.

In most circumstances, the collection should be performed with query files instead
of entering commands in the Hive shell. Query files have a couple of advantages:
they enable the collection to be executed in one or more batches, and the query files
serve as documentation of the collection process. Manually entering the collection
queries using the Hive shell is acceptable; however, documentation of the queries
should still be captured.

All three query collection methods are available with Hive: complete, subset, and
sampled. Performing a complete collection is the most straightforward. In SQL, the
`SELECT *` clause selects all fields from the specified table. By selecting all fields and
not applying any filter criteria, the investigator can collect all records from the table.
For a complete collection, this type of query is run for every database and every
table in the source system. The queries are run from the list of databases and tables
discovered during the identification step.

HiveQL script files are text files that contain the Hive queries that should be run.
Create a text file, insert the following query, and save the file as `NYSEexport.sql`:

```
SELECT * from NYSE;
```

Run the following command from the client to export the entire NYSE table to the host operating system's /home directory:

```
hive -f /home/scripts/NYSEexport.sql > /home/NYSEexport.tsv
```

 An alternative method is the Hive INSERT OVERWRITE LOCAL command, which creates an output file in the local filesystem based on the specified query.

A tab-separated value file that contains the table's column headers along with every record in the table is created in the /home directory. The output file's format matches that of the input file. An issue that sometimes arises with data extraction is that the delimiter matches a character inside a field. This commonly occurs with tab- and comma-separated value files because tab and comma characters are normal characters. Typically, TSV and CSV files use text qualifiers to denote the beginning and end of a field, so any characters within the field that match the delimiter do not cause issues when exporting or importing the data. Double quotes are sometimes used as text qualifiers, as are infrequently used characters, such as the paragraph symbol. Unfortunately, Hive does not handle text qualifiers, so a custom delimiter that does not match any text in the table must be chosen.

If this issue is a concern, the investigator can export the data to a text file with custom-specified delimiters and text qualifiers. The following query selects all of the columns from the NYSE table with the custom delimiter | :

```
SELECT CONCAT_WS('|', exchange1, stockSymbol, CAST(dateVal as
string), CAST(stockPriceOpen as string), CAST(stockPriceHigh as
string), CAST(stockPriceLow as string),
CAST(stockPriceClose as string), CAST(stockVolume as string),
CAST(stockPriceAdjClose as string)
FROM NYSE;
```

This query uses the concat_ws() function to concatenate the strings with the pipe character between each field. Note that each numeric and date field has to be cast as a string. This is required because the concat_ws() function requires string values as inputs. Because the pipe character is rarely used, this is an effective delimiter.

The first row of output from this command is:

```
NYSE|ASP|2001-12-31|12.55|12.8|12.42|12.8|11300|6.91
```

> If a custom delimiter is used, the investigator should examine the properties of each table's fields via the DESCRIBE <TABLE> command to identify the non-string fields that need to be cast as strings. Failing to do so will result in errors.

Script files are the ideal method for collecting multiple tables. Because the investigator wants to collect each table into a separate file, the query files should be created separately, but they can still be executed from a single script. For example, if 100 tables need to be collected, one query file should be created for each table. Then, a single Bash script file can be created that runs the following command for each of the 100 query files:

```
hive -f /home/scripts/table1.sql > /home/table1_output.tsv
```

If all tables need to be collected, the process can be automated through a HiveQL script and a Bash script. First, create a HiveQL script named `tableExport.hql` using the following line of code. This selects all rows of a table, with the table name being passed in through a variable named `tablename`:

```
select * from ${hiveconf:tablename}
```

Next, create a Bash script named `HiveAllTableExport.sh` with the following code:

```
#!/bin/bash
hive -e "show tables;" > hiveTables.txt
for line in $(cat hiveTables.txt) ;
do
hive -hiveconf tablename=$line -f tableExport.hql > ${line}.txt
done
```

This script generates a file called `hiveTables.txt`, which is a listing of all tables in the current database. The script then iterates through the table listing to generate a full export file for each table. If multiple databases need to be collected, the script can be modified to include an outer loop that iterates through the listing of databases via the SHOW DATABASES command.

Hive query control totals

Control totals can be collected for Hive in a number of ways. The simplest and most common method is to collect row counts for each table. Typically, row counts are the only control totals required. However, in cases where questions may arise about the quality of the collection, computing field-level control totals may be necessary.

The following should be considered when deciding whether field-level control totals are necessary:

- How many fields are being collected?
- Is one or more field particularly critical for the analysis?
- Does a particular field contain numeric data or data that otherwise lends itself well to aggregation?
- Will the value from a field be called into question?
- Does an alternative method exist for validating the collection of that field?

Similar to the process for batch collection via queries, the control totals can be captured by creating one query file for each table that captures the row count:

```
SELECT count(*) from table1
```

The same Bash batch script file can be created that executes each query file and stores the output in a separate file—or in a single file if the table name information is generated in the queries.

Another control total method is to compute the numeric totals of key fields. These computations can be the sum value of a numeric field, the number of unique values, or the min/max values. Because a collection can have many fields, the investigator should select a handful of key fields—usually one or two per table—that demonstrate the values were collected properly. Alternatively, if reports are available that represent all records for the key fields from Hive, which is also a viable control total approach.

The following Hive query commands can be used to compute these values on selected fields:

Command	Description
Sum(field1)	This computes the sum total of field1 for all records
Min(field1)	This computes the minimum value of field1 for all records
Max(field1)	This computes the maximum value of field1 for all records
Count(distinct field1)	This computes the number of unique values in field1

Control totals are typically collected in a single file, with the table name being included. Because Big Data collections can involve a large number of tables, the fastest method for collecting control totals is to include the table name and total—along with the type of control total and applicable field, if necessary. Collecting the data into a single file is easiest because that file can be loaded into an analysis repository and then quickly compared to the calculated control totals of the collected data in the analysis repository. This saves the effort required to manually verify each control total.

Hive metadata and log collection

Collecting Hive data through the Hive application does not provide access to metadata, log, and configuration information. While a Hive application collection enables the investigator to capture records from Hive, it does not capture the file metadata, logs, or configuration information, which is available in a Hive data filesystem collection. If Hive is configured to retain audit trail information or data updates to a Hive table, that information can be collected. However, the full set of file metadata, log file, and configuration information can only be collected by acquiring the data through the filesystem. If an investigator decides to collect Hive records through the application, he should consider whether to collect the metadata, log, and configuration file information from the filesystem to supplement the collection.

The Hive script collection

HiveQL is the main language for Hive collections, but other script-based languages are available to collect data. Hive makes available several libraries that enable various languages to access a Hive data set. The three types of libraries are:

- ODBC
- Java
- Thrift

Each of these libraries can be used to access the data. To do this, the investigator must have the script call its language-specific library to access the data. Scripting the data collection offers several benefits, such as the following:

- Automation of the collection process
- Control of the data flow
- Streamlined generation of control totals in parallel to the collection

The two primary drawbacks to script-based collections are: 1) most script-based methods are slower than the use of backups or queries, and 2) developing scripts that collect the right data at a granular level can be time consuming. In addition, the Hive scripting libraries, whether ODBC, Java, or Thrift, must be available on the client machine accessing the data.

The following Python script creates a connection to Hive and exports the results to the supplied output file. Information about the table is exported to the supplied log file, with the collection date, number of records, and query also being written to the log.

```
import pyhs2
import datetime
```

```
outputFile = open('/home/extract/outputFile.txt', 'w')
logFile = open('/home/extract/logFile.txt', 'w')
logFile.write(str(datetime.date.today())+'\n')
with pyhs2.connect(host='localhost',
 port=10000,
 authMechanism="PLAIN",
 user='root',
 password='pwdVal',
 database='default') as conn:
with conn.cursor() as cur:
logFile.write(cur.getDatabases()+'\n')
cur.execute("select * from table")
logFile.write('select * from table\n')
logFile.write('Number of rows: ' + str(cur.rowcount) + '\n')
logFile.write(cur.getSchema()+'\n')
#Fetch table results
for i in cur.fetch():
outputFile.write(i + '\n')
outputFile.close()
logFile.close()
```

Executing this query generates the output file and the log file. The log file and script are sufficient for demonstrating the process used to perform the collection. If, however, errors exist in the script, the entire collection can be called into question. The acquisition log and chain of custody documentation should still be completed.

 For more information about Hive libraries, visit `https://cwiki.apache.org/confluence/display/Hive/HiveClient`.

Collecting HBase evidence

HBase differs from Hive in a number of ways. First, HBase is not a relational database. Unlike Hive, HBase does not support SQL-like queries, because SQL is a language for relational databases. Second, HBase does not have a metastore database. Instead, HBase is a nonrelational database based on Google's BigTable that works with HDFS for data storage and access. Third, HBase data is distributed to various nodes in regions, or to data blocks that store column-oriented chunks of related data. It is far easier to collect HBase evidence through HBase rather than collecting from each node due to the distributed nature of the data.

Given the complexity of carving out data from HFiles, collecting HBase evidence through the HBase interface has an advantage over a filesystem collection. HFiles are distributed file structures that need to be collected from each node. Once collected, HFiles must be carved in order to extract the column-oriented data and metadata and then convert this data into a usable format. This can be overly burdensome during an investigation. Instead, the HBase data can be collected more easily through the application. The output of this data is either flat files or HBase database backups. Both formats are significantly easier to work with during the analysis phase.

The following concepts are important for understanding how HBase operates:

- **HBase data storage**: The type and location of data stored and accessed by HBase, which includes HDFS, Amazon S3, and other locations
- **Tables**: The logical containers of HBase data
- **NoSQL (Not only SQL)**: The type of non-SQL database that provides nonrelational data storage and retrieval
- **Key-pair values**: The scheme in which data values are stored and retrieved; keys are queried to retrieve their corresponding values
- **HBase shell**: The shell interpreter for HBase
- **Master node and regionservers**: The distributed storage and analysis nodes
- **ZooKeeper**: The software that manages the assignment of regionservers
- **HFile**: The MapFile-like file type stored in HDFS by HBase - HFiles are the file containers for HBase table data and metadata
- **Memstore**: The in-memory storage of HBase data that is held in memory until the storage threshold is met and the data is written to HFiles
- **-ROOT- table**: The table that stores the list of .META. table regions
- **.META. table**: The table that stores the list of all user-space regions
- **HBase Clients**: The mechanisms for connecting to an HBase server

The data can be accessed via the HBase shell, or HBase clients can be used to access the data. HBase clients are scripts or programs that utilize Hive's drivers to access the data. The main types of HBase clients are:

- MapReduce
- Java

- REST
- Thrift

These clients operate similar to the Hive clients. Each offers programmatic means for interfacing with HBase and performing data operations. MapReduce is the most common method data analysts employ for running HBase analysis, whereas Java, AVRO, REST, and Thrift can be used for data extract, transform, load (ETL), data export, or analysis. The following figure shows how an HBase application-based collection operates, with the HBase service used to represent the use of the HBase shell or HBase clients to request and collect data:

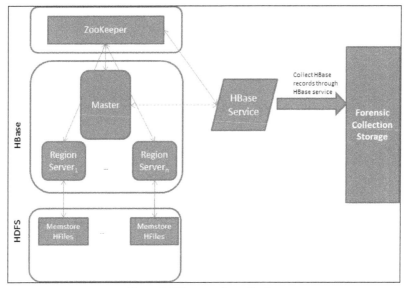

Figure 3: HBase service collection

HBase has a number of robust backup mechanisms that can also be used for a forensic collection. These include the following:

- Full backup
- Online table export

Each of the backup methods is a viable and sound method for collecting HBase data. They also do not require significant configuration for data restoration, making the HBase backup options more advantageous than the Hive backup methods. HBase also offers other backup methods, such as incremental backups and replication, but those are not as valuable or expeditious as the two types mentioned in the preceding list.

Loading HBase data

Data can be loaded into HBase in a number of ways. HBase clients can be used to programmatically push data into HBase. The simplest method is to load HBase data through the HBase shell. The HBase shell is started via the following command:

```
hbase shell
```

Next, the HBase table is created with the following command:

```
create 'testTable', 'account', 'address'
```

This creates a table called testTable with account and address as column family.

Finally, the table is populated using put commands:

```
put 'testTable', 'record1', 'account:name', 'John Doe'
put 'testTable', 'record1', 'account:ID', '100'
put 'testTable', 'record1', 'address:street', '123 Main St'
put 'testTable', 'record1', 'address:country', 'USA'
put 'testTable', 'record2', 'account:name', 'Jane Doe'
put 'testTable', 'record2', 'account:ID', '101'
put 'testTable', 'record2', 'address:country', 'UK'
```

Each put command loads a new value into an HBase cell. The first put command inserts the value John Doe into testTable for record1 in the account:name cell. The record1 value is the unique identifier for the table. Both the account and address column families can have multiple values. In this case, name and ID are part of the account column family and street and country are part of the address column family. Four values are inserted into record1. Only three values are inserted into record2, though HBase does not require every record to populate the same number of columns.

The data load can be tested by first counting the number of rows:

```
count 'testTable'
```

This returns the following output:

```
2 row(s) in 0.0210 seconds
```

The table can also be queried from the HBase shell using the scan command:

```
scan 'testTable'
```

The scan command produces the following output:

```
record1 column=account:ID, timestamp=1427229190902, value=100

record1 column=account:country, timestamp=1427229218748, value=USA

record1 column=account:name, timestamp=1427228899101, value=John Doe

record1 column=account:street, timestamp=1427229207080, value=123
Main St

record2 column=account:ID, timestamp=1427229237904, value=101

record2 column=account:country, timestamp=1427229246303, value=UK

record2 column=account:name, timestamp=1427229008616, value=Jane Doe

2 row(s) in 0.8620 seconds
```

Identifying HBase evidence

HBase evidence is stored in tables, and identifying the names of the tables and the properties of each is important for data collection. HBase stores metadata information in the -ROOT- and .META. tables. These tables can be queried using HBase shell commands to identify the information about all tables in the HBase cluster.

Information about the HBase cluster can be gathered using the status command from the HBase shell:

```
status

2 servers, 0 dead, 1.5000 average load
```

For additional information about the names and locations of the servers, as well as the total disk sizes for the memstores and HFiles, the status command can be given the detailed parameter.

The list command outputs every HBase table. The one table created in HBase, testTable, is shown via the following command:

```
list

TABLE

testTable

1 row(s) in 0.0370 seconds

=> ["testTable"]
```

Information about each table can be generated using the `describe` command:

```
describe 'testTable'

'testTable', {NAME => 'account', DATA_BLOCK_ENCODING => 'NONE',
BLOOMFILTER => 'NONE', REPLICATION_SCOPE => '0', VERSIONS => '3',
COMPRESSION => 'NONE', MIN_VERSIONS => '0', TTL => '2147483647',
KEEP_DELETED_CELLS => 'false', BLOCKSIZE => '65536', IN_MEMORY =>
'false', ENCODE_ON_DISK => 'true', BLOCKCACHE => 'true'}, {NAME =>
'address', DATA_BLOCK_ENCODING => 'NONE', BLOOMFILTER => 'NONE',
REPLICATION_SCOPE => '0', VERSIONS => '3', COMPRESSION => 'NONE',
MIN_VERSIONS => '0', TTL => '2147483647', KEEP_DELETED_CELLS =>
'false', BLOCKSIZE => '65536', IN_MEMORY => 'false', ENCODE_ON_DISK
=> 'true', BLOCKCACHE => 'true'}

1 row(s) in 0.0300 seconds
```

The `describe` command yields several useful pieces of information about each table. Each of the column families are listed, and for each family, the encoding, number of columns (represented as versions), and whether the deleted cells are retained are also listed.

Security information about each table can be gathered using the `user_permission` command:

```
user_permission 'testTable'
```

This command is useful for identifying the users who currently have access to the table. As mentioned earlier, user accounts are not as meaningful in Hadoop because of the distributed nature of Hadoop configurations, but in some cases, knowing who had access to tables can be tied back to system logs to identify individuals who accessed the system and data.

The HBase backup collection

HBase provides a number of backup mechanisms that can be used for forensic collection of HBase data. The HBase snapshot and export utilities are the best methods for forensic collection. The snapshot utility generates a complete backup of the HBase database. The file can be loaded into an HBase instance in the analysis repository via the `restore_snapshot` command during the analysis phase. The export utility creates SequenceFiles that are stored in HDFS. The SequenceFiles can be forensically copied from HDFS to forensic storage after the export utility process completes.

To create a snapshot, first ensure that the `hbase-site.xml` file's `hbase.snapshot.enabled` property is set to `true`. If it is set to `false`, snapshots cannot be created. From the HBase shell, type:

```
snapshot 'testTable', 'snapshotName'
```

This creates a snapshot in the `./hbase/snapshot` directory. Once created, the snapshot directory should be copied along with the files in the following directories:

- `./hbase/<tableName>/<regionName>/<familyName>/`: This directory houses files that are still in use by HBase
- `./hbase/.archive/<tableName>/<regionName>/<familyName>/`: This directory houses files no longer in use by HBase

The MD5 hash values of the files can be computed from the snapshot files and then compared to the MD5 hash values of the forensically copied snapshot files. If the size of the files is prohibitive for the use of MD5, control totals can be captured immediately after the snapshot is generated.

The export utility can be used to export an individual HBase table to SequenceFiles. The advantage of this method is that complete backups of tables can be generated to a common Hadoop file format. To generate an export backup, run the following command from the client operating system (not HBase shell):

```
hbase org.apache.hadoop.hbase.mapreduce.Export 'testTable'
/home/ec2-user/testTable
```

This generates the following output that serves as both a log and record count control total for the export:

```
File System Counters
FILE: Number of bytes read=18233900
FILE: Number of bytes written=18644961
FILE: Number of read operations=0
FILE: Number of large read operations=0
FILE: Number of write operations=0
Map-Reduce Framework
Map input records=2
Map output records=2
Input split bytes=101
Spilled Records=0
Failed Shuffles=0
Merged Map outputs=0
GC time elapsed (ms)=8
CPU time spent (ms)=0
Physical memory (bytes) snapshot=0
Virtual memory (bytes) snapshot=0
```

```
Total committed heap usage (bytes)=238354432
HBase Counters
BYTES_IN_REMOTE_RESULTS=336
BYTES_IN_RESULTS=336
MILLIS_BETWEEN_NEXTS=327
NOT_SERVING_REGION_EXCEPTION=0
NUM_SCANNER_RESTARTS=0
REGIONS_SCANNED=1
REMOTE_RPC_CALLS=5
REMOTE_RPC_RETRIES=0
RPC_CALLS=5
RPC_RETRIES=0
File Input Format Counters
Bytes Read=0
File Output Format Counters
Bytes Written=508
```

The SequenceFile for this export is found in the `/home/ec2-user/testTable` directory:

```
-rw-r--r-- 1 ec2-user ec2-user  496 Mar 25 15:03 part-m-00000
-rw-rw-r-- 1 ec2-user ec2-user   12 Mar 25 15:03 .part-m-00000.crc
-rw-r--r-- 1 ec2-user ec2-user    0 Mar 25 15:03 _SUCCESS
-rw-rw-r-- 1 ec2-user ec2-user    8 Mar 25 15:03 ._SUCCESS.crc
```

These files should be forensically copied to the forensic destination drive, with an MD5 hash value, if feasible.

The HBase query collection

HBase offers a very basic query language that is accessible from the shell. The query language enables filtering and aggregation to be performed, but the language is not as robust and flexible as a SQL variant. Collections are possible using the HBase shell language; however, the queries require some data manipulation to ensure that the results are returned correctly. The following command can be run from an HBase client to execute the HBase shell `scan` command and exclude any output that does not start with a space. That is, this command's output only includes HBase records and excludes summary information and Java output:

```
echo "scan 'testTable'" | hbase shell | grep "^ " >
./outputDir/testTable.txt
```

The output file, `testTable.txt`, contains the records from `testTable`:

```
record1 column=account:ID, timestamp=1427286384337, value=100

record1 column=account:name, timestamp=1427286375900, value=John Doe

record1 column=address:country, timestamp=1427286409638, value=USA

record1 column=address:street, timestamp=1427286400653, value=123
Main St

record2 column=account:ID, timestamp=1427286437526, value=101

record2 column=account:name, timestamp=1427286427052, value=Jane Doe

record2 column=address:country, timestamp=1427286447013, value=UK
```

The use of the HBase shell's `scan` utility is useful for extracting all values for a table, but its filtering capabilities are not as well-suited for filtering data for a collection as SQL methods. Another limitation of `scan` is that the output is limited to the format shown in the preceding output file. Also, because of the lack of data type enforcement and the incapability to create multiple columns for each column family, the output of `scan` cannot be easily imported into a relational database without data transformations. An investigator should determine how many tables need to be extracted and whether data filtering needs to be applied before deciding whether to use `scan`.

Apache Phoenix is a SQL-wrapped layer over HBase that provides SQL-like access to HBase, and Hive can be connected to HBase for SQL querying. If Phoenix or Hive is part of the HBase environment in question, Phoenix or Hive queries can be run in place of HBase queries for the collection.

HBase collection via scripts

HBase data can also be exported using scripts that connect to HBase via the HBase client libraries. The HBase client libraries offer mechanisms for connecting to HBase data stores and then programmatically exporting data. Most scripting languages and Java offer granular data controls and filtering, methods for exporting data to a desired location, and performing other steps (for example, MD5 calculation). The script-based approach requires a strong understanding of the Hadoop architecture and the effect a script has on the Hadoop cluster.

Pig is a common scripting language for querying and extracting data from Hadoop applications. For HBase, the `HBaseStorage()` method can be used to connect to a particular table and extract the specified column families and/or columns.

The following Pig script can be run to collect the results from the `testTable` using the `HBaseStorage()` method into pipe-delimited records:

```
dataOutput = LOAD 'hbase://testTable' USING
org.apache.pig.backend.hadoop.hbase.HBaseStorage('account:ID
account:name address:street address:country', '-loadKey=true') as
(id, accountID, accountName, addressStreet, addressCountry);

store dataOutput into 'results/extract' using PigStorage('|');
```

> For more information about writing Pig scripts for HBase, visit https://pig.apache.org/docs/r0.9.1/api/org/apache/pig/backend/hadoop/hbase/HBaseStorage.html.

HBase control totals

Control totals can be collected in two ways with HBase. First, the HBase shell command `count` can be used to capture the number of records for a particular table. This method can also be scripted from the HBase client operating system:

```
echo "count 'testTable'" | hbase shell >
./outputDir/testTable_recCount.txt
```

The alternative is to collect the control totals through a Pig or MapReduce script at the time of data collection. This method is best because of the automation and the combined step of data collection and validation collection.

HBase metadata and log collection

HBase metadata is limited and not relevant to most investigations. The `.META.` and `-ROOT-` tables, which are described as metadata tables, only contain information about data regions and the locations of the data blocks. These tables are useful for HBase's internal operations but not relevant for most investigations. The primary sources of information about HBase can be found in the data tables, the `hbase-site.xml` configuration file, and HBase log files. Typically, HBase log files are found in the `/var/log/hbase` directory. In this directory, the HBase and ZooKeeper log files about all system activity are available. In addition, investigators can collect the `SecurityAuth.audit` file in the `/var/log/hadoop` directory for information about application login attempts.

Collecting other Hadoop application data and non-Hadoop data

Not all relevant Hadoop data is always stored and accessed within Hive, HBase, or even HDFS. Hadoop clusters are typically part of a larger data analysis ecosystem. This means that data flows into and out of Hadoop from other systems. Inside Hadoop, and at the Hadoop data ingress and egress points, data transfers and transformations may occur. These changes to the data may be relevant, and as such, the investigator may need to collect data from these systems.

Many other Hadoop applications are available for data analysis and storage. The Apache Foundation currently lists many projects and incubator projects that are deployed in production environments. Applications such as Cassandra, Chukwa, and Spark may be found in the course of an investigation as well as new ones (for example, Drill and Tajo). When a new or uncommon application is identified, the investigator can apply the same collection process for each application, which first requires determining whether the collection should be performed in HDFS or the application. If the collection should be performed through the application, the investigator should first become well versed in the methods for collecting the data and review documentation to ensure that critical evidence is not overlooked. If possible, work with the system owner to understand the application. Otherwise, consider employing an expert in that system to assist with the collection process.

> For more information about typical Hadoop implementations and the various Apache Hadoop applications in use, visit `https://wiki.apache.org/hadoop/PoweredB`.

Hadoop is often designed to be part of a larger data environment. Data flows into Hadoop from various sources, such as web servers and customer relationship management (CRM) systems. Data can also flow into Hadoop from other databases or data warehouses as part of the analysis flow. Hadoop performs actions on the data, such as data aggregation, transformation, and reporting. Hadoop then outputs the data into reports or as data flows into other systems.

The following figure illustrates a simplified environment and how data flows into and out of Hadoop:

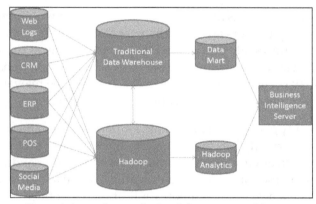

Figure 4: A sample organizational data system architecture

This environment shows five major systems that serve as inputs to both the traditional data warehouse environment and the Hadoop cluster. The data warehouse and Hadoop share data, and all output flows to a business intelligence server by way of a data mart and Hadoop analytics environment. In real-world environments, subsets and various versions of data are distributed to the data warehouse and Hadoop environments, near-line and offline versions of the data are stored, and some or all of the various components are deployed in a cloud environment.

Some of the common solutions that interface with a Hadoop cluster include:

- Hadoop reporting and visualization solutions
- Hadoop data warehouse solutions
- Records management and compliance solutions
- Traditional data warehouses
- Business intelligence software

Understanding how data flows into and out of Hadoop is important for the following reasons:

- The other systems may be easier to collect
- The other systems may retain data that was purged by Hadoop
- Data was transformed inside or outside of Hadoop, and the form of data outside of Hadoop is relevant to the investigation
- Data from the other systems are valuable for data validation

Each of these points highlight the fact that data can be found in various locations and that an investigation does not always rely on a single system. Rather, Big Data can be part of a larger organization-wide investigation. In some cases, only a single system is required. In other investigations, such as fraud investigations and cases involving data manipulation, multiple systems need to be analyzed. The key is for the investigator to understand the requirements of the investigation and clearly identify the available systems and the data they store.

Summary

Collecting evidence through Hadoop applications instead of HDFS offers a number of benefits. The applications offer a quicker, easier means to access the data. Rather than collecting data from each node of the cluster, applications bridge all of the nodes and offer a means to collect data from a single point. Many application-based collection methods also offer an up-front method to cull out the data and limit it to only the relevant data. This is a huge benefit when dealing with terabytes or petabytes of data. In the case of petabytes, a full collection is not currently feasible for most investigations. Application-based collections also make the analysis phase easier. Collecting data from applications enables the investigator to begin the analysis more quickly, instead of spending a large amount of time carving out data and piecing together the data.

Regardless of the application, the same process and concepts can be applied. This chapter focused on Hive and HBase, which are the two most prominent Hadoop data storage and analysis packages. However, many other open source, commercial, and proprietary applications exist. The same concepts and principles can be applied to any other application. First, determine which collection methods are available (for example, query or backup) and then assess which of those best meet the needs of the investigation. During the selection process, the investigator needs to be mindful of the impact of that collection process on the source system and the output format of the evidence. The collection should be documented, and control totals or other validation information must be collected.

The next two chapters cover the analysis phase. The evidence that has been collected can now be put into a format for analysis, and the analysis can be conducted utilizing known techniques, such as fraud detection algorithms and descriptive statistics.

6
Performing Hadoop Distributed File System Analysis

The previous two chapters covered the data collection process. *Chapter 4, Collecting Hadoop Distributed File System Data* discussed filesystem data collection, with a focus on how to collect **Hadoop Distributed File System** (**HDFS**) data in several different ways. *Chapter 5, Collecting Hadoop Application Data*, went through the process of collecting application-level Hadoop data. The analysis phase begins after the collection process, and the type(s) of analysis chosen depend on the collection method that was selected. This chapter covers examples of the main types of analyses that are conducted against the filesystem-level data collection, which was covered in *Chapter 4, Collecting Hadoop Distributed File System Data*.

Evidence collected from the HDFS filesystem can be analyzed in several ways. First, evidence can be reconstructed into its original format for analysis. This is typically the case when a Hadoop cluster is offline during collection and each node is forensically imaged. This process requires data reconstruction—such as file carving—and is the most time-consuming one. A second method is analyzing the logical files collected from a Hadoop cluster. Metadata analysis and data reconstruction can be performed on the logical file collection. A third method is log and configuration file analysis to determine how the cluster was set up and what events occurred. These analyses can be run independently or, more typically, in concert as part of a larger investigation.

The forensic analysis process

Forensic analysis is a process. Investigations are rarely solved in a linear manner. Typically, an investigation begins with a hypothesis that is tested against the data. During the analysis, additional clues or details are uncovered that change or add to the original hypothesis. The process continues iteratively until the investigator can determine exactly what occurred and can provide supporting evidence from the data. This iterative process applies to both traditional computer forensics and Big Data forensics. The following diagram illustrates the steps of the analysis phase:

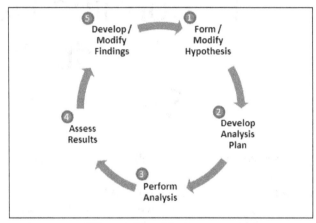

Figure 1: The analysis process

The starting point of the analysis phase is the investigation hypothesis. The hypothesis is based on the facts of the case and is often developed well in advance of the analysis phase. One example of a hypothesis is, "Former employee X stole trade secrets from Company Y, and then implemented a solution based on those trade secrets for his new employer, Company Z."

An analysis plan is developed based on the hypothesis and a combination of factors. The following are the key considerations for developing a plan in the analysis phase:

- The requirements of the investigation
- The available evidence
- The relevant non-Big Data evidence

Analysis plans are useful for planning and directing the analysis. In highly complex investigations, the analysis can involve hundreds or thousands of analyses. Organizing those analysis steps into a plan is critical for ensuring that all analysis is completed. A plan can be as simple as, "Identify all financial transactions from employee X on January 2 in the Hive table trades." Or, the analysis can involve comparing multiple data sources to identify anomalies that indicate a particular pattern. Regardless, analysis plans are developed that address the key points of the hypothesis vis-à-vis the available evidence. They also incorporate additional evidence that can corroborate or be used to cross-validate the results. Additionally, analysis plans account for time limitations and the type of analysis that is admissible in the presentation phase.

The analysis itself takes on many different forms. In some cases, information about the data is critical, such as file date modifications, system configurations, and the volume of data. In other situations, the content of the data is what requires analysis. Most Big Data investigations focus on the data contents. The data is loaded into an analysis repository, and queries are run against the data to identify the characteristics of the data using anomaly detection, descriptive statistics, and/or inferential statistics.

The results of the analysis are reviewed, and based on those results, the analysis is concluded or the analysis is modified based on the findings, or lack thereof. Investigators take the analysis findings and determine whether the findings are sufficient, unbiased, and complete. The results should tell a compelling story that is free of bias. If contradictory results are found, those results should not be discarded. Rather, they should be analyzed further.

Forensic analysis goals

There are a number of goals in the analysis phase. No two investigations are the same, so the goals will vary by investigation. One goal that is common among most investigations is properly scoping the evidence. The investigator may not know what information can be found in the evidence or what the smoking gun even is. Scoping the evidence is the process of surveying the evidence and getting a better understanding of the overall set of evidence. Another goal is extracting evidence. Collected evidence may not be in a format that is conducive to further analysis. The evidence must first either be further extracted or converted into a format that can be reviewed by the investigator.

The obvious goal of the analysis phase is the actual analysis. The analysis should determine what the facts contained in the evidence mean and how they relate to the other facts of the investigation. The analysis should be:

- **Timely**: The analysis is performed within the time constraints of the investigation

- **Complete**: All relevant evidence is analyzed

- **Accurate**: The analysis is performed correctly and without bias

- **Meaningful**: The analysis is conducted in a way that tells a logical story that can be understood by others

Forensic analysis concepts

Several concepts are important in the analysis phase. They ensure the investigation is performed properly and within the practical realities of an investigation. These analysis concepts are defined in the following list:

- **Anomaly/Outlier**: A result or data point that is unexpected and/or not of a normal pattern.

- **Bias**: Any form of prejudice for, or against, a party; or a preconceived fact that is not backed by evidence (for example, confirmation bias).

- **Completeness**: The relevant evidence was analyzed fully.

- **Cross-validation**: The validation of results from one data set against another.

- **Data reduction**: The minimization or culling of irrelevant data to make the analysis data set a more manageable size. This process is important in the early stages of Big Data analysis to ensure the analysis can be performed in a timely manner.

- **False negative**: An analysis result that incorrectly indicates the absence of a condition or attribute.

- **False positive**: An analysis result that incorrectly indicates the presence of a condition or attribute.

- **Hash analysis**: The verification and comparison of hash values against source evidence or against a list of known hash values for common files.

The challenges of forensic analysis

Several difficulties can arise during the course of a Big Data investigation. The system may have been intentionally altered in an attempt to thwart the investigation, or security measures may be in place that hamper or prevent the investigation. These issues can be addressed in a number of ways and should be tested for during the analysis phase.

Anti-forensic techniques

Anti-forensic techniques are intentional steps taken to defeat forensic analysis. Anti-forensic techniques are problematic because they are aimed at destroying evidence and/or creating false or misleading evidence. If an investigator does not control for anti-forensic techniques or perform analysis to determine whether anti-forensics was applied, the analysis could be completed using flawed data. Some advanced techniques include steganography and secret data channels. However, the most common anti-forensic techniques that apply to Big Data investigations include the following:

- Log deletion/modification
- Record deletion/modification
- Injecting large volumes of data around key data

The best methods for combating anti-forensic techniques are 1) cross-validation of existing evidence with other Big Data evidence as well as evidence from other sources, and 2) anomaly detection. Several methods for doing this include comparing log file entries against data sources and comparing sets of mirrored data sets. For example, comparing the Sqoop application log files against the data imported into Hive via Sqoop is one method for determining if records were deleted from Hive or if the logs were modified. The anti-forensic techniques can span multiple data sources, so the investigator should be aware of the possibility of getting a false-positive when validating only two data sources.

Data encryption

Hadoop and its applications support end-to-end encryption. When encryption is configured and turned on, the cluster's data is encrypted at rest and in transit. At-rest encryption means that the data stored in the cluster is encrypted, which is problematic if the evidence was collected via a forensic image with the cluster powered off. In-transit encryption means that the data is encrypted while it is being transferred across the network. Encryption is not an issue when the data is forensically collected from an HDFS client or directly through Hadoop.

If the evidence is encrypted, the forensic investigator should request the encryption keys. The **Hadoop Key Management Server** (**KMS**) is the proxy server that manages Hadoop encryption keys and would be the location of the keys for the cluster. Encryption keys are required to be turned over in criminal and civil litigation cases in the US, and most other courts also require that the party who holds the encryption keys turn them over if they are the only means to decrypt the data.

 For more information about Hadoop encryption, visit `http://hadoop.apache.org/docs/current/hadoop-project-dist/hadoop-hdfs/TransparentEncryption.html`.

Analysis preparation

Several steps are taken at the onset of the analysis phase to prepare the forensic environment for the analysis. The first step is to attach a copy of the evidence to the environment in a read-only manner. Because the amount of forensic data is large in a Big Data investigation, the hard drives containing the evidence should be attached to a sufficiently large storage device in the read-only mode. The Big Data analysis environment should be attached to a **network-attached storage** (**NAS**), or other large-scale storage solution. Cloud environments are becoming increasingly common in forensic investigations, but the investigator must ensure that proper security measures are in place and that such storage is acceptable for the investigation.

 Cloud computing has several advantages for Big Data investigations. These include distributed computing and less of an infrastructure burden being placed on the investigator. However, data upload speeds to many cloud computing environments are slow, and loading data to a cloud raises security issues. The investigator should ensure that cloud storage is allowed for that investigation and that proper security and data privacy controls are in place.

The analysis environment also needs to include the software for performing the analysis. One or more analysis machines need to be set up with the analysis software and connected to the copied read-only evidence. A standard tool for Big Data investigations is database software. These software packages, such as Microsoft SQL Server, MySQL, and Oracle, are valuable tools for loading and analyzing large volumes of Big Data evidence. Programming languages and data visualization tools are also useful for these purposes.

Databases are excellent for analyzing transactional data, but other tools may be required for analyzing HDFS data. HDFS data can require extensive data preparation and the use of other tools before the data can be loaded into a data repository. The subsequent section in this chapter, *Analysis*, covers this topic and several of the available tools used by investigators.

Evidence should be re-inventoried at this stage to ensure that all data has been brought into the analysis environment. Information from the documentation about which information was collected during data collection is compared to the evidence in the analysis environment. Control totals should also be validated at this point, if possible.

Evidence can be culled at this stage in some cases. If a known subset of data is all that is needed for the analysis phase, the other data can be moved out of the analysis repository. The moved data, often referred to as culled data, should still be available should a need for it arise later, but moving that data out of the analysis repository can make the analysis process smoother and faster.

Analysis

The file-level analysis is the analysis that is performed on logical files or forensic images. This analysis differs from data content analysis, because the focus of this analysis is to extract, or piece together, data containers or collect metadata information. For Big Data investigations in which nodes were individually imaged, this is the type of analysis whereby the images are analyzed and the contents of the cluster are pieced back together for further analysis.

Because no two investigations are the same, analysis techniques serve as tools in a toolbox and can be combined or run in various orders and combinations. The primary file-level analyses are:

- Keyword searching
- File and data carving
- Metadata analysis, such as file modification timeline analysis
- Cluster reconstruction

Keyword searching and file and data carving

Two methods for analyzing HDFS evidence are keyword searching and file and data carving. Keyword searching is the technique of identifying sections of data that contain a particular keyword or set of keywords. File and data carving is the process of extracting files or data containers out of a forensic image. A forensic image is just a large data file, but by carving the files and data containers out of the image, the investigator can analyze the evidence in their original structures and formats.

Bulk Extractor

Bulk Extractor is a keyword search and file carving tool that can extract text, graphics, and other information from forensic images. This tool is an excellent method for previewing data by way of searching entire dd images or a logical file collection without needing to reconstruct data or carve files. To extract text using Bulk Extractor, perform the following steps:

1. Download Bulk Extractor version 1.5 from `http://digitalcorpora.org/downloads/bulk_extractor/`.

2. Run Bulk Extractor Viewer, and load the Bulk Extractor tool via **Tools | Run bulk_extractor**.

3. Load the directory of files or dd image to be scanned by selecting the **Image File** option and providing the path to the dd image file. Note that Bulk Extractor provides a number of built-in scanners that look for forensic artifacts and text strings that match known patterns. Additional words or text patterns can be provided to Bulk Extractor:

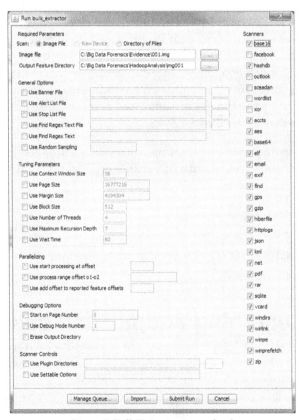

Figure 2: Bulk Extractor image load

4. Click **Submit Run**. After the process completes, the following summary screen is shown as illustrated in the following figure which includes the MD5 hash value and total amount of evidence analyzed:

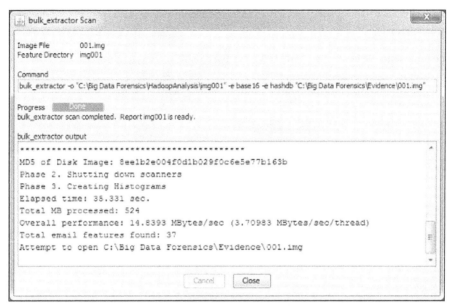

Figure 3: Bulk Extractor processing

5. Bulk Extractor outputs a report for each scanner option selected. The reports include a copy of the string matches and a histogram report of the most frequent results, such as the most frequent email addresses or domains.

Bulk Extractor works well when relevant evidence is unencrypted and uncompressed. The tool is an excellent method for the investigator to search for relevant text strings and also to look at the frequency of text strings to get a better understanding of the data without needing to structure and load the data to an analysis repository. If the data is encrypted and/or compressed in a nonstandard format, Bulk Extractor cannot extract the text and provide results.

Investigators should be careful when relying on this analysis to gain a complete understanding of the text in the evidence collection. If a forensic image was performed on the node's local operating system and Hadoop storage, the HDFS data may not be extracted by Bulk Extractor, depending on the Hadoop configuration settings. For more information about Bulk Extractor, read the documentation available at `http://www.forensicswiki.org/wiki/Bulk_extractor`.

Autopsy

Autopsy is a freeware forensic tool that provides a number of useful functions, including keyword searching and file and data carving. Autopsy is a graphical version of the Sleuth Kit, another freeware forensic tool that is widely used in investigations.

To carve files and data using Autopsy, perform the following steps:

1. Download and install Autopsy version 3.1 from `http://www.sleuthkit.org/autopsy/`.

2. Run Autopsy, and select **New Case**.

3. On the **New Case Information** screen, as illustrated in the following figure, enter the **Case Name** and **Base Directory** to indicate where to store the Autopsy output, and click **Next**:

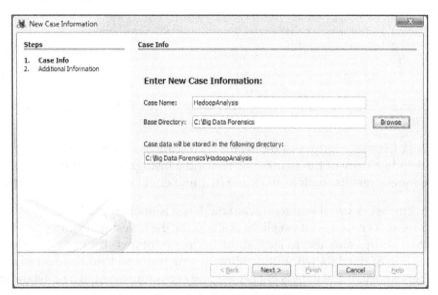

Figure 4: Autopsy case setup

4. Enter the **Case Number** and **Examiner** information, and click **Next**. The **Case Number** is typically a sequential, numerical identifier for each set of evidence. The following figure shows a configuration with **Case Number** 001:

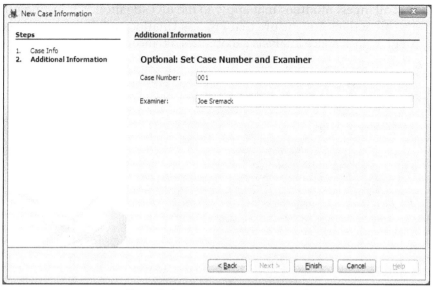

Figure 5: Autopsy case setup continued

5. At this point, the new case has been opened and the evidence can be added. Click on **Add Data Source** to add the forensic image or directory of evidence files.

6. Enter the data source information, as illustrated in the following figure. Select either **Image File** or **Logical Files**, and enter the path to the image file or logical files. Click **Next**:

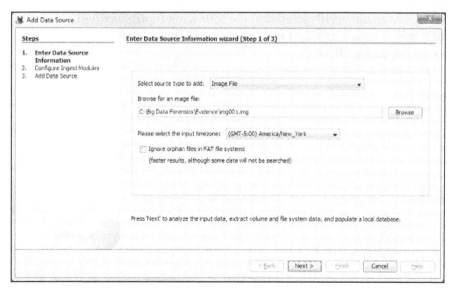

Figure 6: Autopsy evidence input

7. Select all ingest modules that apply to the investigation. For testing purposes, select all options and ensure that **Process Unallocated Space** is checked. That provides slack space analysis capabilities, including deleted file recovery:

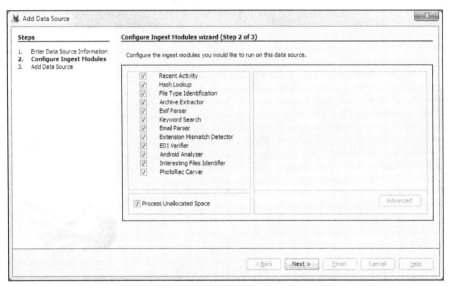

Figure 7: Autopsy evidence input continued

The carving tool provided by Autopsy file view enables the investigator to view audio, video, picture, document, and other file types from the source filesystem and slack space. After the evidence has been ingested into Autopsy, the investigator can view the files under the **Views** menu, where the list of images, videos, and other files is available. The menu, as illustrated in the following figure, is divided into several different types of views: 1) **File Types**, 2) **Recent Files**, 3) **Deleted Files**, and 4) **MB File Size** (grouped by file size).

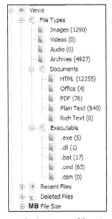

Figure 8: Autopsy file viewer

Files can be extracted through the file carver by right-clicking on the file and selecting **Extract File(s)**. Any type of file, deleted or not, can be extracted using this method. The files are then extracted to the location specified by the investigator.

Files can also be tagged in Autopsy for later extraction or further analysis. The investigator can right-click on a selected file and select **Tag** to save the file with tag information for later analysis.

Autopsy also provides keyword searching capabilities. In the top-right corner, Autopsy has the **Keyword Search** and **Keyword Lists** menus. Click on **Keyword Search** to run a one-time search. The search can run the following three types of searches:

- An exact word match
- A substring match
- A regular expression match

When the search is run, Autopsy searches all extracted text from the evidence and returns the list of files with one or more matches and all associated metadata.

Multiple search terms can be searched in a batch via the **Keyword Lists** menu. Clicking on **Keyword Lists | Manage Lists** brings up the search settings, where the investigator can add a list of multiple search strings. A list is created and saved after all terms have been entered. Then, the investigator can search the evidence using that list by clicking on the dropdown menu next to **Keyword Lists** and selecting the list to use.

The results of keyword searches can be exported as a report file that shows the file that matched and the search term. Let's see the steps to generate a report file:

1. Click **Tools | Generate Report**.
2. Select **Results | Excel** or **Results | HTML**.
3. Select **All Results** or **Tagged Results**, and click **Finish**.

A report file is generated that displays which files match the search terms.

 Reports that are generated by forensic software are preferable over manual notes, unless the reports do not capture the details required for the analysis.

Metadata analysis

Analyzing metadata is typically not as important or relevant for a Big Data investigation. Because HDFS data is distributed and the data is created, modified, and accessed using shared or system accounts, the metadata is not as valuable as it is in typical forensic investigations, where a single user's activity is important and discernible. Metadata can still be important, though. Information about when files were last accessed or created can be retrieved.

Autopsy has a number of powerful metadata analysis tools for understanding when data was created, modified, and accessed; who created the data; and the types of events that occurred. Metadata can be updated by various mechanisms and can reflect the local operating system's timestamps and permissions, or it can reflect application's information about the data.

File activity timeline analysis

Autopsy's timeline feature generates graphical, interactive timelines based on the evidence's **Modified, Accessed, and Created (MAC)** metadata times. To create a timeline, click **Tools | Timeline**. Autopsy generates a timeline based on the loaded evidence. If MAC times are not available for a file, the file is not represented in the timeline.

The following figure shows the timeline feature:

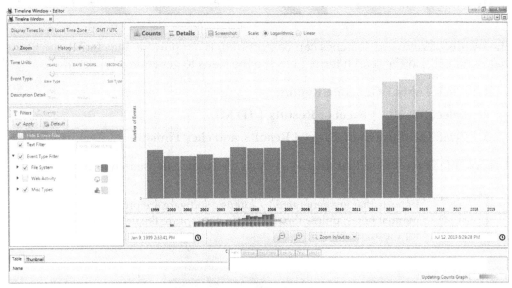

Figure 9: Autopsy timeline viewer

The Autopsy timeline is an interactive tool that gives the investigator the ability to review events in a number of ways:

- **Zoom**: The time units, event type, and description can be adjusted to show more or less information on the timeline; the investigator can zoom in on specific dates and times down to the second.

- **Filters**: Text filters, known files, and types of events can be included or excluded from the timeline, reducing noise events.

- **Table/Thumbnail Preview**: The list of files and thumbnail previews of the files can be viewed, and the list of strings and metadata are also provided when an investigator selects a file.

Timeline analysis is performed by one or more of the following approaches:

- Identifying key epochs and reviewing events in the same time period
- Looking for key clusters of events and homing in on those
- Tracing key events to related events to build a timeline of key events

Other metadata analysis

Other forms of metadata can be analyzed with the help of Autopsy and Excel (or a database). Autopsy stores the available metadata for every file, and that metadata can be extracted to a tab-delimited text file for analysis in another program:

1. Select **Tools | Generate Report**.
2. In the **Report Module** screen, select **Files | Text**.
3. Select the metadata to extract (select all for this example).
4. Click **Finish**, and note the location of the output file.
5. Open Excel, select the **Data** tab from the ribbon, and click **From Text**.
6. Navigate to and select the Autopsy-generated text file.
7. Import the text file as **Delimited** with the **Tab delimiter**.
8. Click **Finish**.

The following metadata can now be analyzed:

- Filename
- File Extension
- File Type

- Deleted/Not Deleted
- Last Accessed/Created/Modified
- Size
- Hash
- Permissions
- File Path

Depending on the nature of the investigation, several types of metadata analysis may be useful and include:

- Identifying anomalies or outliers based on the number of such files or having an extremely large or small size
- Locating files that meet a key characteristic, such as deleted files or files accessed during a key time period
- Identifying patterns within the data, which could involve determining file activity during normal business hours and then locating outliers
- Finding files related to known relevant files to see if additional clues or information can be spotted from files of a certain related characteristic (for example, the same file path or extension)

The number of files that are listed by Autopsy in the export may exceed the limits for Excel analysis and may require the use of a database. Any tool that can aggregate large sets of data and lets the investigator work with individual records is sufficient for this type of analysis.

The analysis of deleted files

One form of analysis is to specifically analyze deleted files for indications of certain actions or behavior that arose. Deleting files before the investigator performs a collection is a common technique to thwart or interfere with an investigation. The files can also be deleted accidentally or as part of an automated data purging process. Regardless, the deletion of files, also called **spoliation**, is an issue investigators regularly encounter in the course of analyzing evidence.

There are several types of file deletions that can occur for a Big Data investigation:

- Files were deleted from the node's local operating system
- Files were deleted from HDFS
- Hadoop data was deleted from inside a file

Recovering files that were deleted from the node's local operating system is a straightforward process when a forensic image of the node was collected. In Autopsy, select the **Deleted Files** view, and expand the list to see the list of all deleted files that were identified. This list shows the files that were deleted and the deletion date. The files can be sorted by filename, directory, MAC times, file size, and other metadata.

The following analyses and steps can be performed against deleted files in Autopsy:

- **Matching hash value analysis**: Right-click on the file and select **Search for files with the same MD5 hash**.
- **Keyword searches**: Run a keyword search and sort the results by the **Flags(Dir)** to find the unallocated files.
- **Tagging for reporting or further analysis**: Right-click on the file and select **Tag File**.
- **File preview**: Right-click on the file and select **Open in External Viewer**.
- **File date filtering**: Right-click on the file and select **Show only rows where**.

The recovery of HDFS deleted files from a forensic image of a node requires additional steps to first identify the HDFS data blocks and files. After they have been reconstructed, analysis can be performed on the HDFS deleted files and data. If the Hadoop files were copied logically, the only deleted data that can be recovered are the files from the .Trash directory. If files were collected from the .Trash directory, those can be analyzed in the same manner as non-deleted files, because no additional steps are required to recover the files.

HDFS data extraction

When a node's operating system and Hadoop storage is imaged, the HDFS data is embedded in the image. Those HDFS files need to be extracted from the image for analysis to be performed. The process for extracting the files is to carve out the DataNode data and then extract the data blocks from the DataNode data to piece together records or HDFS files. Currently, no software packages exist for this, so the process is manual and requires careful analysis. This process is not ideal for large Hadoop clusters but may be necessary if no other options exist.

There are a number of HDFS files that will be encountered in an HDFS data extraction process:

- Hadoop log files (for example, application and MapReduce logs)
- Input data files
- Hive and HBase files
- Job configuration files

Some or all of these files can be relevant depending on the investigation. Being able to locate and extract these types of files is important for analyzing relevant data.

The process for extracting HDFS data from a forensic image has several steps:

1. Identify the location of the DataNode data in the local operating system.
2. Locate the DataNode data block files in the local operating system using that path.
3. Analyze the data blocks to identify the relevant files.
4. Extract the data into a file for analysis. The process is similar to any other type of file carving, except the local operating system layer requires an extra step for identifying the data.

To identify the location of the DataNode data in the local operating system, find the `hdfs-site.xml` file in the forensic image. Using Autopsy, this can be done in two ways: 1) navigate to the standard directories where `hdfs-site.xml` is stored, 2) run a keyword search for `hdfs-site.xml` and sort the results by filename for that file. After the file is located, open the file, and find the value of the `dfs.data.dir` property. That location is the root directory where the DataNode block files are located.

Next, go to that directory in the mounted forensic image in Autopsy. The directory should contain a `VERSION` file and a directory with this structure, `BP-<random integer>-<IP address>-<creation time>`. Navigate to the `BP` directory, and then navigate to the `BP` directory's `current` subdirectory. Inside this folder is data that can be analyzed. The following should be located in the current subdirectory:

- `dfsUsed`: The storage report file.
- `VERSION`: The information about the namespace and current block pool ID.
- `finalized`: The HDFS data blocks that have been written.
- `rbw`: The `rbw` directory with data blocks still being written to the filesystem.

The `current`, `finalized`, and `rbw` subdirectories can contain DataNode block files that were deleted in the local operating system. These files can be recovered and analyzed, similar to DataNode block files that are active and visible in the live system. Autopsy can be used to recover these deleted files. Note that these files are automatically deleted by Hadoop during the data writing process, so the presence of deleted files does not necessarily mean that the files were intentionally deleted by someone.

The files in the `finalized` and `rbw` directories should now be extracted for analysis. There are two types of files. The files with the `.meta` file extension contain checksum information that is used by Hadoop to verify the integrity of data blocks. The files without an extension are the data blocks, which are the valuable files for an investigation. The finalized directory should contain the most data, and unless the Hadoop cluster was particularly active, the `rbw` directory may not contain data, although it probably contains deleted files.

The following screenshot shows a subset of the files from the DataNode's `finalized` directory for a single node forensic image:

Name	Modified Time	Change Time	Access Time	Created Time	Size
[current folder]	2015-03-31 16:47:10 EDT	2015-03-31 16:47:10 EDT	2015-04-05 06:53:48 EDT	2014-09-12 22:40:43 EDT	4096
[parent folder]	2015-04-05 07:13:03 EDT	2015-04-05 07:13:03 EDT	2015-04-05 07:33:08 EDT	2014-09-12 22:40:43 EDT	4096
blk_1073741825	2015-02-17 10:05:45 EST	2015-02-17 10:05:45 EST	2015-04-03 14:58:38 EDT	2015-02-17 10:05:44 EST	6322
blk_1073741825_1001.meta	2015-02-17 10:05:45 EST	2015-02-17 10:05:45 EST	2015-04-03 14:58:38 EDT	2015-02-17 10:05:44 EST	59
blk_1073741826	2015-02-17 10:07:58 EST	2015-02-17 10:07:58 EST	2015-04-03 14:58:35 EDT	2015-02-17 10:07:58 EST	6322
blk_1073741826_1002.meta	2015-02-17 10:07:58 EST	2015-02-17 10:07:58 EST	2015-04-03 14:58:35 EDT	2015-02-17 10:07:58 EST	59
blk_1073741827	2015-03-12 14:28:51 EDT	2015-03-12 14:28:51 EDT	2015-04-03 14:58:35 EDT	2015-03-12 14:28:37 EDT	44005963
blk_1073741827_1003.meta	2015-03-12 14:28:51 EDT	2015-03-12 14:28:51 EDT	2015-04-03 14:58:35 EDT	2015-03-12 14:28:37 EDT	343807
blk_1073741839	2015-04-02 17:04:59 EDT	2015-04-02 17:04:59 EDT	2015-04-02 17:04:59 EDT	2015-04-02 17:04:59 EDT	64
blk_1073741839_1015.meta	2015-04-02 17:04:35 EDT	2015-04-02 17:04:35 EDT	2015-04-02 17:19:37 EDT	2015-04-02 17:04:35 EDT	4096
blk_1073741840	2015-04-02 17:04:35 EDT	2015-04-02 17:04:35 EDT	2015-04-02 17:04:35 EDT	2015-04-02 17:04:35 EDT	2604
blk_1073741840_1016.meta	2015-04-02 17:04:35 EDT	2015-04-02 17:04:35 EDT	2015-04-02 17:04:35 EDT	2015-04-02 17:04:35 EDT	5084

Figure 10: DataNode block files

Next, select all of the DataNode block files for extraction. Right-click on the selected files, and select **Extract file(s)** to extract the files for analysis. Typically, the best method is for the investigator to extract all files and analyze each. If the number of DataNode block files makes this infeasible, the investigator can preview the files using Autopsy to locate the potentially relevant files, or focus on data block files from a specific period of time if they know the date ranges of interest.

The next step is to analyze the files using a hex editor.

Hex editors

Hex editors are a part of every forensic investigator's toolbox. Hex editors are applications that display the binary contents of a file in a number of display formats, most commonly represented in hexadecimal values. These applications are important for forensic investigations because forensic investigators can look into the contents of a file. Unlike a text editor, the investigator can use a hex editor to see non-text values, such as file header signatures and binary file formats. Hex editors also give the forensic investigator the ability to copy binary chunks of data and create new files with that data. This means that an investigator can manually carve out files or data records from a filesystem or image file.

To begin working with a hex editor, download and install the free HxD hex editor from http://mh-nexus.de/en/hxd/.

Open one of the DataNode block files in HxD. The following screenshot shows the first ten lines of the hex editor data for one of the DataNode block files, which contains the data imported into HDFS earlier in this chapter:

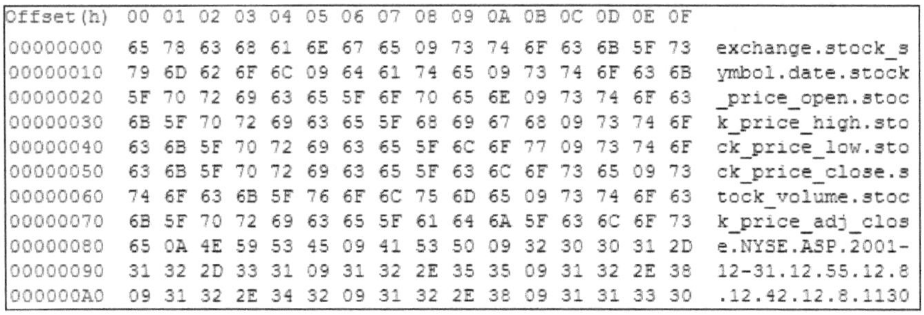

```
Offset(h)  00 01 02 03 04 05 06 07 08 09 0A 0B 0C 0D 0E 0F

00000000   65 78 63 68 61 6E 67 65 09 73 74 6F 63 6B 5F 73   exchange.stock_s
00000010   79 6D 62 6F 6C 09 64 61 74 65 09 73 74 6F 63 6B   ymbol.date.stock
00000020   5F 70 72 69 63 65 5F 6F 70 65 6E 09 73 74 6F 63   _price_open.stoc
00000030   6B 5F 70 72 69 63 65 5F 68 69 67 68 09 73 74 6F   k_price_high.sto
00000040   63 6B 5F 70 72 69 63 65 5F 6C 6F 77 09 73 74 6F   ck_price_low.sto
00000050   63 6B 5F 70 72 69 63 65 5F 63 6C 6F 73 65 09 73   ck_price_close.s
00000060   74 6F 63 6B 5F 76 6F 6C 75 6D 65 09 73 74 6F 63   tock_volume.stoc
00000070   6B 5F 70 72 69 63 65 5F 61 64 6A 5F 63 6C 6F 73   k_price_adj_clos
00000080   65 0A 4E 59 53 45 09 41 53 50 09 32 30 30 31 2D   e.NYSE.ASP.2001-
00000090   31 32 2D 33 31 09 31 32 2E 35 35 09 31 32 2E 38   12-31.12.55.12.8
000000A0   09 31 32 2E 34 32 09 31 32 2E 38 09 31 31 33 30   .12.42.12.8.1130
```

Figure 11: The hex editor analysis of a DataNode block file

The hex editor shows the hexadecimal value of the bytes based on the offset (in the far-left column) and the location (in the top row). The ASCII value is shown on the far right.

The file in the previous screenshot is easily recoverable from the DataNode block because the file was stored as plaintext in HDFS. The entire file can be analyzed in a database without further carving from this format. If a subset of the file is needed, highlight the sections of the file that need to be extracted, and select **File | Save As**. If the amount of data for a single HDFS file is greater than the HDFS block size, the data will be found in multiple DataNode block files.

The data shown in the previous screenshot is actually found in two different DataNode block files. The data was loaded into HDFS, which was stored in a block. Earlier in this book, the HDFS file was loaded into Hive during an example completed in *Chapter 2, Understanding Hadoop Internals and Architecture* which created a new copy of the data in the HDFS ./hive directory. If multiple copies of the same data are found during this DataNode analysis, the investigator can infer that the data may have been loaded into a Hadoop application, such as Hive.

Hex editors are valuable tools when investigating binary formats of data. Compressed and other binary formats cannot be viewed and directly loaded into a database for analysis. Instead, the files can be extracted and then converted into text format. Common formats that require this are SequenceFiles and MapFiles. Both types have header and trailer information, metadata, and sync blocks—and they can be compressed. The data requires conversion to a text format, but before the data can be converted, the file type must be identified. This is accomplished by reviewing the file header. SequenceFiles have headers that begin with SEQ4 or SEQ6.

The following screenshot illustrates a SequenceFiles header:

```
Offset(h)  00 01 02 03 04 05 06 07 08 09 0A 0B 0C 0D 0E 0F
00000000   53 45 51 36 6F 72 67 2E 61 70 61 63 68 65 2E 68    SEQ6org.apache.h
```

Figure 12: An example SequenceFiles header

Cluster reconstruction

Cluster reconstruction can be performed on different levels and in different ways. The simplest way is reconstructing the cluster from an HDFS logical file collection. These are the files from the node's HDFS that were copied to storage. The method for reconstruction is to build up the collection of HDFS files into a single repository and de-duplicate files based on MD5 hashes. This method gives the investigator a static snapshot of the files available in the cluster. It does not give a snapshot of Hadoop data that was not yet written to the filesystem, and it may not yield all of the Hadoop application's data.

 Forensic reconstruction refers to reconstructing the forensically-collected data, not creating a replica Hadoop cluster using the data. The goal of cluster reconstruction is to piece together the acquired data into a usable format for analysis.

The second method is reconstructing the cluster using the forensically-imaged node data. This is a complex process by which the following steps are taken:

1. Analyze the NameNode `edits` and `fsimage` files to determine the files and application data required and the corresponding block ID information.

2. Extract the DataNode data blocks based on the block IDs identified in the previous step.

3. If the file is spread across multiple blocks, piece together the blocks.

4. If necessary, recover deleted data to identify the cluster's status at specific points in time.

The reconstruction begins by reviewing the `edits` and `fsimage` files. Both files are run through the Hadoop Offline Image and Offline Image Viewer to convert them into a readable format. Once converted, the files will contain the directory names and filenames, along with the corresponding block IDs. The DataNode block files that correspond to the relevant block IDs are extracted, and the contents can be put into the analysis repository with the correct directory name or filename. Because DataNode blocks can be replicated across multiple nodes, the investigator should be careful not to introduce duplicative data to the analysis repository.

The following figure illustrates the process for reconstructing the cluster's data:

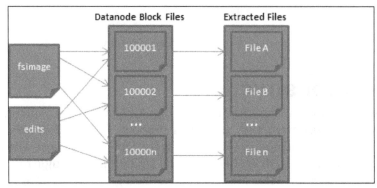

Figure 13: A cluster reconstruction of allocated data blocks

In some cases, the investigator is only required to analyze one application or a specific type of data. The entire cluster does not need to be analyzed to achieve this. Instead, the edits and fsimage files should be reviewed to identify the relevant data blocks. Those data blocks should then be targeted.

As an example, the following steps can be performed to locate and reconstruct a file named wiki_page_hits.txt.

First, the edits file is reviewed to identify the relevant data blocks:

```
<RECORD>
  <OPCODE>OP_ADD></OPCODE>
  <DATA>
    <TXID>18</TXID>
    <LENGTH>0</LENGTH>
    <INODEID>16937</INODEID>
    <PATH>/wiki_page_hits.txt._COPYING_</PATH>
  </DATA>
</RECORD>
<RECORD>
  <OPCODE>OP_ALLOCATE_BLOCK_ID</OPCODE>
  <DATA>
    <TXID>19</TXID>
   <BLOCK_ID>1073741825</BLOCK_ID>
  </DATA>
</RECORD>
```

Next, the `fsimage` file is reviewed to verify the relevant data blocks and determine the replication factor:

```
<inode>
  <id>16397</id>
  <type>FILE</type>
  <name>wiki_page_hits.txt</name>
  <replication>1</replication>
  <mtime>1424185545147</mtime>
  <atime>1424185543359</atime>
  <perferredBlockSize>134217728</perferredBlockSize>
  <permission>root:supergroup:rw-r--r--</permission>
  <blocks>
    <block>
      <id>1073741825</id>
      <genstamp>1001</genstamp>
      <numBytes>6322</numBytes>
    </block>
  </blocks>
</inode>
```

Both the `edits` and `fsimage` files confirm that only one DataNode block file must be extracted. Block number `1073741825` needs to be extracted, and given that the replication factor is set to `1` in `fsimage`, the investigator does not need to concern himself with potential data block duplication, because only one DataNode block file would exist.

Next, the corresponding block file is identified. That file is found in the DataNode `./finalized` directory, as illustrated in the following screenshot:

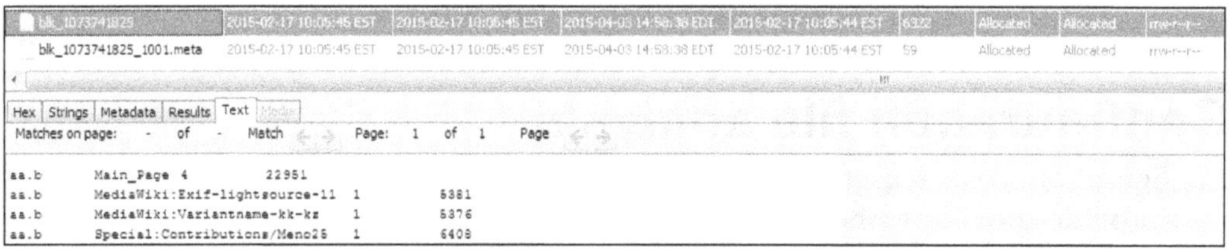

Figure 14: The DataNode block file

If the replication factor was set for 2 or more, only one of the DataNode block files would be required; however, the investigator would first need to compare the hash values of all duplicate files to ensure that they are true duplicates.

The file is then extracted and saved with its filename and relevant metadata for subsequent analysis.

Unallocated files can also be recovered using this method if a specific point-in-time snapshot of the cluster is needed. Because the local operating system may still have the previously deleted DataNode block files, archived versions of the `fsimage` and `edits` files can be analyzed vis-à-vis the unallocated DataNode block files recovered by Autopsy. Using the same method as described earlier, the information in the entries in `fsimage` and `edits` are applied to the unallocated DataNode block files, and the files are extracted. Hadoop rarely reuses block IDs, so the investigator can reliably determine if a DataNode block file corresponds to the `fsimage` and `edits` file entries for that block ID without concern about a mismatch. The filename of the archived version of the `fsimage` file has the maximum block ID contained in the file, and the filename of the archived version of the `edits` file has the block ID ranges contained in the file. This means that for a given block ID, the investigator can identify both the `fsimage` and `edits` files that apply. The following diagram illustrates the process for extracting unallocated DataNode block files:

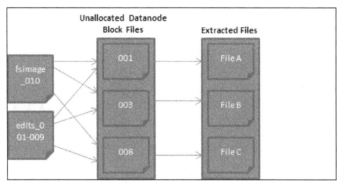

Figure 15: Unallocated DataNode block files

Configuration file analysis

Configuration files are useful for forensic investigations because of the information they provide about how the system was set up, including how the configuration is unique and where data sources are located. Configuration file analysis, a form of static analysis, is typically only performed when the investigator needs to know more about how a cluster was configured and operated, and the types of Hadoop applications and services that were used. Configuration file analysis is sometimes an overlooked part of a forensic investigation, and it can be performed in both the identification and analysis phases.

The following types of configuration files can be analyzed:

- The local operating system
- Hadoop
- Hadoop application

The goal for analyzing configuration files is to build a map of the various layers of a cluster's configuration, and then fill in the relevant information about how Hadoop is configured.

Linux configuration files

Currently, the local operating system for Hadoop clusters is Linux, unless the system is a non-production development server. This means that the local operating system configuration files are Linux files. There are many different Linux configuration files, and the following is a list of some of the most useful for Hadoop forensic investigations:

Filename	Description
`/etc/hosts`	This contains list of known hosts in the local network
`/etc/hosts.allow` `(deny)`	This contains access control that permits or blocks specific hosts from accessing the system
`/etc/rc.d/rc/rcX.d`	This contains the scripts that are run at startup based on the run level "X," where "X" ranges from 1-5
`/etc/fstab`	This contains the list of filesystems currently mounted by the system
`/etc/group`	This contains the valid group names and users included in each group
`/etc/syslogd.conf`	This contains the syslogd daemon configuration file, which controls the system logging received from applications

The following are some of the types of information an investigator can glean from these configuration files:

- They can identify data flows into and out of Hadoop
- They can identify user accounts that can access Hadoop
- They can identify the hosts that can or can't access the node

Hadoop configuration files

Hadoop configuration files are stored in the local operating system but control how Hadoop and HDFS are structured and operate. These configuration files are stored in the local operating system, typically in the /etc/hadoop directory. The following is the list of configuration files useful in Hadoop:

Filename	Description
core-default.xml	This contains general default system variables and data locations
hadoop-default.xml	This contains site-specific settings for all Hadoop daemons and MapReduce jobs
hdfs-default.xml	This contains HDFS-specific configuration settings
job.xml	This contains job-specific configuration parameters

Each of the configuration files shown in the preceding list are the default versions. System configuration changes are made to the -site.xml versions of the files (for example, hdfs-site.xml). The investigator can quickly determine if the system was configured with non-default settings by searching for -site.xml files.

In addition to those Hadoop configuration files, the Conf/log4j.properties file is the customized Hadoop daemon's logging configuration file. This controls default logging by Hadoop and its applications. The output of the logging is specific in the ${HADOOP_LOG_DIR} directory. Job history logs (for example, MapReduce job logs) are stored in the ${HADOOP_LOG_DIR}/history directory.

Analyzing Hadoop configuration files enables the investigator to identify data flows into and out of Hadoop, locate where MapReduce and other job files are stored, and identify the structure of NameNode(s) and DataNodes.

Hadoop application configuration files

Hadoop application configuration files are similar to Hadoop configuration files but are specific to the applications. These configuration files are valuable because of the information they provide relating to where each application stores data, security settings, logging settings, and data transfer configurations. Both HBase and Hive have configuration files, hbase-default.xml and hive-default.xml, respectively, and cluster-specific settings are saved to the -site.xml files. The presence of other application configuration files is a good way for the investigator to determine which applications were installed and configured in the cluster.

Log file analysis

Log files can be valuable for investigations where the events on the cluster are relevant or the investigator needs information about how the cluster operated. There are different types of Hadoop logs. The local operating system maintains its own set of logs about Hadoop's operations. There can also be logs for data transfers that occur into or out of Hadoop, which would be maintained by the system that interfaces with Hadoop. Log files about databases connected to Hadoop may need to be examined (for example, Hive). Finally, some log files about Hadoop's operations are maintained inside of HDFS.

Log file analysis can be performed from logical file collections or forensic image collections. In the latter situation, any HDFS logs first need to be extracted from the DataNode block files before the analysis can be performed.

Several types of log files can be analyzed such as:

- Local operating system logs
- Hadoop logs
- Application logs (for example, Hive and HBase)

The local operating system maintains a variety of log files that can be relevant to an investigation. Linux, by default, stores log files in the /var/log directory. Several of the useful log files include:

- **Audit events**: Auditable event logging, which is stored in the /var/log/audit directory.
- **Cron events**: Scheduled job logs.
- **User logins**: User login attempts and location information. The secure and btmp/utmp/wtmp files store this information.

Hadoop clusters can generate large volumes of log file entries across a number of different types of logs. Log files can be found on the NameNode and the DataNodes, depending on the type of log. Hadoop clusters can process billions of records per day and generate millions or billions of log entries in the process, so the investigator should only analyze the relevant logs. The following types of Hadoop log files can be found in the /var/log/hadoop and /var/log/mapred directories:

- **Daemon logs**: These include the NameNode, JobTracker, and secondary NameNode daemons. The logs have either a .log or .out extension, with the .log files storing the events of the running daemon and .out storing the daemon startup events.

- **Job configuration**: The logged events from the JobTracker jobs, which are stored as XML files.

- **Job statistics**: The JobTracker log for runtime statistics, including start times, attempts, and shuffling.

- **log4j**: The log4j output submitted by task processes. These log files are given a filename that matches the corresponding application. For example, Hive and HBase both use the log4j service for their logs, and the logs are stored as `hive.log` and `hbase.log`.

- **Standard error**: The TaskTracker log for job errors.

- **Standard out**: The TaskTracker log for job output.

Analyzing Hadoop logs requires an analysis tool or a greatly reduced set of log files and entries that are analyzed. The large number of Hadoop events is best analyzed in a structured database or a large spreadsheet application. Since millions of events may exist, the investigator should either cull the data or load the information into a large-scale analysis repository.

The main types of log analysis are:

- **Cross-validation**: A comparison of the results of data found in Hadoop to logged events.

- **User activity analysis**: An inspection of logins by specific users or at specific times.

- **System change analysis**: A review of changes to events and data systems during the history of the cluster, such as changes to scheduled Hadoop data transfers or data input sources.

Summary

In this chapter, we covered the elements of performing filesystem-level analysis and data carving. The topics we discussed included taking the data from a forensic image or performing a logical file collection, various analysis techniques, and data extraction methods. The analysis techniques, such as timeline analysis and keyword analysis, may be sufficient for an investigation where a key event or a small set of data is required for the investigation. In other cases, the analysis performed in this chapter can be part of a larger investigation that includes both Hadoop data and data from other systems.

Regardless of the role of the analysis, the information must be presented. Taking the analysis and putting that into an illustrative and accessible presentation format is critical for conveying the results. The presentation of this type of information is covered in *Chapter 8, Presenting Forensic Findings*.

Some of the data extraction methods are performed in order to prepare data for analysis in a database for quantitative and further qualitative analysis. The next chapter details some of the main analysis techniques used for large-scale data investigations and how to prepare voluminous data sets for such analysis.

7
Analyzing Hadoop Application Data

The analysis of Hadoop application data is often the primary objective in a Big Data forensic investigation. Hadoop application data is valuable in a Big Data investigation because of the informational content of the data. Unlike traditional forensic investigations, issues such as metadata and file carving are not often applicable to the investigation. Instead, analysis of the data in the context of the investigation is the investigator's primary concern.

Every investigation is different, so the types of analyses performed first depends on the available data and the nature of the investigation. In fraud investigations, the investigator is analyzing data for signs of data manipulation or anomalous conditions shown in the data. In fact-based litigation where Big Data is used to show what occurred such as complaints involving retail sales, the data is analyzed to show that certain events or conditions existed. The investigator must choose the right types of analyses based on the facts of the case, the type of investigation, and other practical considerations (for example, available time).

Analyzing application data requires different tools than analyzing HDFS data. Hadoop application data are the transactional records, so metadata and forensic artifacts are not part of this form of analysis. Instead, the investigator relies on large-scale database systems to load, transform, and analyze the data to reach his findings. The investigator sets up the analysis environment and prepares the data for analysis before beginning any analysis. The data transformation or preparation is the process of converting and standardizing the data from Hadoop applications into a form that can be readily analyzed. After the data is prepared, the analysis can begin. This is done utilizing the same process flow discussed in *Chapter 6, Performing Hadoop Distributed File System Analysis*.

The following diagram illustrates this analysis process:

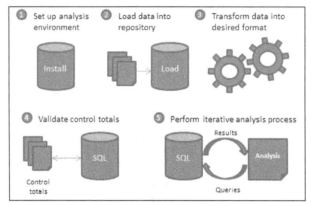

Figure 1: The analysis process

This chapter covers the steps necessary to prepare and analyze Hadoop application data for forensic investigations. The main analysis techniques are discussed, along with the types of investigations for which they are typically employed.

Preparing the analysis environment

The first step of the analysis process is to prepare the data analysis environment. Large volumes of data require a large-scale analysis tool, and that tool is a database system. Relational databases are typically used for the analysis because of the ease and power of the SQL language, and those systems work well with data visualization tools and other software packages. Nonrelational databases can be used, but those are not preferred by most investigators.

Any relational database software that can handle large data volumes can be used. Commercial packages, such as SQL Server and Oracle, are the most common. Free packages, such as MySQL and PostgreSQL, can also be used. In this book, SQL Server is discussed because of its user-friendly interface and powerful features.

First, download and install SQL Server 2014 Express LocalDB and SQL Server 2014 Management Studio, which are available from `http://www.microsoft.com/en-us/server-cloud/products/sql-server-editions/sql-server-express.aspx`.

Next, attach the evidence to the analysis environment, and copy the data to the analysis environment's storage. During the copy, verify that all source evidence data is copied to the analysis environment. This data will be loaded into SQL in subsequent steps. Retain the original source evidence because the data copied to the analysis environment will be deleted after the data has been loaded into SQL Server and verified.

On average, the analysis environment storage should be at least 2.5 times the cumulative size of the evidence. This is because the analysis environment will have both the original evidence and analysis copies of the data. In cases involving very large amounts of evidence, the number of copies of the data can be reduced.

Pre-analysis steps

Several steps are performed before the analysis can be started. The data is first imported into the database. Some data is structured in a manner that cannot be imported and requires pre-load transformations. The data should be surveyed after the data has been loaded to understand the structure of the data, detect any anomalies, and determine which data require transformations. Based on the results of the data survey process, the data may require transformations before it can be analyzed.

This process can be iterative. The data may require a series of transformations, and after each transformation, a data survey needs to be performed to assess whether any further transformations are required. The following figure illustrates the steps and iterative nature of the pre-analysis process:

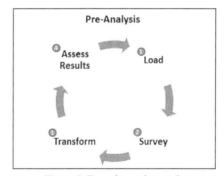

Figure 2: Transformed records

Loading data

The collected evidence is next loaded into SQL Server. Relational databases systems store data in databases comprised of tables. With forensic evidence, the original evidence should be loaded into tables representing the original structure and values, if possible. The source database will contain the unaltered data and can be referenced should there be a need to review the original data.

The following diagram illustrates the relationship between the source and analysis databases:

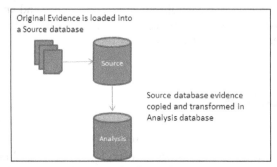

Figure 3: The data architecture

The following are the steps for loading the data into the source database:

1. Create source database.

2. Create table structures in the source database.

3. Load source data.

4. Verify the loaded data.

New databases can be created in **SQL Server Management Studio (SSMS)** by right-clicking on `Databases` in the `Object Explorer screen` and selecting **New Database**. The following screenshot illustrates this process:

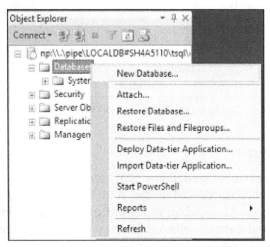

Figure 4: Creating a new database in SSMS

The database should be created with a name that uniquely describes that case—especially if multiple investigations are conducted on the same database server. A best practice for naming an investigation database is to include the unique investigation number, the name, and the database's type. For the data collected in *Chapter 5, Collecting Hadoop Application Data*, create a database called `1001-NYSE-Source`. This naming convention denotes that the investigation number is `1001`; it is related to NYSE data, and the data loaded into the database is source evidence and not analysis.

> Source evidence and analysis data can be stored in the same database so long as the tables and/or schemas used are well labeled.

The underlying tables need to be created before the data can be loaded. The table structures should be identified using the information about the collected data. The structure needs to map to the columns in the collected data. In addition, the data types for each column need to be defined. If the data types are known, those data types should be used when creating the table. If the columns are known but the data types are not, the tables should be created with loose data types, such as SQL Server's maximum-length Unicode string data type (nvarchar(max)) or the Unicode text data type (ntext). With these loose data types, the data is not altered and can be analyzed later to determine the correct data types.

The NYSE data collected in *Chapter 5, Collecting Hadoop Application Data*, is loaded into a table by first creating the table structure. The columns should be created with the original column names for ease of reference. The table can either be created using the SQL Server CREATE TABLE command or the SSMS **New Table** option in the **Graphical User Interface** (**GUI**). To create the table using the GUI, go to **Databases** in the Object Explorer. Next, select the database for which you want to create a new table, in our example, this is `1001-NYSE-Source`. Right-click **Tables**, and then select **Table**. This creates a new table for the NYSE data. The following figure illustrates this process:

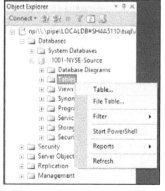

Figure 5: Creating a new table

Next, enter the field names exactly as they appear in the source data and set the data type to nvarchar(max), which is the variable-length Unicode character field with the maximum number of allowable characters. The data types can be set to their actual values, but those can be updated later in the transformation process. Setting those fields to nvarchar(max) ensures that the import will not result in conversion errors so long as none of the values are greater than the system-allowed number of characters, which is typically 4,000 for nvarchar. The following figure illustrates this process:

Column Name	Data Type	Allow Nulls
exchange	nvarchar(MAX)	✔
stock_symbol	nvarchar(MAX)	✔
date	nvarchar(MAX)	✔
stock_price_open	nvarchar(MAX)	✔
stock_price_high	nvarchar(MAX)	✔
stock_price_low	nvarchar(MAX)	✔
stock_price_close	nvarchar(MAX)	✔
stock_volume	nvarchar(MAX)	✔
stock_price_adj_close	nvarchar(MAX)	✔

Figure 6: Setting column names and data types

After the column names and data types are set, save the table, and give it a descriptive name that contains the evidence ID number from the collection process. For this example, the table is named 001_NYSE.

The table structure can be automatically created by SQL Server via the SQL Server **Import/Export** wizard when the data contains the column headers.

Next, the data is loaded into the table. SQL Server offers several methods for importing data, but the BULK INSERT command is the preferred method in forensic investigations. BULK INSERT is a script-based approach to loading the data into an existing table by defining the location of the data and the source data's properties. Investigators should retain copies of the BULK INSERT scripts that are executed during the data load process for process validation. The following is an example of loading data using BULK INSERT:

```
BULK INSERT dbo.[001_NYSE]
FROM 'C:\Evidence\NYSE-2000-2001.tsv'
WITH
(
   FIRSTROW = 2,
   FIELDTERMINATOR = '\t',
   ROWTERMINATOR = '0x0a'
)
```

This command loads the data from the `NYSE-2000-2001.tsv` file into the `001_NYSE` table. The command further specifies that the first row should be skipped because it is the header row, the fields are separated by tab characters, and the rows are terminated by UNIX line breaks.

The following is the output from the `BULK INSERT` command:

```
(812989 row(s) affected)
```

This process can be validated in two ways. First, the number of records should be validated against the evidence file by opening it, using a text editor that can handle large files, and identifying the number of rows. Alternatively, a line-counting utility can be used to return the number of lines in the file without opening the file in a text editor. The second method is to compare the number of records to the control totals collected in the collection phase. The control totals can include the number of records and the calculated control totals of key fields.

Sample records should also be manually reviewed to ensure that the data was loaded correctly. Run the following command to view the first twenty records of the NYSE data set:

```
SELECT TOP 20 *
FROM [001_NYSE]
```

In some cases, the data loading method may result in an improper data load. For example, delimiters can be used without text qualifiers, and the delimiter is a part of a field's value. This kind of issue requires correction, either by reloading the data or correcting the issue manually. Typically, this kind of issue can be easily identified by reviewing sample records and running several types of tests, such as:

- Querying the minimum and maximum length of each field to determine if fields are empty or are the same length as the maximum-defined length of the field (indicating that the data in the field exceeds the length of the field in SQL)
- Identifying outliers, such as unexpected values
- Reviewing numeric fields for alphabetic characters, and vice versa

In some instances, the data validation is performed after data transformations are performed. The data may not be in a format that can be easily verified, such as a numeric field that has a character data type or multiple files that need to be consolidated before they can be compared to the control totals. The transformation steps can be performed before the data validation if this is the case. The validation should, however, be performed before the analysis is started.

Preload data transformations

In some cases, data cannot be immediately loaded into the database and requires transformations outside of the database. Some forms of data, such as key-value pairs, object-oriented data, and other forms of data not in a two-dimensional relational structure, cannot easily be loaded into the database. In other cases, it is easier or faster to transform data before loading it into a database. Regardless, some types of data structures are not conducive to being loaded into a relational database.

The following are several types of files that can require pre-load transformations:

- Key-value pair data
- Report files that include headers and/or footers
- Certain forms of markup files

There are two possible solutions: 1) develop and run custom scripts that transform the data into files with a suitable structure for database import or 2) directly import the transformed data into the database. The goal of a pre-load data transformation is to correct the structure of the data so it can be loaded and analyzed immediately, or analyzed after transformation. Additional transformations can be performed at this stage, but they can also be performed after the data is in the database; the latter is typically faster.

When running pre-load data transformations, keep the following in mind:

- Determine whether the script needs to be run and if running the script is faster than performing transformations in the database
- Have the script generated logs detailing what was transformed and any errors that may have occurred
- Preserve a copy of the script for documentation

Data surveying

Data surveying is the process of running an overview analysis of the data to understand the structure and data contents. Surveying the data allows the investigator to get a base understanding of the full structure of the data and the types of values contained therein. Should any additional data transformation be required, the survey process helps identify those transformations.

Surveying the data provides several benefits; they are as follows:

- Locating data that requires transformations
- Identifying anomalies and data gaps that require immediate attention
- Generating information that can be applied to the preliminary analysis

Surveying is best performed through the use of scripts and a manual review of the results. The first type of surveying is to produce a list of boundary values and counts of distinct values. Rather than running separate surveys for each field in each table, a script can be written to automatically identify all tables and fields and calculate the relevant statistics.

The first step is to create a table to store the results of the script:

```
CREATE TABLE tbl_DB_Survey (tableName varchar(max), colName
varchar(max), minVal varchar(max), maxVal varchar(max), minLen int,
maxLen in, numDistinct int, numNULL int, numNumeric int , numDate
int)
```

The table stores the table and column names; the minimum and maximum values; the minimum and maximum field lengths; and the number of distinct values, NULLs, numeric values, and date values. Next, the following script is run to iterate through SQL Server's `syscolumns` and `sysobjects` table to identify the tables and fields as a cursor and then insert the corresponding `tbl_DB_Survey` values for each table and field:

```
DECLARE @curCol varchar(255)
DECLARE @curTable varchar(255)
DECLARE curSurvey CURSOR FOR
SELECT sc.name, so.name
FROM syscolumns sc, sysobjects so
WHERE sc.id = so.id
AND xtype = 'U'
ORDER BY 2,1
OPEN curSurvey
FETCH NEXT FROM update_cursor
INTO @curCol,@curTable
WHILE @@FETCH_STATUS = 0
BEGIN
   INSERT INTO tbl_DB_Survey (tableName, colName, minVal, maxVal, minLen,
   maxLen, numDistinct, numNULL, numNumeric, numDate)
   SELECT ''@tableName'', ''@colName'', CONVERT(varchar,MIN(@colName)),
   CONVERT(varchar,MAX(@colName)), MIN(LEN(@colName)), MAX(LEN(@colName)),
   COUNT(DISTINCT(@colName)), COUNT(ISNULL(@colName)), COUNT(ISNUMERIC(@
   colName)), COUNT(ISDATE(@colName))
   FROM @tableName
   FETCH NEXT FROM curSurvey INTO @curCol,@curTable
END
CLOSE curSurvey
DEALLOCATE curSurvey
```

This script populates the tbl_DB_Survey table with summary information about each table. The results should be reviewed to identify anomalies and which fields are important. Several examples of the types of issues to review include:

- An expected numeric field's minimum and maximum values are evaluated as strings and not numeric

- An expected date field does not have a majority of values that are considered date values by SQL Server

- The number of distinct values for a field is only one

Other forms of descriptive statistics can be applied to survey the data. Grouping and outlier analysis are two methods that enable the investigator to identify what types of information are contained in the data and how many outliers exist. The simplest form of this analysis is to group data by a single field. The following query returns the number of records for each stock symbol in the descending order:

```
SELECT stock_symbol, COUNT(*)
FROM [001_NYSE]
GROUP BY stock_symbol
ORDER BY 2 DESC, 1
```

The query returns 1,734 results, with the first 508 symbols having 500 records. This large number of records shows that these symbols each have a normal amount of records. The query can then be reordered to display the symbols with the smallest amount of records by removing the DESC clause. As illustrated in the following table, the top five stock symbols with the fewest number of records shows that they each have fewer than twenty records. Depending on the expected values, this type of survey can help get a preliminary understanding of the data and highlight potential outliers:

stock_symbol	Number of Records
PCN	3
KFS	9
PRU	11
HYV	19
AYI	19

Transforming data

Data from Hadoop applications can require transformation into a more readily usable format. Some Hadoop applications, such as HBase, store the data in a key-value pair format, which is not a usable format for SQL Server or other relational databases. The data has to be transformed before it can be analyzed. Even if the data was extracted into a format that is usable for SQL Server, the data may still require transformation to clean up the data values or structure the data for a particular type of analysis.

Transforming data is the process of converting the format of the data to a more readily usable format, but it does not mean the values of the data should be altered. A transformation involves changing the structure of the data. When data is collected from Hadoop, the data is extracted into files with the structure of the original application's format (or into files that were structured in the easiest format for collection). These formats may not be ideal for analysis and need to be converted into a format that can be analyzed in SQL Server. With all transformations, however, the values are not altered. If data needs to be transformed into an aggregated or reduced data set, the data must still reflect the original values.

Transformations can be required for a number of reasons. Some of the common reasons include:

- Data of the same structure needs to be consolidated into a single table
- Data is stored in report files with headers and footers that cannot easily be imported into a relational database
- Duplicative data requires consolidation or normalization
- Data was imported in text field columns and needs to be converted to the actual data types (for example, dates or numeric)
- Extraneous data needs to be removed from the analysis data set for simplicity and data reduction

Many different types of transformations can be performed. Field values can be transformed into a standardized format. For example, date values can be standardized into a single format of DD/MM/YY to provide for uniform values and easier analysis. The name and order of column headers can be structured in a consistent manner. The records can also be reoriented by making horizontal records vertical.

The next two figures illustrate a set of records that are transformed by rotating them from horizontal to vertical. This was done by changing the date column headers into a single date column and making the corresponding values presented vertically into separate records. The following screenshot is an example of data in a horizontal structure:

Item ID	3/1/2010-12/31/2010 Amount	3/1/2010-12/31/2010 Orders	1/1/2011-6/30/2011 Amount	1/1/2011-6/30/2011 Orders
Item 1	$ 27,214.20	36	$ 14,363.05	19
Item 2	$ 61,570.75	97	$ 20,946.75	33
Item 3	$ 55,551.38	62	$ 70,783.21	79

Figure 7: Pre-transformation records

In the next screenshot, the two sets of **Amount** and **Orders** are split into two vertical records and the date range in the column headers is moved into the **Date Range** column:

Item ID	Amount	Orders	Date Range
Item 1	$27,214.20	36	3/1/2010-12/31/2010
Item 1	$14,363.05	19	1/1/2011-6/30/2011
Item 2	$61,570.75	97	3/1/2010-12/31/2010
Item 2	$20,946.75	33	1/1/2011-6/30/2011
Item 3	$55,551.38	62	3/1/2010-12/31/2010
Item 3	$70,783.21	79	1/1/2011-6/30/2011

Figure 8: Transformed records

This type of transformation is useful for aggregating fewer sets of columns and restricting records to a particular date range rather than aggregating multiple columns together, or not being able to easily restrict the records to a specific date range.

Several types of techniques can help the investigator prove that the data was not altered during the transformation process. The primary mechanism is the use of control totals. If a control total was captured during the collection phase, that control total can continue to be used to verify that the transformation did not alter the records. In the previous screenshot, if a control total was captured for the number of orders or total amounts, the control total can be compared to the transformed data's order or amount values. The other method is to perform the transformations using queries that are retained as part of the records. All alterations to the data must be carefully documented.

Using the NYSE data, the field's data types can be updated for faster analysis. The numeric fields can be updated to numeric data types, and the date field can be updated to SQL Server's datetime data type. Updating these data types in SQL Server saves analysis time because the conversion is performed once instead of during every query, enabling the investigator to run numeric computations and date analysis functions faster. First, the field's data types should be tested to determine if the conversion can be performed.

The following command returns any records in `001_NYSE` that cannot be converted into SQL Server's `datetime` data type:

```
SELECT *
FROM [001_NYSE]
WHERE ISDATE([date]) = 0
```

This command returns no records, so the data type can be updated using the following command:

```
ALTER TABLE [001_NYSE] ALTER COLUMN [date] DATETIME
```

The `date` column's data type has been converted to `datetime`. The same steps can be applied to the numeric columns using the `ISNUMERIC()` function.

Another common form of data transformation is culling data. Culling is the process of reducing the data set based on specific criteria. The relevant analysis for an investigation may only require a subset of the data. Rather than have extraneous fields or records, the data can be culled to the relevant data set. Culling in a forensic investigation means to create a copy of the relevant subset of the evidence. It does not mean that the source evidence should be deleted or modified.

The first method of culling is to identify and remove nonrelevant tables and columns. This can be done by surveying the fields and reviewing sample records, as well as documentation about the data, to determine whether it could potentially be relevant. The process can either be performed by selecting the relevant tables and columns that should be copied or by selecting the tables and columns that should be culled.

The second method is to apply filtering criteria to the data. Like culling tables and columns, this method can be performed by identifying what should or should not be included. An inclusive or exclusive filter is applied to the data, and the results determine what information should be copied into the analysis data set. For example, a common form of culling is to restrict the data to a date range from the investigation. A filter is created to generate a new table for all records that fall within that date range. The following command provides a simple example of how this is performed:

```
SELECT *
INTO ANALYSIS.[001_NYSE_Filtered]
FROM [001_NYSE]
WHERE [date] between '1/1/2000' and '12/31/2000'
```

This generates a new table in the `ANALYSIS` schema that only includes records between January 1, 2000 and December 31, 2000.

Optimization techniques can be applied to the analysis data. In addition to culling data, standard techniques should be considered if the data set is very large. Several examples include creating a new analysis database with separate data and index files, creating optimized indexes on key fields, and normalizing or de-normalizing data.

Keep in mind, all data test and conversion scripts should be saved and clearly documented to show that the data was not incorrectly modified.

Transforming nonrelational data

Nonrelational data can be transformed in the database. Several Hadoop applications produce key-value pair data, which is not a data structure traditionally handled in relational databases. This type of data can either be transformed into a relational structure or maintained in its key-value pair format and transformed in a way that can be used in SQL. The decision about how to transform the data depends on the structure of the data and the nature of the investigation.

Consider the following sample data that was extracted from HBase:

```
itemID        Key            Value
1             Name           John Doe
1             Address        123 Main St
1             Email          jdoe@zzz.com
2             Name           Jane Doe
2             Phone          555-1234
```

This data can be imported directly into SQL Server with those column names. An example of the difficulty with this format in SQL Server is that querying for all key-value pairs of a particular `itemID` query criteria is cumbersome. For example, identifying all items with an email address with a `zzz.com` domain requires multiple steps. Instead, the data can be transformed in to a more useful structure.

There are several approaches to transform key-value pair data to a standard SQL structure, but the following method is the most straightforward. First, identify all possible keys using the following command:

```
SELECT DISTINCT Key
FROM tbl_keyPair
```

Next, create a table with those keys and the item ID as the column headers:

```
CREATE TABLE tbl_keyPair_transformed (itemID int, [Name] VARCHAR
(255), Address VARCHAR (500), Email VARCHAR (255), Phone VARCHAR
(100))
```

Now insert one record into the transformed table for each `item` ID in the original table:

```
INSERT INTO tbl_keyPair_transformed (itemID)
SELECT DISTINCT itemID
FROM tbl_keyPair
```

Finally, iterate through the original table and insert the corresponding key-value for each item:

```
DECLARE @curKey varchar(255)
DECLARE curSurvey CURSOR FOR
SELECT DISTINCT KEY FROM tbl_keyPair ORDER BY 1
OPEN curSurvey
FETCH NEXT FROM update_cursor
INTO @curKey
WHILE @@FETCH_STATUS = 0
BEGIN
UPDATE output
SET @curKey = input.Value
FROM tbl_keyPair input, tbl_keyPair_transformed output
WHERE input.itemID = output.itemID
AND input.Key = @curKey
FETCH NEXT FROM curSurvey INTO @curKey
END
CLOSE curSurvey
DEALLOCATE curSurvey
```

The following is the resulting table:

itemID	Name	Address	Email	Phone
1	John Doe	123 Main St	jdoe@zzz.com	
2	Jane Doe			555-1234

This type of data is much more conducive to the types of analysis that are covered in the following section, *Analyzing data*. However, in some cases, the key-value pair data may need to be maintained in its original format should the analysis need to mirror how the data was structured and analyzed in the source system.

Analyzing data

Analyzing Hadoop data in a forensic investigation, also known as forensic analytics, is the process of running tests against the data to isolate events, trends, and patterns that relate to the investigation. Investigators have a large set of techniques for performing the analysis that meets the needs of the case. Each investigation is different, and each requires its own type of analysis. In some cases, not much is known about how the data relates to the facts of the investigation. In other cases, a single data point that represents an event or fact is believed to reside in the data. The role of the investigator is to understand the data and run an analysis that brings out the facts of the case in a clear, understandable way.

Investigators should begin the analysis with an approach and plan in place. The investigation began with a set of issues and facts that need to be proven or further developed. In addition, the preceding steps of the process, such as interviews and documentation review, should have yielded information about what data has been collected and how to analyze it. Based on this information, the investigator can develop at least an initial plan on how to approach the data and begin the analysis.

The following sections discuss how to approach the forensic analysis and several of the main analysis techniques employed by investigators.

The analysis approach

The analysis approach of the investigation depends on two major factors:

- How much information is known about the events or facts related to the collected data
- The type of investigation

The amount of information known to the investigator impacts how the analysis is conducted. Hadoop data can be used in some investigations to find supporting evidence or examples of a known set of facts. In these cases, the amount of information known is high and the analysis process is largely a matter of further proving what is already known, or highlighting known facts. In other cases, the investigation is performed based on suspicions or evidence that points to some facts. The amount of information known in these cases is low, and the analysis is aimed at locating facts, often called the "smoking gun", and/or establishing patterns.

To develop an analysis plan, the investigator must start with the known facts and theory. This information is generally known because that was the basis for conducting the investigation in the first place. The set of facts may be limited, so the analysis plan may involve surveying the data, further gathering supporting information, and adjusting the investigation theory. If the facts are largely known, the analysis plan should be focused on proving the established theory and bolstering it by identifying key information that will serve as evidence while eliminating the possibility of alternate theories. Finally, the analysis can include steps to further prove that the findings were accurate. This can include validating the information using other analysis techniques or data sources, including the use of publicly-available data sets. The following figure illustrates the phases of the analysis process and several approaches to each step:

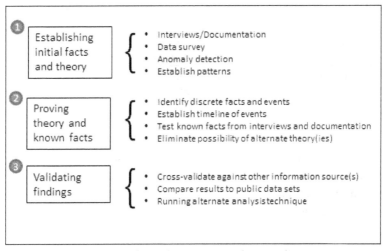

Figure 9: The analysis process and approaches

The analysis process can be highly iterative. The investigation theory and a set of known facts change throughout the process, so the analysis plan is adjusted to account for the changes. The analysis may begin with a set of known facts and the investigator focuses on proving those facts, but in the process, new information may be uncovered that requires the original theory to be modified.

Types of investigation

Forensic investigations are performed for a wide array of issues. The common and well-known ones are fraud investigations; however, there are several different types of fraud. Data breach or other forms of improper access are common types of investigations, but many other types of investigations are also performed. Each type of investigation has its own unique issues and requirements.

The following table lists the various types of investigations and the unique characteristics of each:

Investigation Type	Characteristics
Consumer Fraud	This is a fraud committed by one or more individuals, with their behavior tracked and stored in the system
Corporate Fraud	This is a fraud conducted by an organization, which requires a large volume of data to be analyzed to isolate fraud events from nonfraudulent ones
Employee Fraud	This is a violation of organization's policies and procedures and/or illegal activity by one or more employees that is stored within the system
Government Fraud	This is similar to corporate fraud, but perpetrated by the government or an organization involved with the government
Intellectual Property	This is a comparison of common data structures or informational contents with another system or data set
Unauthorized Access (for example, Data Breach)	This is an analysis of event-based evidence (for example, web logs) indicating that an unauthorized access occurred
Class Action	This is a litigation analysis whereby common characteristics or set of facts affecting a set of individuals are analyzed

The type of investigation being conducted should be considered when developing the analysis plan and performing the analysis. This serves to better direct the approach and findings to match the requirements of the investigation. The analysis should align with the characteristics of the type of investigation.

 Several of the investigation types may apply to a complex investigation. In such cases, the combined characteristics of all applicable types should be considered.

Analysis techniques

While the identification and collection of forensic data is a well-defined process, forensic analysis requires some level of creativity. This is needed to match the requirements of the investigation to the analysis techniques that should be run. The analysis techniques employed for forensic investigators range in scope from identifying individual transactions to performing inferential statistics to describe the contents of the data. Multiple analysis techniques can often achieve the same result, so the investigator needs to be aware of which analysis techniques best meet the requirements of the investigation.

The following sections detail some of the main analysis techniques used in forensic investigations. Countless techniques exist, but the key ones covered here are frequently used in investigations and can be applied to virtually any Big Data investigation.

Isolating known facts and events

The investigator can approach the data with a set of known facts and events that need to be identified in the data. In these cases, the facts and events can be identified by querying the data using information about the data to pinpoint where the data exists. Big Data investigations are complicated by the fact that the data set can contain billions of records, so the investigator cannot manually review all records for the specific data points of interest. Instead, the investigator can apply a series of techniques to reduce the potentially relevant data to a manageable subset of records.

The first technique is is to apply data filters. A set of known facts or events will have information associated with it that can be applied to the data to reduce the number of potential records. The events may be within a specific date range or on a specific date. The facts may be limited to a specific person or for records with a specific code value. These filters can be added as SQL WHERE clauses to ignore nonrelevant data.

The second technique is to sort the data by a key field or set of fields to assess the filtered records. Sorted data can be reviewed more easily, and if the set of returned records is small enough, the investigator can review them to assess whether the different sorted field values are relevant. This sorting not only helps the investigator identify the potentially relevant records quicker, but it also allows for an easier data review to identify additional filter criteria.

Using the NYSE data set, the following query can be run to limit results to a single date in question:

```
SELECT *
FROM [001_NYSE]
WHERE date = '2/1/2001'
AND stock_volume BETWEEN 100 and 200
ORDER BY stock_symbol
```

The query returns three records. The investigator should manually review the records to ensure that the query results include desired information. The query can be adjusted to include additional filter criteria if too many records are returned.

Once the facts or events have been located, the filter criteria can be loosened to look for supporting or related records that can help the investigation. One or more of the facts may be supported by additional related records, or the scope of the investigation may need to be expanded if a larger pattern of events is found.

Grouping and clustering

Cluster analysis is a powerful statistical technique for analyzing large sets of data. Clustering can be achieved by running a number of algorithms to group data, assess the distribution, and identify outliers. A cluster is a grouping of like subsets of data for the purpose of classifying them. Cluster analysis typically shows multiple clusters from a data set, and these clusters can be devised and structured in a number of ways. Cluster analysis is useful in Big Data investigations because it provides a means for grouping data into sets for analysis (for example, relevant versus nonrelevant data or legitimate versus fraudulent data).

A basic technique for grouping data is to create pseudo-clusters to group data and define groups from the results. Using the NYSE data set, the following query can be run to group trades into clusters based on the size of the trades:

```
SELECT grouping, SUM(stock_volume), COUNT(*)
FROM
(SELECT stock_volume
CASE
WHEN stock_volume BETWEEN 1 and 25000 then 1
WHEN stock_volume BETWEEN 25001 and 50000 then 25001
WHEN stock_volume BETWEEN 50001 and 75000 then 50001
WHEN stock_volume BETWEEN 75001 and 100000 then 75001
ELSE 100001
END AS grouping
FROM [001_NYSE]) AS Z
GROUP BY grouping
ORDER BY 1
```

The results from the query can be plotted in a bubble chart to show the relative size of the five groups, as shown in the following figure. The x-axis represents the grouping of the records based on the `stock_volume` value of each record. The y-axis represents the cumulative number of `stock_volume` values, and the size of the circle represents the number of records in that grouping:

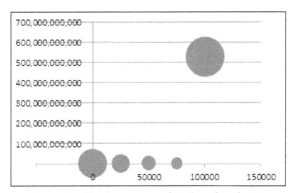

Figure 10: A basic grouping of stock trade volumes

Numerous cluster analysis techniques exist in the field of data mining. The two primary algorithms used for data clustering are k-means and **expectation-maximization** (**EM**). The approaches an investigator can take to perform clustering are:

1. Select a distance measure.
2. Select a clustering algorithm.
3. Define the distance between two clusters.
4. Determine the number of clusters based on the data.
5. Validate the analysis.

The most common distance measure is the Euclidean measure, which computes the distance using spatial coordinates. Here, the Euclidean measure can be applied to calculate distance using the values from a numeric field. The following example calculates the distance for the first three non-zero values of the `stock_volume` field:

Record	stock_volume
A	100
B	200
C	300

The following is the output generated:

```
Distance

B vs. A: 200 - 100 = 100

C vs. A: 300 - 100 = 200

C vs. B: 300 - 200 = 100
```

Additional fields can be added to the distance calculation, if required. The formula for adding fields is:

$$\text{sqrt}((\text{Record A}_{field\ 1} - \text{Record B}_{field\ 1})^2 + (\text{Record A}_{field\ 2} - \text{Record B}_{field\ 2})^2)$$

Next, the clustering algorithm is selected. The k-means clustering algorithm is a well-known clustering algorithm and is computed as follows:

1. Define the number of clusters, k.
2. Assign each data point to its closest cluster center.
3. Recompute the cluster centers.
4. Repeat these steps until there are minimal or no changes to the cluster centers.

The clusters can be defined to meet the needs of the clustering. Here, three clusters are selected based on the following values: second smallest (200), second largest (153,932,600), and mean (672,237).

Next, each record's `stock_volume` is assigned to one of the clusters based on the distance to each:

Cluster	Starting Center	Number of Records	Avg stock_volume
2nd Smallest	200	561,501	79,047
2nd Largest	153,932,600	13	127,766,500
Mean	672,237	241,993	2,041,798

This result shows that a majority of records have a `stock_volume` value closest to the minimum, while very few records have a `stock_volume` value close to the maximum. The result also shows the mean of the values assigned to each cluster and how far the centers for each cluster have shifted after just one iteration.

After the initial calculations are run, the cluster's centers are recalculated, and the data point calculation is rerun until there are no significant changes to the number of records and starting center after multiple iterations. If the results are too skewed, the investigator can return to the first step, select a different number of clusters, and select different center values for each cluster to better distribute them.

Histograms

The frequency of particular events or ranges of values appearing in the data is an important metric for investigators. Histograms plot the frequency of events, or ranges of values, in a visual that can be used to further analysis or as part of the findings. To create a histogram, data is classified into a preset list of bins, and the number of data points per bin is summed. The number of data points per bin is called the frequency. The following is an example of plotting a histogram based on the `stock_price` field, using bins in increments of 10, with everything greater than 100 represented in the `More` bin:

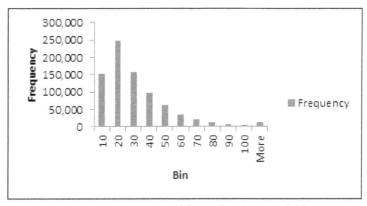

Figure 11: A histogram of the stock_price_open field

Histograms are useful for quickly showing the distribution of data in a format that can be easily understood by most audiences. For an investigation, showing normal patterns within normal distributions of events and highlighting abnormal events or characteristics is important. Histograms provide a quick and accessible method for showing the distributions in a way that is easily understood.

The time series analysis

Events in the data can be plotted to establish a chronology, highlight key pattern changes, or establish what the normal patterns are in the data. Time series analysis computes specific metrics using a sequence of data points based on a defined date interval. The date interval can be chosen by the investigator, and the time period can either be the entire date range of the data or a selected subset of the dates.

The first step is to select the date range and date interval. In the NYSE data, there are 519 individual dates spanning a two-year period. The investigator can plot every single day, plot a subset of days, or plot the data using an aggregated interval (for example, by months or years). Given the large number of days, the data can best be reviewed when aggregated by month and year:

```
SELECT MONTH(date) + "-" + YEAR(date), SUM(stock_volume)
FROM [001_NYSE]
GROUP BY MONTH(date) + "-" + YEAR(date)
ORDER BY 1
```

The plotted data is shown in the following figure:

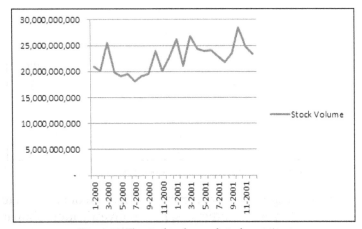

Figure 12: The stock volume plotted over time

Plotting the data to show chronology can help establish when events occurred and demonstrate basic data patterns. More advanced techniques can be applied to explain the chronology.

Measuring change over time

Changes in the data can be measured to show key changes that occurred. One such measure is the single moving average, which is the mean of successive past events. The mean for all preceding time periods is calculated for each time period, which shows the change in average caused by each successive time period. The first two time periods do not receive a single moving average value. Starting with the third time period, the mean is calculated using all values from that time period and the previous two time periods. The process is repeated for all N time periods.

The following table shows the stock volume single moving average for the first four time periods:

Date	Stock Volume	Single Moving Avg
1-2000	21,011,437,800	N/A
2-2000	20,137,095,500	N/A
3-2000	25,565,580,900	22,238,038,067
4-2000	19,879,493,700	21,860,723,367

The single moving average can be plotted along with the actual monthly values to show the effect that each month has on the mean for that month and all preceding months. This is illustrated in the following figure:

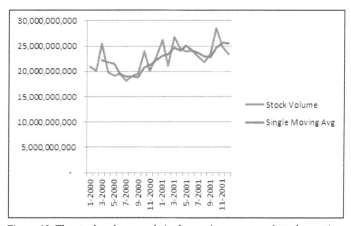

Figure 13: The stock volume and single moving average plotted over time

Time series analysis helps to establish normal patterns and can conditionally help identify anomalies. The time series represents the patterns within the data over time. Perhaps a key event or change in procedure resulted in a change that is reflected in the data, or perhaps the data contradicts what was believed to have happened. Running time series analysis is a fast method for visually creating a chronology of what happened and determining whether a repeating or consistent pattern exists in the data. If there are spikes or dips in the time series, or a pattern is not followed, that indicates an issue that needs to be explored and explained.

Normal behavior can also be tested by comparing the data set to a trusted data set, such as a public data set, to determine if the data set comports with the trusted data set. A common technique in financial fraud investigations is to compare financial performance to other organization's performance via public data sets.

Anomaly detection

Data anomalies are a major issue. Anomalies can be natural occurrences due to data being incorrectly entered or imported into a system, or they can indicate or be proof of fraud or other wrongdoing. An investigator can analyze a data set for anomalies to either pinpoint where evidence of wrongdoing exists or to indicate or rule out the possibility of wrongdoing.

There are two major types of techniques for identifying anomalies: rule-based identification and statistical identification. Rule-based identification is where predefined rules for expected values are established and the investigator tests the data for records that violate the rule. These tests are run with specific criteria in mind, and all outliers are segregated for further analysis. Statistical identification is where descriptive or inferential statistics are used to determine normal patterns or distributions of data. The investigator then uses these patterns or distributions to isolate the anomalies for further analysis.

Both rule-based identification and statistical identification are equally valid forms of analysis, but the investigator may choose one over the other based on the requirements of the investigation. Rule-based analysis requires a priori knowledge of the data and what constitutes an outlier. The rules can be developed from earlier phases, from data surveying, or from other information learned about the data and investigation. Statistical analysis can be applied without a priori knowledge and is typically performed when the investigator does not know what constitutes an anomaly or when he wants to prove what the normal behavior and patterns of the data are. Grouping and clustering are forms of statistical analysis, and the output from those forms of analysis can be used for anomaly detection. In addition, analyzing data for duplication and applying Benford's law, topics that are covered in the sections that follow, are useful techniques for identifying potential outliers.

Rule-based analysis

Rule-based analysis is an effective method for isolating specific types of anomalies or key records. This method requires knowing the rules that the data should adhere to and then executing the rules against the data to identify the records that violate the rules.

The rules can take many forms and include multiple criteria, such as:

- Date ranges
- Acceptable values
- Numeric value ranges
- Acceptable combinations of values across fields
- Data values confirmed against known events

Once the rules have been documented, they can be converted into queries. The queries can be run in one of two ways: 1) independently or 2) a table of rules can be created and a script can be executed to run all of the rules from the table, sending the outliers to an anomaly table.

The following query runs a rule-based query to isolate records whose `stock_price_open` value is less than the `stock_price_low` value:

```
SELECT *
FROM [001_NYSE]
WHERE stock_price_open < stock_price_low
```

The query returns a single record whose `stock_price_open` equals to zero and `stock_price_low` equals to 188.6. Obviously, this record is an anomaly, but it may be a data quality issue or an explainable issue.

Multiple rules can also be coded into a rule table in the form of SQL WHERE clauses in order to automate the process. An automated SQL script using a cursor can iterate through the rules table, with all records that violate the rules being stored in a rules violation table, as illustrated in the following figure:

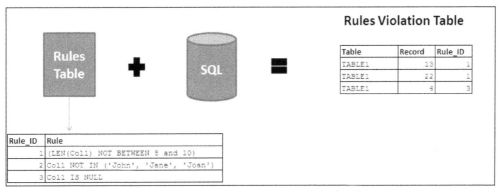

Figure 14: Rule-based analysis using multiple rules

Duplication analysis

One indicator of fraud or intentionally-altered data is higher-than-expected levels of data duplication. Duplication can be normal when a particular type of data is repeatedly entered; however, duplication is not always the norm. When fraud or a cover-up of a certain kind of activity is committed, the values of the data are rarely distributed in a normal manner. Instead, the individual(s) entering or altering the data may enter duplicative data.

Duplication can be found in records, fields, or characters within a field. The set of values of a record, the entire value of a field, or individual characters can repeat at a higher-than-expected level. To identify duplicates, the data should be grouped or split into the units to be analyzed. The simplest form is to analyze the entire field. The data is then aggregated to identify the counts. For example, the following query aggregates the stock_volume field and the number of results, with the results sorted in descending order:

```
SELECT stock_volume, count(*) as recCount
FROM [001_NYSE]
GROUP BY stock_ volume
ORDER BY 2 DESC
```

The five stock_volume values with the highest number of records are:

stock_volume	recCount
0	9,482
200	1,783
1,000	1,661
2,000	1,660
600	1,551

This type of query is typically a starting point and requires an understanding of the expected counts. The results are reviewed for any anomalies or unexpected values, such as too much or too few records for each value. Then, the investigator can continue the analysis in one of two ways: 1) by adding additional criteria to the aggregation query in order to review a specific subset of the records (for example, the date range in question) or 2) by further reviewing the types of records with higher-than-expected duplication. In this case, the records with a stock_volume equal to zero should be reviewed for possible issues:

```
SELECT *
FROM [001_NYSE]
WHERE stock_volume = 0
ORDER BY stock_symbol
```

Reviewing the individual values that contain duplication may identify an issue based on suspicious records, or there may be an explanation for why the duplication was normal. If other possible duplication remains, the analysis can be refined to home in on the remaining duplicates. The following query adds the `stock_symbol` to the aggregation and excludes records with a `stock_volume` equal to zero:

```
SELECT stock_volume, stock_symbol, count(*) as recCount
FROM [001_NYSE]
WHERE stock_volume <> 0
GROUP BY stock_volume, stock_symbol
ORDER BY 3 DESC
```

This query first returns the following top five rows:

stock_volume	stock_symbol	recCount
800	KUB	54
1,200	KUB	47
100	CDR	42
100	GMK	42
200	CSS	41

This query then provides more refined results that can be interpreted against the expected distribution. Here, both the volume and symbol can be examined together, and the false positive (`stock_volume = 0`) is eliminated.

Another method is to include the relative percentage of duplication for each aggregated set. In the previous query, the KUB stocks returned the first two results, but what if that stock has the highest number of overall records? The query can be modified as follows to include the percentage for any `stock_volume` and `stock_symbol` combination with more than 10 records:

```
SELECT a.stock_volume, a.stock_symbol, a.recCount,
a.recCount/b.totalCount
AS percentOfSymbol
FROM
(SELECT stock_volume, stock_symbol, count(*) as recCount
FROM [001_NYSE]
WHERE stock_volume <> 0
GROUP BY stock_volume, stock_symbol) a,
(SELECT stock_symbol, count(*) as totalCount
FROM [001_NYSE]
WHERE stock_volume <> 0
```

```
GROUP BY stock_symbol) b
WHERE a.stock_symbol = b.stock_symbol AND a.recCount > 10
ORDER BY 4 DESC, 3 DESC
```

This query returns the following top five results:

stock_volume	stock_symbol	recCount	percentOfSymbol
100	EXM	30	0.278
100	CDR	42	0.251
100	ALY	12	0.245
200	EXM	19	0.176
100	GMK	42	0.163

As evidenced from these results, the top results do not appear to be an issue because of how common stock purchases in blocks of 100 and 200 are and the relatively small size of blocks of 100 and 200. However, there may still be issues in other duplicative values that could require analysis.

Duplication analysis can also be performed on digits within certain fields. In fraud investigations and cases where the data may have been altered, an investigator can look into the duplication of values to determine if specific digits have been used. As an example, an accountant accused of manipulating the books may enter nonexistent transactions using a standard value to mask the fraud.

To perform this analysis, one or more digits from a field are aggregated and the results are plotted to represent the distribution of the data. The following query analyzes the two left-most digits of stock_price_open field, excluding records having stock_price_open equal to zero:

```
SELECT LEFT(CONVERT(VARCHAR, stock_price_open), 2), COUNT(*) AS
recCount
FROM [001_NYSE]
WHERE stock_price_open <> 0
GROUP BY LEFT(CONVERT(VARCHAR, stock_price_open), 2)
ORDER BY 2 DESC
```

The query returns the following top five results:

Digits	recCount
13	35,508
14	33,929
12	31,079
11	29,388
10	27,478

This analysis can be augmented by analyzing the days in which each set of digits was entered at the highest percentage using the following query:

```
SELECT A.digits, date, dateCount/totalCount as datePercentage,
totalCount

FROM

(SELECT date, LEFT(CONVERT(VARCHAR, stock_price_open), 2) AS digits,
COUNT(*) as dateCount

FROM [001_NYSE]

WHERE stock_price_open <> 0 AND LEN(stock_price_open) > 1

GROUP BY date, LEFT(CONVERT(VARCHAR, stock_price_open), 2)) AS A,

(SELECT LEFT(CONVERT(VARCHAR, stock_price_open), 2) AS digits,
COUNT(*) as dateCount

FROM [001_NYSE]

WHERE stock_price_open <> 0 AND LEN(stock_price_open) > 1

GROUP BY LEFT(CONVERT(VARCHAR, stock_price_open), 2)) AS B

WHERE A.digits = B.digits

ORDER BY 3 DESC
```

The query returns the following results:

Digits	date	datePercentage	totalCount
98	2000-11-14	0.15	394
99	2000-12-13	0.12	335
88	2000-11-20	0.11	610
95	2001-04-11	0.11	445
95	2000-12-15	0.10	445

This analysis, or analyzing the two right-most digits, can be used to expose whether certain digits were entered on a single date, pointing to the likelihood of manual entry and possible data manipulation.

Benford's law

Benford's law is a principle that defines the expected distribution of digits in natural data sets. Similar to duplication analysis, Benford's law enables the investigator to break down the data to determine the distribution of digits and their positions to assess whether any digits may have been intentionally altered. Numerous studies have been performed on the distribution of digits related to real-life phenomena, and the findings from most studies comport with Benford's law. While no one has been able to give mathematical justification for why Benford's law is true, the principle itself is a widely accepted method for testing whether data appears natural.

The applications of Benford's law to forensic analytics are numerous. Financial statements are perhaps the most widely known application of Benford's law. The distribution of certain types of financial data has been tested many times, and Benford's law is virtually always true when the data is unaltered. When Benford's law does not comport with data, forensic investigators know that the data requires further analysis because of the likelihood of fraud or data manipulation. Other fields, such as marketing, natural sciences, and user online activity have also been studied in relation to Benford's law.

The requirement for applying Benford's law to a data set is to confirm that the data set is a geometric sequence. When the data set of digits is ordered, the data should form a geometric sequence. If the data set forms a geometric sequence, the digits relative to their position should conform to the previous position's value multiplied by a common factor. The following table shows an example of the distribution of digits that obeys Benford's law (source: *Nigrini, M. J. "A taxpayer compliance application of Benford's law." The Journal of American Taxation Association 18 (1996): 72-91.*):

Digit	1st Position	2nd Position	3rd Position	4th Position
0	N/A	.11968	.10178	.10018
1	.30103	.11389	.10138	.10014
2	.17609	.10882	.10097	.10010
3	.12494	.10433	.10057	.10006
4	.09691	.10031	.10018	.10002
5	.07918	.09668	.09979	.09998
6	.06695	.09337	.09940	.09994
7	.05799	.09035	.09902	.09990
8	.05115	.08757	.09864	.09986
9	.04576	.08500	.09827	.09982

Certain types of data sets are known to obey Benford's law. Accounting data, by and large, obeys Benford's law because it contains nondeliberate human decision making. The following types of data, however, are not believed to obey Benford's law:

- Data directly influenced by human decision making (for example, negotiated prices)
- Numbers that are typically rounded or set to end in specific amounts (for example, prices ending in 99 cents instead of arbitrary values)
- Sequentially-ordered number assignment
- Data with a predetermined floor and/or ceiling value

Several techniques have been developed to determine whether a data set obeys Benford's law. The simplest is calculating the mean, median, and skew of the data. As a rule of thumb, if the mean is greater than the median and the skew is positive, Benford's law is obeyed. Additionally, the data can be plotted and then overlaid with the expected distribution based on Benford's law.

To apply Benford's law to the NYSE data, the field in question should be queried to isolate and aggregate the first digit. The following query does this and excludes the 3,370 records that have a `stock_price_open` value of zero:

```
SELECT LEFT(CONVERT(VARCHAR, stock_price_open), 1), COUNT(*)
FROM [001_NYSE]
WHERE stock_price_open <> 0
GROUP BY LEFT(CONVERT(VARCHAR, stock_price_open), 1)
ORDER BY 1
```

The results of this query can be plotted to visually inspect the distribution in relation to Benford's law, as shown in the following figure:

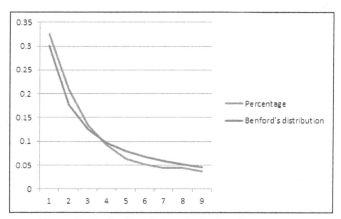

Figure 15: The leading digit analysis of stock_price_open

This diagram illustrates that the distribution of the first digit of `stock_price_open` obeys Benford's law. This finding can be used by the investigator to potentially rule out the likelihood that the leading digit was intentionally altered. The data may have still been manipulated for a small set of records; however, this shows that at least the majority of records have a natural distribution of the first digit.

Note that all digits in `stock_price_open` are positive. If the digits in a set are both positive and negative, the positive digits should be evaluated separately from the negative digits.

The digits for additional positions can be analyzed in certain cases, but typically the first digit is sufficient for determining whether a significant amount of the data was altered. Modifying the lesser digits is rarely performed as the amount of effort required is often too great compared to simply modifying the first digits of select records.

In the U.S., evidence based on Benford's law has been admitted in both civil litigation and criminal cases, so the method is legally accepted. The investigator should ensure that he is well versed in the mathematics of Benford's law and be able to prove 1) the digits of the data set form a geometric sequence and 2) the nature of the data set is sufficiently natural. If both these points can be proven, Benford's law is a powerful tool for the investigator to identify instances of data manipulation.

> Before applying Benford's law to an investigation, the investigator should spend time understanding the mathematics behind it. At a minimum, he should understand how to identify whether there is a geometric sequence and how to compare the results to determine if the data set obeys Benford's law.

Aggregation analysis

Data can be analyzed using aggregation to establish the distribution of data and isolate anomalies. In a Big Data investigation, analysis can be simplified by using aggregation to assess the distribution of data, rather than analyzing potentially billions of records individually. Aggregation reduces the number of observations that are required and can help pinpoint anomalies more quickly.

Aggregation can be performed across a single field or across multiple fields. The investigator can start with a single field when the analysis requires learning more about the data; they can then add more fields as they learn about the data. One test that can be applied to identify the largest groups of values from a particular field is the largest subset test. This test takes one or more fields, aggregates a related numeric field, and sorts the data in descending order. The following query calculates the stock symbols with the highest total stock volume:

```
SELECT stock_symbol, SUM(stock_volume), COUNT(*)
FROM [001_NYSE]
WHERE stock_volume <> 0
GROUP BY stock_symbol
ORDER BY 2 DESC
```

stock_symbol	Total Stock Volume	Total Records
GE	9,625,312,600	500
JNPR	8,003,694,300	500
EMC	7,920,856,300	500
MOT	7,218,593,300	500
NOK	7,145,176,100	500

The quantified aggregation can be expanded to include other metrics, such as average, minimum, and maximum values. In addition, other fields can be added to the aggregation. The following query adds the trade date's year to the aggregation to refine the results:

```
SELECT stock_symbol, YEAR(date), SUM(stock_volume), COUNT(*)
FROM [001_NYSE]
WHERE stock_volume <> 0
GROUP BY stock_symbol, YEAR(date)
ORDER BY 3 DESC
```

This changes the results to show the stock that had the highest volume in a year in the data set:

stock_symbol	Year	Total Stock Volume	Total Records
JNPR	2001	5,652,752,300	248
GE	2001	5,449,695,500	248
EMC	2001	5,146,650,000	248
GE	2000	4,175,617,100	252
MOT	2000	4,147,971,600	252

When performing multiple analyses, be sure to use the same filtering criteria if results from the separate analyses are to be compared. In this case, the WHERE clause stock_volume <> 0 is used throughout to exclude those records. If the WHERE clauses are different across analyses, be sure to note where and how they differ.

The aggregation can also be refined by adding WHERE clauses that restrict the data to a particular subset of data. For example, if the investigation of the NYSE data is specific to small lot orders of stocks, the aggregation can restrict all records having stock_volume values of 1,000 or less:

```
SELECT stock_symbol, YEAR(date), SUM(stock_volume), COUNT(*)
FROM [001_NYSE]
```

```
WHERE stock_volume <> 0 and stock_volume <= 1000
GROUP BY stock_symbol, YEAR(date)
ORDER BY 3 DESC
```

stock_symbol	Year	Total Stock Volume	Total Records
SNS	2000	58,600	82
MTR	2001	56,700	100
MLP	2000	51,000	109
ALX	2001	50,400	106
KTH	2001	50,300	87

Plotting outliers on a timeline

Outliers can be identified and plotted on a timeline to assess whether the outliers form a pattern or are restricted to a specific time period. The investigator first sets an outlier threshold and then queries all records that are above or below that threshold. The resulting list of anomalies can be plotted by date. The following figure illustrates an example outlier timeline:

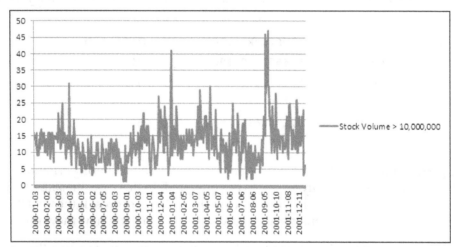

Figure 16: Identifying stock_volume outliers on a timeline

The anomalies in this case are the large sets of daily stock volume. Any one of the records could be a key data point; however, the investigator can begin by looking at the dates in which the highest number of anomalies occurred, especially those that are immediately preceded by a low number of anomalies.

The timeline can also plot relative percentages of anomaly types to show the trend relative to the total number of records per day, as illustrated in the following figure:

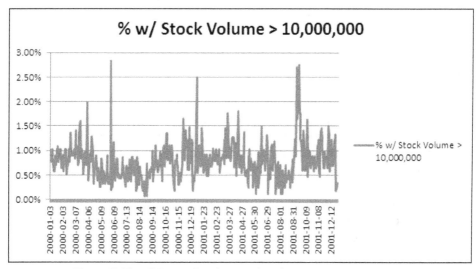

Figure 17: Identifying stock_volume outliers by percentage on a timeline

This analysis can be compared to the previous analysis to assess whether the large number of anomalies was due to the large number of transactions, or if there was a disproportionately large number of anomalies. For example, June 2, 2000 shows an anomaly rate of 2.84 percent, which was the day with the highest percentage of anomalies but not the day with the most anomalies. This type of finding can be significant in a fraud investigation to pinpoint when fraudulent events occurred and to show that those types of events were not normal across the time period in question.

Analyzing disparate data sets

Big Data investigations can involve multiple, disparate data sets. One set of data may include social media data and another may be accounting data. These data sets come from different sources, and there may not be a natural way to link the data or easily compare the values. To get around this issue, the investigator can take several steps to address the disparate data sources.

First, data transformations can be run on both sets to identify whether certain values (for example, addresses or names) can be standardized. Because the data sets may not have the same types of values between them, data transformation enables the results to be compared. If the data sets do have the same types of values, steps should be taken to standardize the values.

Other techniques can also be applied to disparate data. These include:

- Identifying duplication and data overlap, possibly with subsequent corrective measures being applied
- Linking data on one or more common fields
- Performing transaction mapping

Transaction mapping is a set of techniques for creating links between data sets that do not have a natural link between them. Transaction mapping is an important concept in Big Data investigations as Big Data information is often unrelated and fairly unstructured. Investigators may not find good data links between multiple data sets. Instead, the investigator may need to map sets of transactions across multiple data sets using one or more criteria. An example of this in financial fraud investigations is tracing the order of a stock to its point of execution and then tracing the point of execution to an account portfolio. All three data sets could have originated from different systems that do not share a common identifier or link. This prevents the investigator from running a SQL JOIN query.

Transaction mapping becomes necessary in such cases where disparate data sets are a factor. To create links between these disparate data sets, the investigator must perform the following steps:

1. Identify all fields that could be linked.
2. Test the possible links and determine whether any data variances need to be addressed in order to link the data.
3. Test the links to determine the percentage of transactions that can and cannot be mapped.
4. Codify the links as part of a query or within the table by assigning shared ID values to form primary key and foreign key relationships.

In the case of the stock order and execution example, the first step is to find the links between the stock order and execution data sets. Stock orders may be represented by a single record that maps to multiple, smaller execution records. An order of 10,000 shares can be executed in two blocks (for example, 6,000 and 4,000 shares), so the investigator should look to other fields to help form the data map. The customer account number, the date and time of the order, the stock symbol, and the type of order can all be possible fields used to help map the data. If both data sets are complete and are expected to include all orders and executions, the investigator can use these fields to find all records in the execution data that form a sum value equal to the order amount. The same process can then be applied to map the execution data to the account portfolio.

Transaction mapping is rarely a perfect process, and not all transactions may be able to be mapped. The investigator can manually review key records or create a subset of data that is not mapped. The key to the process is to identify the data that should be mapped and carefully assess the mapping to avoid false positives when linking the data sets.

Keyword searching

Big Data investigations can involve data from unstructured sources that are converted into a structured format. This information can contain keywords or specific numeric amounts that need to be identified. The simplest method is to run searches using matching algorithms, either with wild cards or pattern searches. SQL has built-in text wildcards that can be used to search data:

- %: Matches for zero or more of any character
- _: Matches to any single character
- [0-9]: Matches to a single digit between 0 and 9
- [a-z]: Matches to a single character between a to z and A to Z
- [^a-z] or [!a-z]: Matches to any character not between a to z or A to Z

The following query returns all stock symbols that contain the letter z:

```
SELECT *
FROM [001_NYSE]
WHERE stock_symbol LIKE '%z%'
```

The results of the query include BEZ, LZ, ZTR, and others.

More complex pattern searching can be created using multiple WHERE clauses. The following example returns records with a stock_symbol value that contains the following features: a letter z, a length of three characters, and no letter a in the second position:

```
SELECT *
FROM [001_NYSE]
WHERE stock_symbol LIKE '%z%'
AND LEN(stock_symbol) = 3
AND stock_symbol NOT LIKE '_a_%'
```

Patterns can also be searched in the SQL server using PATINDEX(). This function returns the starting position of a matched pattern or 0 if the pattern is not found in the field. PATINDEX() functions are entered as WHERE clauses and are similar to regular expression pattern matches.

The investigator may not know exactly which fields contain the keyword, so multiple fields within the data set need to be searched. This can be achieved by running a cursor across several or all of the fields. The cursor structure is the same as the cursor shown earlier in this chapter and simply includes the keyword or pattern in the WHERE section of the matching query.

The SQL server is not always the most efficient method for running keyword searches. An alternative method is to load the data into an indexing and searching tool to run more efficient keyword searches. Tools such as dtSearch are excellent for indexing data and locating keywords and strings of text using advanced search strings.

Validating the findings

The investigator should take steps to validate the findings. Validation helps to confirm that the analysis methodology was sound, all key findings were found, and no unknown biases influenced the findings. This step is important for proving both the correctness and completeness of the analysis.

The analysis findings can be validated by employing different analysis techniques or comparing the results to data from other sources. The first technique is to thoroughly review and test the analysis that was performed. This includes reviewing the data sources used and the queries that were executed. The output of the queries should also be reviewed to ensure that the correct results were captured.

A second technique is to perform similar analyses on the evidence using different techniques. This is a so-called quality control, or QC, method for validating that the analysis was correct and that the results are accurate. For example, if a histogram is a component of the analysis, the results of a SQL GROUP BY query using the same data can be compared to the histogram to confirm that the distributions match.

Another technique is to compare the findings to another data source. In some cases, the data may be able to be verified against another data source, either data from the organization or a third-party (for example, government data). From within the organization, the data could be a copy of the data that originated from outside Hadoop, or it may have come from Hadoop. This data can be used as a baseline from which the analysis can be validated. If there is an expectation that the other data source should comport with the evidence, this data serves as a general benchmark for the data. Otherwise, the other data source could also be used as part of the analysis findings to highlight the ways in which the evidence differs.

Documenting the findings

The analysis process can become complex when the theory requires multiple analyses and the data set is voluminous. Big Data investigations are complex, and the analysis process is the stage where the information needs to be understood and multiple facts must be combined to prove the theory. Unlike other types of investigations, Big Data investigations often involve billions of records and many different data sets. The analysis process of such investigations requires careful organization of the learned facts and thoughtful structuring of the analysis steps. Likewise, each step of the investigation should be properly documented by the investigator.

Best practices for a Big Data investigation include careful documentation of each step taken by the investigator. In the analysis phase, this requires documenting two important stages: the data transformations and the analysis steps. Documenting the data transformations is critical when describing the data set that was analyzed. Whether the transformations were changing the data types of fields, changing key-pair values to relational records, or culling the data, all of these can be called into question by an opposing party. As such, it is important that the investigator properly document each step of the process.

To document the data transformations, the investigator should note the following in his documentation:

- The summary data counts of each data set and for each derived data set, accompanied by all scripts used to transform the data

- The explanations for why each transformation was performed

- The descriptions of any data sets not included in the analysis, such as data characteristics and the total number of records

The analysis steps should also be documented. Many different analyses may have been run, and remembering all of the criteria and techniques applied for each finding may not be feasible. Instead, the investigator should document the analysis in such a way that it includes the following information:

- Listing each finding with its query scripts or providing a detailed explanation about how the findings were derived

- Carefully adding comments to complex queries that explain why each technique and criteria was applied

- Listing the data source(s) for each finding

The analysis usually yields a large number of findings, but not all of the findings may be relevant. To determine which analyses are critical to the findings, the investigator creates documentation about each theory and lists every analysis, in the order of the logical story, to organize the findings and document which ones are necessary. Findings that are not relevant should still be retained because they may help provide further backing to the findings at a later stage.

Summary

The analysis process is both an art and a science. The pre-analysis steps of loading, surveying, and transforming data are a well-defined process that prepares the data for the analysis. The analysis itself, however, is a creative process whereby the investigator matches the requirements of the investigation to the data in order to determine which analyses should be performed. Many different types of analyses can be performed, and it is up to the investigator to identify which techniques should be applied in order to build the case and arrive at the findings.

The next chapter will cover how to present the analysis findings and how to provide a clear and compelling case based on Big Data evidence.

8

Presenting Forensic Findings

The final phase of an investigation is to present the findings to those who will evaluate and rule on the outcome of the investigation. This process is crucial to the success of the investigation because any actions taken regarding the issue depend on the clarity, completeness, and accuracy of the findings. The investigator will most likely present the findings to a non-technical audience, but that audience may also seek input from other forensic experts. This means the findings should be presented in a clear and understandable manner that is accessible to a non-technical audience, and technical details should be provided with the findings for a technical expert who may evaluate the findings.

A report is the most common method for presenting the findings of an investigation. It is the account of the investigation that will be read by the audience. Almost no one else will access the data, except for an opposing forensic expert and attorneys, so the report is all that the audience has to learn about the data and how the investigation was conducted. The investigator is responsible for educating the audience about all phases of the investigation. If the report does not properly convey the findings and describe the steps performed, the entire investigation can be dismissed or discredited.

Investigation findings can be presented in several other ways. They can be presented in person, either as part of a legal proceeding or in other presentations outside of court. The in-person presentation can be in the form of a deposition or trial testimony for a legal proceeding. These presentations can make use of reports and other forms of documentation entered as evidence. The findings can be presented in any number of ways for investigations taking place outside of the court system. The findings for an internal investigation, government inquiry, or other types of investigations can be presented in-person using presentation software, remotely during a phone call, or in any other agreed upon manner.

This chapter covers the most common ways to present findings and the standard approaches used to build a presentation that can be understood by a general audience.

Types of reports

Findings are typically presented in writing, but they can also be accompanied by various types of in-person presentations. There are several types of reports, depending on the nature of the investigation. The first is an internal report. These reports are formal but do not require specific legal formatting or standard language. The second is an affidavit, which is a sworn statement that can be admitted as evidence in court. The third is a declaration. Declarations are intended as statements of facts that are submitted to a court. The fourth is an expert report, and this is evidence that can be submitted by a subject matter expert about a particular set of facts and findings in a case. The forensic investigator can also be called to provide an in-person presentation based on the report, which can be in the form of a deposition, testimony, or a non-legal, question-and-answer meeting.

The following table summarizes the types of reports an investigator may be asked to write:

Report	Description
Internal investigation	This is a detailed report for an investigation of an internal matter (for example, a data breach or employee misconduct) that is not part of a legal proceeding
Affidavit	This is a sworn, notarized statement of fact about the investigation used to put facts into evidence in a case
Declaration	This is a statement of fact about the investigation—similar to an affidavit but not notarized—used as a clarifying document by the court
Expert report	This is a report detailing the investigation for a legal proceeding that is admitted as evidence

Sample reports

Reports are written in a standardized way depending on the type of report. The reports presented here show the standard structure of documents for US-based investigations. Each legal system has its own requirements and individual jurisdictions may differ, so the investigator should base his report on the standards for that legal system.

Internal investigation report

Internal investigation reports have several standard components but can vary in structure. The goal of an internal investigation is to determine findings within an organization, so the decision makers within that organization can decide on what actions to take. The report should contain an executive summary, an explanation about what prompted the investigation, a list of steps that were taken, and the findings. The following figure provides a sample structure for an internal investigation report:

Internal Investigation of Issue X for ABC Corporation
Prepared by Joe Sremack on June 15, 2015

Executive Summary
    I, Joseph Sremack, was hired by John Smith, ABC Corporation's General Counsel, to investigate instances of suspected fraud committed by current and former employees of ABC Corporation. [...]

    Based on the evidence reviewed and my analysis, I have concluded that the fraud did, in fact, occur at least six times from November 7, 2014 through May 3, 2015. [...]

I. Background
    On May 9, 2015, an instance of fraud involving current and former employees was reported to Bob Jones, ABC Corporation's VP of Compliance. The fraud is believed [...]

II. Collection of Key Evidence
    My analysis was based upon the following sets of data acquired from ABC Corporation's systems: [...]

III. Analysis of Hadoop Server
    [...]

Figure 1: An internal investigation report

Internal investigation reports are typically only used within an organization to determine the cause and outcome of an event. The organization can use the report to terminate employees, remediate against data theft, or any number of other actions. The internal investigation may also lead to civil litigation or a criminal case, so the investigator has to be thorough and specific in his report. Every opinion should be supported by verifiable fact.

Affidavit and declaration

Affidavits and declarations are reports that are submitted to the court by attorneys to purport to facts that support a set of facts in the investigation. The primary differences between an internal investigation report and expert affidavits and declarations are 1) the expert submitting the affidavit or declaration must be recognized by the court as an expert in forensics, 2) an affidavit or declaration has a more defined purpose and format to be entered into a case, and 3) once submitted, an affidavit or declaration cannot be revised.

Declarations and affidavits are reports used to support motions put forth by attorneys to support a particular claim. The investigator submits a declaration or affidavit to support those motions; however, the investigator's opinions should be objective and not simply reiterate the attorneys' motions without substantiation. The facts and opinions in the affidavit or declaration can be rebutted by an opposing expert. There are at least two sides to every legal case, so the investigator should develop this report with the understanding that the document will be carefully reviewed and critiqued by the opposing side.

In an affidavit or declaration, the forensic investigator first states his educational background and the major factors that make him an expert who can opine on the matter under investigation. This section is critical for explaining to the court why it should trust his opinion. Courts have strict standards for assessing whether an investigator is qualified to be recognized as an expert, and if the investigator cannot prove that he is an expert, his reports and testimony can be excluded from the case. Investigators typically list several points about themselves to show the court that their opinions can be trusted, and these include their educational background, applicable technical certifications, current company, the number of years in their field, and any additional factors or training such as being a college professor or having taken a certain number of hours of training in the past several years.

 Investigators submitting expert opinions should be familiar with Daubert requirements for being recognized by the court as an expert.

Affidavits and declarations are written using a similar structure. The following figure provides a sample structure for a declaration:

I, JOSEPH SREMACK, declare under penalty of perjury that the following is true and correct:

1. I am a citizen of the United States and am over the age of eighteen years old. I am not a party to the above-captioned action. My business address is [...]. I have personal knowledge of the facts set forth in this Declaration and, if called as a witness, I could and would competently testify to them.

Scope of Engagement and Summary of Conclusions

2. I was retained by [Law Firm], counsel for plaintiff [Client], as an expert to review and provide comments in response to the motion filed on [Date], by [Party's name] [...]

3. Specifically, I was to explain (1) in general terms the efforts performed to conduct the investigation of the Hadoop system; (2) review and assess the findings related to the matter [...]

4. Through my review of the data collection, and my understanding of the facts of the case, I have come to the following conclusions, which are more fully explained below in this Declaration:
    *   [Findings]

Qualifications

5. I am a Director with [Consulting firm].
6. My job duties regularly involve providing advisory and investigatory services regarding complex data systems. [...]
7. I have over a decade of experience in the litigation and technology consulting profession. [Education and professional experience]
8. My CV is attached as Exhibit "A" hereto.

Opinions and Conclusions

I. Data identification and collection

9. The following sets of data were identified and collected in the process of [...]

II. Analysis of [Party's] Hadoop system

[...]

20. Based on my understanding of the relevant data and my experience, I have concluded the following: [...]

Figure 2: Declaration

Expert report

Expert reports are typically required of anyone offering expert testimony in a trial. Investigators who serve as expert witnesses submit expert reports to 1) disclose all opinions and the bases for those opinions, 2) provide information disclosed for pretrial discovery, and 3) give the court information so it can decide whether the expert's testimony is admissible. The report is a complete set of facts and opinions from which the expert can testify.

The expert report is not required to adhere to a standard format, but several sets of information are required. Generally, investigators write their reports in a narrative style that tells the story of the investigation and how the conclusions were drawn. This style is helpful to judges and juries because it reads better and is more understandable than other formats. The investigator must include required information in the expert report. As per the US Federal Rules of Civil Procedure Rule 26 (a)(2)(B), the expert report is required to contain the following sections:

- A full and complete statement of all opinions expressed and the reasons for them

- The qualifications of the witnesses, which includes a list of all publications authored within the preceding ten years

- The compensation to be paid to the expert

- The information used by the expert to form his opinions (for example, data and publications upon which the methodology was based)

- A full list of all cases in which the expert testified in the previous four years

The following figure provides a sample structure for an expert report:

I.	**OVERVIEW** I have been retained [Overview of involvement …]
II.	**QUALIFICATIONS** [Education, work experience, and training]
III.	**PRIOR EXPERT WITNESS EXPERIENCE** I have been designated and served as an expert witness in the following matters: […]
IV.	**COMPENSATION** I have been retained by [Law Firm], counsel for plaintiff [Client], and compensated on an hourly basis at the hourly rate of […]
V.	**ITEMS REVIEWED** The following evidence was reviewed to form my opinion […]
VI.	**ANALYSIS** I have reviewed the evidence collected from the Hadoop cluster to determine whether […] It is my expert opinion that the following event occurred […]
VII.	**CONCLUSION** Based on my review and analysis of the evidence collected, it is my opinion that […]

Figure 3: An expert report

Developing the report

All types of reports serve the same goal: explaining the findings and the steps that were applied to arrive at the findings. Forensic investigations are complex, and the results of an investigation are typically reported to a non-technical audience, whether it is an internal investigation or an investigation involving the legal system. A report is a tool that summarizes the salient points of the entire forensic investigation in a logical and accessible way. While Big Data investigations are complex, the report should be simple and understandable by any audience, so they understand the steps performed from identification through collection and analysis and the findings are supported by the investigator's interpretation of the results. The report should be developed with the audience in mind and an awareness of how to explain the technical concepts to a non-technical audience.

Reports can be made more accessible and understandable for a general audience by including certain types of information and explaining technical concepts. The following concepts can be applied to a report to simplify and clarify the report:

- Use charts and diagrams to explain steps performed or logical connections between findings

- Include technical detail as exhibits or appendices so as not to muddle the main sections of the report

- Explain technical concepts that need to be included in general, plain language

- Use professional language and avoid informal or colloquial language

- Only include relevant and factual information, not speculation

Explaining the process

The report structure typically includes one or more sections detailing the evidence considered and the steps the investigator took to arrive at his findings. The investigator must clearly list all evidence he considered. This is typically done by identifying the name, type, and characteristics of the data source. The steps taken by the investigator can be explained in several ways. A standard approach is to describe the process in chronological order, from identification through analysis. This approach is well-suited to reports intended for a general audience, because it allows the reader to follow the steps in the same order in which the events occurred.

The data identification process should be explained in plain language, with descriptions about why certain data sources were included or excluded. Most audiences will understand how evidence was identified; however, some explanation about how each type of system operates and why some data was not deemed relevant may be required. The investigator does not need to describe every data source that was considered, but he may want to discuss key data sources if he expects that questions will arise during testimony.

The collection process, likewise, should be explained in plain language. This process is highly technical, so the investigator should adhere to very basic descriptions of the collection. For example, rather than describing the collection as, "a bit-wise collection of the 40 nodes was collected into dd image files and restored to a single image using [...]", the investigator may prefer to simplify the language to a statement more like "the distributed system's data was collected and restored using forensic means". Depending on the case and the preference of the attorneys, the latter approach may be preferable, and any questions about the exact methods can be raised during trial.

A key point in Big Data forensic investigations is to explain the concept of a distributed system and how Hadoop operates. Distributed systems are not new, but the investigator cannot assume that the audience of the report understands the concept of distributed systems.

Supporting documentation and complex, technical detail can be presented as an appendix or exhibit in the report. Documentation, such as chain of custody forms and logs from the collection process, can muddle the body of the report, making it less readable. Similarly, technical detail, such as source code, can be excessive or confusing to a general audience. Instead, the investigator can use plain language to describe the process and explain what occurred in the body of the report, while citing the detailed information and including it as an exhibit or appendix. This method helps the investigator to provide a report that is readable while ensuring that all backing information is available to a reader who wants to understand more about the investigation.

The analysis phase is the most complicated phase, so the investigator should explain his findings in a logical and coherent manner. The focus should be on the relevant analyses performed, the results, and the interpretations of those results, not necessarily the investigator's thinking, hypotheses, or reasons for performing the analysis. The analysis can either be presented in a separate section or in the findings section.

Showing the findings

The findings section is where the investigator presents the findings and his interpretation of the findings. The findings are presented in a logical order to demonstrate how and why the findings were reached. The findings should be explained in clear, concise language that can be understood by a general audience. The key points should be highlighted, and unnecessary detail should be excluded.

The following are several key points for the investigator to consider when drafting the report:

- Be objective, not an advocate for a particular scenario. Present the results clearly, concisely, and objectively.

- Avoid conjecture or hedge words such as "could" or "possibly."

- Do not draw legal conclusions. The investigator should stick to what was asked of him and avoid legal language, such as discussing negligence.

- Do not provide opinions for which the reasons were not supplied.

The findings of an investigator should be organized in a logical way. There are several approaches to organizing the findings section of a report. First, the findings can be organized by the chronological order of events that occurred. This method for organizing the findings is quite common and can be presented either according to the order of the events that are being investigated or the order of events performed by the investigator. The former is typically preferred, because it tells the story of what actually happened.

A second method is to organize the findings by the relation of the facts. Rather than focus on a chronology, this method organizes the findings by the importance of the events and how they are related. For instance, in a fraud investigation, many less significant events may have occurred, but two events that did not occur near to one another may be the most important and what the investigator wants to stress. Rather than detail those findings apart from one another, the investigator can present them together to highlight their importance.

Another method is to present the findings according to a theory. In this case, the investigator details why a particular theory appears to be true, and the subsequent findings are presented to support that theory. The investigator may also include findings that disprove potential alternative or contradictory theories. This method requires careful organization and wording, because the investigator is required to be an expert on the case. He cannot appear to have been led down a particular line of reasoning or appear to be an advocate for a particular theory. Instead, he needs to show that he had a solid basis for a particular theory and carefully explain how and why his findings prove that theory.

The following figure illustrates how these methods for organizing the findings can be structured:

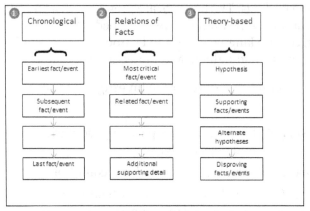

Figure 4: Approaches for organizing the findings

The investigator has a great degree of freedom in how the individual findings are presented. The findings can be shown as:

- Textual descriptions
- Numerical representations
- Charts
- Sample data records

A good report does not need all of these elements, but combining multiple types of presentation can be helpful in detailing the findings. Textual descriptions are a part of all reports. These are the narratives and explanations of the facts of the investigation. They form the bulk of the report because this is how the findings are described, and they present how the investigator interpreted the results. Numerical representations are the facts presented numerically, such as aggregate computations and statistical analyses. Charts and other graphics are useful for visually imparting the findings. A general audience may not fully appreciate the raw numbers, so a visual can further clarify and elucidate the significance of the numerical findings or a timeline.

In traditional digital forensic investigations, the findings are described in narrative form and screenshots can be included. In Big Data investigations, screenshots and sample data are not as valuable. Big Data investigations are based on large volumes of data, and while sample records can help explain the structure of the data, the findings are typically based on identifying a subset of records or performing aggregate calculations. This is a major difference in how the findings are presented between Big Data and traditional investigations.

Using exhibits or appendices

Reports are written in a narrative form. An investigator may find the supporting information and large graphics that are necessary to fully explain a concept or fact may interfere with the readability of the main sections. This information can be cited in the main sections and placed at the end of the report. The main types of appendix and exhibit content include:

- Graphics (for example, charts and screenshots)
- Forms (for example, chain of custody)
- Source code or other technical detail

The investigator should follow these general principles when considering whether to include an exhibit or appendix:

- Each exhibit or appendix should be labeled in the sequential order in which it appeared in the report
- The investigator should avoid providing an extraneous exhibit or appendix (for example, chain of custody documentation when there are not questions about the evidence's handling)
- The exhibit or appendix should be adequately described in the text of the report or be self-explanatory

Testimony and other presentations

The investigation can also be presented orally. The investigation may need to be presented in an interactive manner with one or more parties being present and asking questions. For internal investigations, the investigator may be called to present his findings to explain what he did and answer any questions that the client may have. For legal proceedings, this can take the form of depositions or testimony. Both of these types of oral presentations involve one or both sides of the investigation having a chance to ask the investigator about his report and ask further questions about his findings and interpretations.

Internal investigations take place outside of the legal system, so there are no fixed rules for how those are conducted. The investigator may be called to answer questions and explain the report in a way that can be understood by the organization. In this setting, the investigator may wish to present the findings using a presentation software or by using graphics that were not in the report to explain his findings. The investigator should answer questions truthfully and avoid speculation.

In addition, the investigator should be aware of how the organization intends on memorializing the findings. Should the organization reserve the right to use the findings as evidence, or if a legal case may arise out of the investigation, the investigator should prepare all materials and limit statements to only those for which he would be able to support in court for a later legal proceeding.

Depositions and testimony are two distinctly different forms of legal presentation. Expert witness depositions are sworn testimony that are conducted in a question-and-answer manner, usually outside of the court. An attorney will ask questions—either based on the expert's affidavit or declaration or not—and the investigator answers the questions to the best of his knowledge. The investigator does have an opportunity to later correct any statements for a fixed period of time, but he should aim to limit the corrections as much as possible in order to maintain credibility. The deposition is considered testimony by the court, so that information will be seen by the court as part of the proceedings. Transcripts of the testimony can also be introduced as evidence and read to the court or jury in a later trial.

Testimony, on the other hand, is sworn testimony that is taken in the court as part of a trial. Testimony is preceded by the expert report being submitted. The investigator will not have an opportunity to correct any mistakes he says. The investigator should present himself professionally and be able to recall the facts of the investigation. He must also have a keen legal sense and refrain from speculation or interpreting questions.

- Answer only the questions asked; avoid giving long narratives
- Do not guess; "I don't know' or "I don't remember' are acceptable responses
- Ask to see document that would refresh one's memory, if one exists
- Couch opinions in terms of the underlying facts and the methods used to come to them
- Be prepared to answer potentially hostile background-related questions regarding academic and professional background as well as publications

 Investigators who have not served as an expert witness before should seek out expert witness training and literature before serving as an expert. Experts are expected to be well versed in the legal system and how to conduct themselves in that role.

Summary

The final step of the investigation is to present the findings. The investigator should already have all of his findings and documentation when beginning this process. Depending on the nature of the investigation, the investigator may need to write a number of different reports and present the findings in person—or he may only need to draft a single document. The goal for any investigation is not only to perform a sound data collection and complete analysis, but also to present the findings in an intelligible and accurate way. By knowing the requirements of the investigation and the forms of presentation required, the investigator can successfully present the findings.

Big Data forensics is a new and rapidly evolving field. Many of the technologies presented in this book will continue to evolve and possibly disappear. The concepts and best practices in this book, however, will remain and can be applied to investigations in the future. Data storage will continue to expand, which means that forensic investigations will continue to expand in turn. Distributed systems, NoSQL databases, and other Big Data concepts require these new forensic techniques to keep pace with the rapid changes in the size and scope of forensic investigations.

Index

B

backup-based collection 115
Benford's law 205-208
Big Data
  about 12
  architecture 15, 16
  concepts 15, 16
  four Vs 12-14
  requirements 60
  variety 13
  velocity 13
  veracity 15
  volume 13
Big Data forensics
  about 1, 16, 17
  collection methods 18
  collection verification 18
  metadata preservation 17
Bulk Extractor
  about 152, 153
  URL 152, 153

C

chain of custody 79
challenges, forensic analysis
  anti-forensic techniques 149
  encryption 149, 150
Cloud computing
  advantages 150
cluster system
  collecting 83-85
collection phase
  Logical collection 6
  Physical collection 6
  Targeted collection 6
collection, via Sqoop 107, 108
compression formats, Hadoop
  defining 40
computer forensics
  about 2, 3
  forensic process 3, 4
  investigation considerations 10
configuration files
  Hadoop application configuration files 170

Hadoop configuration files 170
  Linux configuration files 169
  types 169
configuration files, Hadoop
  defining 170
  hadoop-default.xml 29
  hadoop-site.xml 29
  job.xml 29
  mapred-default.xml 29
cross-validation 8

D

data
  analyzing 190
  loading, into AWS 52
data analysis
  analysis approaches 190, 191
  analysis techniques 192
  findings, documenting 215, 216
  findings, validating 214
data analysis tools, Hadoop
  about 31
  HBase 33-36
  Hive 32, 33
  Pig 37
database management system (DBMS) 48
data collection
  requirements 69
data collection request 74-78
data collection types
  about 73
  in-house 73
  investigator-led collection 78
  third-party collection 73
data flow, in Hadoop
  considerations 142
data, loading
  defining 177-181
  preload data transformations 182
data model, HBase
  defining 33, 34
data requests
  types 73, 74
data requirements
  compiling 59, 60

data scripting
benefits 130
data source identification
defining 70
data sources
considerations 58
identifying, in noncooperative
situations 67-69
data, surveying
benefits 182
data transformation
considerations 185
defining 185-187
nonrelational data, transforming 188, 189
data viability
assessing 65, 66
dd tool
about 89
advantages 90
documentation review process
defining 62-64
Domain Name System (DNS) 51

E

EDRM
about 4
URL 4
Elastic MapReduce (EMR) 49
evidence
identifying 55-58
expectation-maximization (EM) 195

F

features, tools 89
fields, file header
blockCompression 41
Compression 41
Compression Codec 41
keyClassName 41
Metadata 41
Sync 41
valueClassName 41
Version 41
File Allocation Table (FAT) 28
file deletion

types 160
file-level analyses
cluster reconstruction 165-167
configuration file analysis 168
deleted files, analysis 160, 161
file and data carving 151
HDFS data extraction 161-163
keyword searching 151
log file analysis 171, 172
metadata analysis 158
file permissions, HDFS
Execute (x) 38
Read (r) 38
Write (w) 38
files, Hadoop
data serialization 44
defining 37
file compression and splitting 40
file permissions 38
Hadoop archive files 42, 43
JAR files 45
log files 39, 40
packaged jobs 45
SequenceFile 41, 42
trash feature 38, 39
forensic analysis
challenges 149
concepts 148
goals 147, 148
forensic analysis process
defining 146, 147
forensic data, Hadoop
record evidence 46
supporting information 46
user and application evidence 46
forensic process
analysis phase 7, 8
collection phase 5-7
identification phase 4, 5
presentation phase 9
FUSE
URL 93

G

Graphical User Interface (GUI) 179

H

Hadoop
  Amazon Web Services (AWS) 49-51
  components 24, 25
  configuration files 28-30
  defining 21
  forensic evidence ecosystem 45-47
  Hadoop data, loading 51, 52
  LightHadoop 48
  running 47
  working 22
Hadoop application backup methods
  defining 117
Hadoop application data
  collecting 141-143
Hadoop architecture
  about 22, 23
  application layer 23
  DBMS layer 23
  Hadoop layer 23
  operating system layer 23
Hadoop Archive (HAR) files 42
Hadoop daemons 30
Hadoop data
  about 114
  collecting 114
  sample data, importing for testing 52, 53
Hadoop data, collecting
  advantages 114
Hadoop Distributed File System (HDFS)
  about 26-28, 56, 81, 145
  advantages 81
  collecting, ways 82
  need for 26
Hadoop encryption
  URL 150
Hadoop evidence
  collecting, from host operating system 87
Hadoop implementations
  URL 141
Hadoop Key Management Server
    (KMS) 150
Hadoop log files
  Daemon logs 171
  Job configuration 172

Job statistics 172
  log4j 172
Hadoop Offline Image Viewer
  defining 105
  Inode 105
  NameNode 105
Hadoop shell command collection
  about 99-101
  Edits Viewer 104-107
  Hadoop Offline Image Viewer 104-107
  HDFS files, collecting 101-103
  HDFS targeted data collection 103, 104
HAR format
  defining 43
HBase
  .META. table 132
  -ROOT- table 132
  about 33-36
  HBase Clients 132
  HBase data storage 132
  HBase shell 132
  HFile 132
  Key-pair values 132
  Master node and regionservers 132
  Memstore 132
  NoSQL (Not only SQL) 132
  tables 132
  ZooKeeper 132
HBase data, accessing
  Avro 36
  Java program 36
  MapReduce 36
  REST 36
HBase evidence
  collecting 131-133
  HBase backup collection 136-138
  HBase collection, via scripts 139
  HBase control totals 140
  HBase data, loading 134, 135
  HBase metadata and log collection 140
  HBase query collection 138, 139
  identifying 135, 136
HDFS
  advantages 100
  built-in commands 51
  mounting 87

S

sample data, for testing
  URL 52
sample reports
  affidavit and declaration 220, 221
  expert report 221
  internal investigation report 219
script-based collection 115
Secure File Transfer Protocol (SFTP) 77
Secure Shell (SSH) 49
semi-structured data 14
SequenceFile
  Blocked-compressed 41
  Record-compressed 41
  Uncompressed 41
serialization frameworks, Hadoop 44
software-based collection 115
sources of data
  locating 58
spoliation 160
SQL 131
SQL Server 2014 Express LocalDB
  URL 176
SQL Server 2014 Management Studio
  URL 176
SQL Server Management Studio
  (SSMS) 178
Sqoop
  about 107, 108
  data, importing in databases 107
staff interview
  defining 62-64
staff types
  defining 67
structured data
  defining 14, 71, 72

structure, directories and files 96
subset
  collecting 117
system architecture
  reviewing 61, 62

T

testimony 227, 228
timeline analysis
  performing 159
time series analysis
  about 197, 198
  change over time, measuring 198, 199
tools, Hadoop
  Flume 26
  HBase 25
  Hive 25
  Pig 26
  Sqoop 26

U

unstructured data
  defining 14, 71, 72

V

virtual machine (VM) 48

W

write-ahead log (WAL) 35

Z

ZooKeeper 35

Thank you for buying
Big Data Forensics – Learning Hadoop Investigations

About Packt Publishing

Packt, pronounced 'packed', published its first book, *Mastering phpMyAdmin for Effective MySQL Management*, in April 2004, and subsequently continued to specialize in publishing highly focused books on specific technologies and solutions.

Our books and publications share the experiences of your fellow IT professionals in adapting and customizing today's systems, applications, and frameworks. Our solution-based books give you the knowledge and power to customize the software and technologies you're using to get the job done. Packt books are more specific and less general than the IT books you have seen in the past. Our unique business model allows us to bring you more focused information, giving you more of what you need to know, and less of what you don't.

Packt is a modern yet unique publishing company that focuses on producing quality, cutting-edge books for communities of developers, administrators, and newbies alike. For more information, please visit our website at www.packtpub.com.

About Packt Open Source

In 2010, Packt launched two new brands, Packt Open Source and Packt Enterprise, in order to continue its focus on specialization. This book is part of the Packt Open Source brand, home to books published on software built around open source licenses, and offering information to anybody from advanced developers to budding web designers. The Open Source brand also runs Packt's Open Source Royalty Scheme, by which Packt gives a royalty to each open source project about whose software a book is sold.

Writing for Packt

We welcome all inquiries from people who are interested in authoring. Book proposals should be sent to author@packtpub.com. If your book idea is still at an early stage and you would like to discuss it first before writing a formal book proposal, then please contact us; one of our commissioning editors will get in touch with you.

We're not just looking for published authors; if you have strong technical skills but no writing experience, our experienced editors can help you develop a writing career, or simply get some additional reward for your expertise.

Hadoop MapReduce v2 Cookbook
Second Edition

ISBN: 978-1-78328-547-1   Paperback: 322 pages

Explore the Hadoop MapReduce v2 ecosystem to gain insights from very large datasets

1. Process large and complex datasets using next generation Hadoop.

2. Install, configure, and administer MapReduce programs and learn what's new in MapReduce v2.

3. More than 90 Hadoop MapReduce recipes presented in a simple and straightforward manner, with step-by-step instructions and real-world examples.

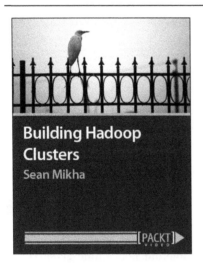

Building Hadoop Clusters [Video]

ISBN: 978-1-78328-403-0   Duration: 02:34 hours

Deploy multi-node Hadoop clusters to harness the Cloud for storage and large-scale data processing

1. Familiarize yourself with Hadoop and its services, and how to configure them.

2. Deploy compute instances and set up a three-node Hadoop cluster on Amazon.

3. Set up a Linux installation optimized for Hadoop.

Please check **www.PacktPub.com** for information on our titles

Hadoop Beginner's Guide

ISBN: 978-1-84951-730-0   Paperback: 398 pages

Learn how to crunch big data to extract meaning
from the data avalanche

1. Learn tools and techniques that let you
   approach big data with relish and not fear.

2. Shows how to build a complete infrastructure
   to handle your needs as your data grows.

3. Hands-on examples in each chapter give the
   big picture while also giving direct experience.

Big Data Analytics with R and Hadoop

ISBN: 978-1-78216-328-2   Paperback: 238 pages

Set up an integrated infrastructure of R and Hadoop
to turn your data analytics into Big Data analytics

1. Write Hadoop MapReduce within R.

2. Learn data analytics with R and the
   Hadoop platform.

3. Handle HDFS data within R.

4. Understand Hadoop streaming with R.

Please check **www.PacktPub.com** for information on our titles